Ronald Hutton is a leading authority on the history of the British Isles in the sixteenth and seventeenth centuries, as well as ancient and medieval paganism and magic, and the global context of witchcraft beliefs. He is author of the definitive *The Pagans: A History* as well as *The Rise and Fall of Merrie England, The Restoration* and a biography of Charles II. His expert opinion is frequently sought on TV and radio.

Highlights from the series

A BRIEF HISTORY OF

BRITAIN 1485–1660

RONALD HUTTON

ROBINSON

Constable & Robinson Ltd
3 The Lanchesters
162 Fulham Palace Road
London W6 9ER
www.constablerobinson.com

First published in the UK by Robinson,
an imprint of Constable & Robinson, 2010

A copy of the British Library Cataloguing in Publication
Data is available from the British Library

ISBN 978-1-84529-704-6

1 3 5 7 9 10 8 6 4 2

CONTENTS

ACKNOWLEDGEMENTS

Back in 1988, my friend Jeremy Black invited me to write a textbook for a series that he was editing on key episodes in British history. He wanted me to supply the volume on the years 1649 to 1660, and I was happy to do so, as it gave me the opportunity to try my hand at a new kind of historical authorship and to plug a chronological gap in the areas that I had covered before then. The result was published in 1990 under the title of *The British Republic*. Almost two decades later, he returned with an invitation to contribute a larger general survey, of what are conventionally called the Tudor and Early Stuart periods, and the Interregnum, to a series of volumes on British history as a whole. Once again, the moment has seemed opportune, as the commission enables me to write, however concisely, upon a range of topics about which I have thought and lectured with great pleasure for over thirty years. My first textbook for Jeremy has remained my one and only exercise of its kind, a book about a relatively short period of national events which synthesised the thoughts of other experts with my own. This second one may well be my only contribution to the larger textbook format, a sustained piece of writing that sums up my thoughts and those of colleagues upon national history over a period of almost two hundred years. I referred to the first form of book when I wrote it, rather rudely, as 'microwaved history'; a heap of everything that seemed to be known on the subject, heated through briefly with my own opinions and served up to be as convenient and easy to general readers as possible. I regard this new exercise more as like leading a relatively rapid guided tour through an extensive landscape which is familiar and precious to me, making comments about the surroundings as we progress and pausing in front of features that are of particular interest to me.

I showed one section of the work to an expert reader, Peter Marshall, before submission, and am very grateful to him for his encouragement and advice.

INTRODUCTION

On 22 August 1485, the English king Richard III led a characteristically reckless and courageous charge into the centre of the army that opposed him on Bosworth Field, trying to win the battle at a stroke by cutting down his rival for the throne, Henry Tudor. His gamble failed, and he was killed instead, thereby ending both his reign and his dynasty. Whatever passed through his mind in his final few frantic minutes of life, as steel weapons sliced into his body, we can be certain that one thing did not: that he had just brought to a close in England a period of history called the Middle Ages. Yet, ever since the nineteenth century, that has been regarded as the greatest single significance of that moment.

By contrast, when Charles I stepped out on to a scaffold in Whitehall on a bitterly cold day at the end of January 1649, he must have been very conscious that an epoch would end when he died at the hands of the executioner who awaited him there. Not only was the judicial murder of a king at the hands of his subjects quite unprecedented in European history, but Charles could be sure that with him would perish the English monarchy, the House of Lords and a national church which demanded a monopoly of his subjects' religious loyalties and which was focused on bishops, cathedrals and ceremonies. What happened when the blades carved into Richard was a change of kings; when the one fell on Charles's neck a whole system of government and ideology, in place for a thousand years, died with him. No large span of British history, however, traditionally ends in 1649. This is because the revolution that occurred then is seen as a temporary aberration in the national story, ushering in a short-lived and uncharacteristic experiment which lasted only ten years before monarchy, Lords and church were restored together in 1660 and – the implication runs – British normality with them. That is why this later date is commonly seen as the watershed of the century, and the beginning of the end of the early modern period in England; a commencement of the process of settling down after the huge changes of the previous 200 years.

It may therefore be seen that a book with the prescribed title *Britain 1485–1660*, delineated by its need to fit into a series, immediately imposes certain crucial presuppositions. One is that high politics, and especially the affairs of central government and the monarchs who led it, are going to be the main motivating and determining factor of the book. Another is that British history is essentially organic, conservative and cumulative, with radical change played down. If economic, social and cultural history were to be the main subject matter, then the dates concerned would make no sense at all, and others, such as the blunter '1500–1700' would be chosen instead. The title also ensures that England will be the nation at centre-stage, because in Scottish history the date 1485 has virtually no significance. There was a change of King of Scots in 1488, but it made relatively little difference, and most Scottish historians, even of high politics, would choose a different dividing line, such as 1500. The year 1660 was indeed of considerable significance to Scotland, but initially it played an almost completely passive role, being a conquered and occupied nation completely dependent on the actions of the English for its future. Before 1560, or perhaps even 1603, Scotland and England had relatively little to do with each other, and events in France were far more important for both. Indeed, throughout the whole period from 1485 to 1660, Ireland, which is not part of Britain, usually had far more impact on English affairs than Scotland.

How to do justice to the two British kingdoms, in a book with this title, is therefore a serious problem; and it is worsened by another consideration. In the period concerned, Scotland was a proud and independent kingdom with its own distinctive and very dynamic polity and culture, which were to be of tremendous consequence for later British history. In that sense it deserves to be given half the space of any history of Britain. On the other hand, in the years under review it had only a fifth of the population of England and its share of the island's wealth was even smaller. Even more importantly to an historian, it generated many fewer records, a comparison which has a knock-on effect on what can be written of it. The amount published during the past four decades on any aspect of Scottish history between 1485 and 1560 is far less than that which has appeared in the same time upon the reign of one contemporary English sovereign, Henry VIII. The same difficulties are even greater when considering other British peoples who were included within the English kingdom: the Welsh, who comprised a twelfth of its population, and the Cornish. I have therefore bowed to all this logic. It is my hope that my own admiration and affection for all three peoples, and knowledge of them, comes through in this book, but the Scots play a relatively small part in it, the Welsh have walk-on moments, and the Cornish barely feature.

In other respects I have conformed to the pressure exerted by the dates in the title. This book is mostly concerned with the work of government, and especially of central government and the royal personages in charge of it. Economic, social and cultural factors are mostly treated as auxiliary to that. This format has two advantages: it probably conforms to the expectations of most of its prospective readership; and it matches my own interests and abilities. I could have interpreted the remit of a 'brief history' to provide a summary of what is known in general about Britain in the span of time concerned; but that would, given the word limit, have reduced it at times to a breathless recital of data. Instead I have chosen to play to my own strengths and enthusiasms. There is therefore not much economic history or history of ideas, and the social topics treated are those with which I am most engaged personally, and on which I have formed opinions. There are, however, quite a few of those, and a lot of high and low politics, war and religion, with great importance attached to personality and contingency and more than usual notice taken of the differing and developing views of historians.

Built into many of the arguments made below is a major assumption: that one of the tasks of an historian is to trace developments in the past which relate to features of the present, and show how the latter have their origin in the former. This is not the most important of the responsibilities of the discipline, or even a necessary one, for another way in which history can be written with equal value is to show how different long-dead humans could be from ourselves, and what may be learned from the contrasts. Both assist in the understanding of what is possible to us, and how present systems are limited, regulated and justified by the past. There are considerable dangers in stretching an interest in the origins of the present too far, such as assuming that the way in which history turned out was inevitable, or censuring or praising people in history according to how well they lived up to the standards of the present. To assume that any inhabitants of past ages should have been like those of the current age is itself an attitude which negates a true sense of history. None the less, interest in the past is itself kept alive largely by the changing tastes and needs of the present, and I am perhaps more conscious than many historians (and archaeologists) of the manner in which perceptions of former times are shaped by current cultural preoccupations.

In general, this book is designed for anyone who wants to know about the period, or wants to know more about it, or knew about it once and wants to find out what is thought about it now. More specifically, however, I have written for an amalgam of audiences with which I am well acquainted:

university and school students, school staff, local history societies, and listeners to and viewers of history programmes on radio and television. Most of my knowledge of these is in Britain, but I have also borne in mind those whom I have encountered in America, Australia, New Zealand and Canada. I recognize a duty to provide bread-and-butter facts, and to summarize as fairly as I can what experts currently think of each topic. I do not however regard myself merely as an honest broker, and have loaded the bread and butter with plenty of stylistic and ideological jam, in the form of my own opinions. I want to use this book as my best opportunity to convey the excitement and colour – and the importance – which I myself have found in its subject matter.

Ronald Hutton
Martinmas 2008

I

HENRY VII (1485–1509)

Character and High Politics

The first Tudor monarch is a classic example of a king who ruled at a boundary in history, and it is notoriously hard to achieve agreement about such figures. Since the nineteenth century, some historians have called him the first modern king; which is why, of course, English school courses have generally ended the Middle Ages in 1485. Others have seen him as part of a 'New Monarchy' started by his predecessors, the Yorkist kings, to repair the government after its collapse in the Wars of the Roses. Others still have seen him as the last medieval king, before the English state got remodelled under his son. The trouble is, of course, that all these views have elements of truth; but the problem of Henry VII goes deeper than that. In recent years, Alexander Grant has thought that he was the first English ruler for over three hundred years who solved all of the problems of governing. Christine Carpenter, on the other hand, has concluded that he never understood the English state and made a hash of ruling it.

Both were equally good scholars, with comparable knowledge of the evidence; but both cannot be right.

Certainly Henry has a public image problem. The enduring popular image of the reign is that of a grey interlude between the drama of the Wars of the Roses and the charisma of Henry VIII. He was the only English king to rule between 1377 and 1547 about whom Shakespeare didn't want to write. The British Broadcasting Corporation was less wise, during the 1970s, and found him a ratings destroyer. It had already screened a successful television series on Henry VIII and then another on Elizabeth I. Reckless with this achievement, it ran one on Henry VII, which turned away viewers so completely that it killed historical soap operas on British television for over a decade. The roots of the trouble go down to the most basic conceptual tools of historians: periods and sources. Henry falls on the conventional border between medieval and early modern history, and so is unwanted by specialists in either. His reign is too early for the state papers and other records familiar to experts on the Tudors, but the standard medieval source materials – chronicles, administrative rolls and legal documents – are fewer than before. As a result, it is not an attractive subject for research.

This is a pity, because he had an extraordinary life and reign. He spent most of his formative years on the run from one Continental state to another, sometimes getting across a frontier only just before his current host tried to have him arrested and handed over to the current Yorkist king of England. He won the English throne without having any good claim to it; he was indeed descended from its fourteenth-century kings, but through a family, the Beauforts, which had been explicitly barred from the succession. His main justification for seizing the Crown was simply that as he had overcome the previous king, Richard III, in a fair fight, it should be clear that God had wanted him to do so. There were plenty of people around with more right to inherit the throne than he, so to strengthen his position he had immediately to marry the most eligible Yorkist princess, Elizabeth. The couple were happy together, and produced several children, but she died, leaving only one young son still alive, and for the last seven years of the reign the fate of the dynasty hung on that boy. The fact that Henry survived at all was largely due to amazing luck. At Bosworth Field he faced a bigger army under an experienced soldier king, and only won the battle because Richard gambled everything on what turned out to be a suicidal charge into the middle of Henry's men. As a result, Richard was not only defeated but killed, instead of escaping to carry on resistance. He left no children to avenge him, and the next heir along, Edward, Earl of Warwick, was a child whom Henry captured just after winning the throne. Henry let him grow up in prison and then cut off his head. The next in line was John, Earl of Lincoln, and he did rebel in 1487, but was promptly killed in battle. Henry himself had no brothers or cousins to envy his position, and only one uncle, Jasper Tudor, who was steadfastly loyal and in any case had no claim to the throne.

In managing his kingdom, Henry faced the dual problem of having no knowledge of it and no acquaintance with most of its nobility. Unlike other invaders, such as William the Conqueror, he had owned no land abroad from which to bring experienced administrators. He had to learn on the job. He was not, however, totally inexperienced in royal government; the problem was that he was trained for the wrong kingdom. While in exile in France, he had sat on the royal council and impressed ministers with his intelligence, energy and grasp of business. In 1498 a Spanish ambassador reported that Henry wished he could run England in the same manner as French kings governed their country; but knew that he could not. He set out to learn how English law, Parliaments and finances worked, and did, displaying a huge appetite for just those aspects of government which bored most rulers. In particular, he personally checked most aspects of royal administration, auditing and initialling all accounts and making all grants of land and office. The great lesson of the Wars of the Roses had been that a king needed to keep the nobles happy while allowing none of them to become powerful enough to endanger him. He also had to maintain public order without making local magnates feel bullied or cramped. Henry therefore set out to weaken the English aristocracy without making any direct attack on them as a group.

He let them decrease in numbers by making an absolute minimum of new creations, so that the overall size of the peerage declined from fifty-five to forty-two titles during his reign and those above the rank of baron halved in number. He rewarded the few who had supported him in his bid for the throne with mighty offices, but not huge estates, so that they had no power to hand on to their sons. One by one, most regions were put under formal or informal councils of nobles, gentry and bishops, instead of under a single magnate. Most famously, he made the peerage deposit sums of money as guarantees of good behaviour; by the end of his reign four-fifths of them had been treated like this. The great families who had fought the Wars of the Roses were carefully stripped of power and money, so that no single noble was left wealthy enough to challenge the Crown by himself. He encouraged the nobles to play a full part in both central and local government, but to wear themselves out in dull and routine work. Very few were allowed to have any role in the actual making of policy, and to balance their power in the administration he also upgraded the authority of three other groups: churchmen, lawyers and local gentry. The first two supplied his most trusted servants in central government, while the latter were taken into royal service in the counties, in large numbers.

Henry was no tyrant. He only executed people for outright rebellion, did not take hostages, and cared deeply about law enforcement. Above all, he believed in consultation, working with a larger royal council, with Parliaments, and with less formal gatherings of nobles and townsmen. He kept an exciting court, with tournaments, pageants and dances, built or rebuilt beautiful palaces, at Richmond and Greenwich, and constructed gorgeous chapels, at Westminster Abbey and Windsor Castle. There is absolutely no doubt that his way of ruling was effective; but there is equally little doubt that it made him an unpopular, isolated and rather tragic figure, whose death was greeted with relief. The popular image of him as turning into an old misery is absolutely right, and it seems that his addiction to work broke his health. His eyesight certainly deteriorated under the strain of checking all those records, and he once shot a chicken by mistake, under the impression that it was a wild bird. His portraits show a man pushing himself into premature old age. His fear and suspicion of the world was built into two new royal institutions: the Privy Chamber and the Yeomen of the Guard. The first was a private suite of rooms, into which the king could retire from the rest of the court, staffed only by menial servants. The second was a permanent bodyguard for the king, of a kind unknown before in English history.

What is more, if kingship is a matter of morality (and most people certainly thought so at the time), then Henry could be a bad king. His system of binding people over side-stepped the law courts, because if he believed that somebody had misbehaved he simply pocketed the money deposited. This effectively fined the person without any legal process. When individuals challenged his right to demand feudal dues from them, his agents bullied and bribed juries to return verdicts in his favour. As for his followers, a suspicious, fearful and sometimes inaccessible king created a perfect environment for vicious court intrigues. A succession of his most prominent servants were disgraced and then imprisoned or executed, and these feuds spilled out into the provinces. As Henry rewarded his followers so little with land and money, to get rich they needed to exploit government office for all they were worth, and this increased the intensity of local power struggles. At times areas like the Midlands and the Welsh borders were torn apart by rival politicians as badly as they had been at the opening of the Wars of the Roses.

In many respects, therefore, Henry belongs to the category of unpopular and resented monarchs; but unlike most of those, he managed to die in power. This was partly due to luck and lack of effective rivals, and partly due to his intelligence, but he also had social changes on his side. The traditional power of the English nobility had been badly disrupted by the civil wars. The huge turnover in aristocrats holding power had caused local gentry to separate off from them and form links with each other instead. This made it much harder for nobles to build up regional military bases and much easier for monarchs to employ gentlemen directly as royal servants. More than ever before, the royal court was becoming the centre of political intrigue and power-broking, and royal favour was much more important to local people. Access to the king was therefore crucially important, and more restricted. In manipulating and reinforcing these developments, Henry was adroitly going with the flow of developments. In that sense he was part of a new monarchy that had been produced by the Wars of the Roses. In another, however, his style of government was unique, for nobody else has ever ruled like Henry VII. His whole reign was one usurpation crisis, policed by emergency methods. In yet another sense, he himself introduced a kind of monarchy that was to last as long as his dynasty did: a series of strong and determined rulers who lacked an adult male heir. No Tudor ever broke out of that mould, and England between 1485 and 1603 was to enjoy both the constant rule of unusually able monarchs, and to fear a renewed plunge into civil war at the end of each reign.

Resistance and Rebellion

Henry VII died of old age, enabling his young son Henry VIII to make the first natural and uncontested succession to the English monarchy for eighty years. The previous four kings had all failed in this fundamental achievement. On the other hand, it took almost his entire reign to see off challenges from rival claimants to the throne. He may have died in peace, but he was quite incapable of living in it. In the course of his first sixteen years as king, he survived four invasions, two large rebellions and eight conspiracies. That is a record unsurpassed by any other English monarch.

In large part, Henry's problems were created by the fact that he was a usurper with a weak claim to the throne, and by his inability to be the kind of king who was loved by his subjects. He may have rejoiced in a lack of effective rivals from the genuine royal family, but instead he was challenged by young men pretending to be Yorkist princes who were in fact already either in prison or dead. One of these, Lambert Simnel, claimed to be the Earl of Warwick, and fronted a serious invasion which was defeated at East Stoke in 1487. Another, a Fleming called Perkin Warbeck, pretended to be the younger brother of the Yorkist boy king, Edward V.

These two lads were the tragic 'princes in the Tower', who had disappeared in the Tower of London in 1483 after Edward was deposed, and he and his brother imprisoned, by Richard III. As Henry himself recognized these boys as having a better claim than himself, and as he could not prove that Richard had murdered them, he was in serious trouble if enough people believed Warbeck. The pretender represented a problem for Henry for seven years, both by launching invasions supported by foreign powers and by stirring up plots in Henry's own court, until he was hanged in 1499.

To survive, Henry had to reward the few powerful people who had supported him at Bosworth and to make new friends. The essential trick was to bring in new adherents without offending the old, and Henry proved much better at the former than the latter. He added large numbers of former Yorkists to his government, and won over the most valuable surviving supporters of Richard III. On the other hand, he also alienated Sir William Stanley, a member of the family which, by changing sides at Bosworth Field to defend Henry when Richard charged him, had given Henry the Crown. Stanley was rewarded with the key court office of Lord Chamberlain, but nine years later he was executed for conspiring to murder his royal master. Henry had also to strike a different balancing act, by levying enough taxes from his people to wage successful war and yet not provoking them into rebellion. Here again he was not entirely successful, for Yorkshire revolted in 1489 against taxation imposed to fight France, and the whole of the West Country rose in 1497 against that demanded to attack Scotland. None the less, the regionalism of England meant that neither rebellion was supported by the commons in other parts of the realm, as these did not feel currently overtaxed. As a result loyal forces could crush each one. In victory he blended mercy and severity, killing determined or dangerous enemies, but giving both Simnel and Warbeck chances to redeem themselves once they were captured, and fining the commoners who rose against taxation rather than hanging them.

Henry therefore made some mistakes, but never a fatal one, and this was largely due to his own personal strengths. He was tall, strong and well built, with a regal bearing. He was also energetic, physically brave, conscientious, ruthless and patently clever. The threat to him from pretenders and rebels was serious, but it diminished with time. His greatest knife-edge moment was at Bosworth Field, where he would have been defeated and killed had Richard not made that crucial error. The battle of East Stoke two years later was almost as hard, but nothing in the 1490s was as desperate. His third battle, against the Western rebels of 1497, overcame an enemy which was outnumbered, badly equipped and already demoralized. None of the court plots against him ripened because his system of informers was so effective. The real failures among English kings were those rulers whose problems got worse as their reigns went on; Henry, by contrast, had enough ability to reinforce his advantages and push through to victory. If he never won the love of his subjects, he managed to become accepted by them.

Public Finance
One of the remarkable features of Henry VII is that he is associated more with his financial policies than any other English

monarch. After his death, two prominent intellectuals who had lived during his reign, Sir Thomas More and the Italian scholar Polydore Vergil, published their opinion that his worst failing had been avarice. A century later, Sir Francis Bacon, who wrote what long remained the standard history of Henry's regime, said that greed was its main characteristic.

Henry certainly faced a genuine problem: that the income of the English Crown had dropped by 1485 to about half of what it had been a hundred years before, as a result of civil war, loss of territory, a falling population and trade depressions. One of Henry's tasks as a king was to increase it, and he did so both by trying to reform the system of taxation and by working the existing sources of revenue as hard as possible. He paid minute attention to the process: no other English monarch has personally inspected the Crown's financial dealings as Henry did. During the Wars of the Roses, rulers had taken to using their Chamber, the inner part of the royal household, as their main fiscal institution. This was a natural response of monarchs involved in civil war, who needed to be able to take their financial administration with them on campaign. Henry never felt secure enough to stop doing this, and it suited his anxious, obsessive personality. He got huge grants of war taxation from Parliament, larger in total than Henry V had received for the campaigns with which he conquered a quarter of France. These were sometimes based on new assessments of national wealth and income, and, in addition, he tapped the resources of the Church more than any previous monarch.

The financial records are not good enough for anybody to prove how well Henry did overall. What is certain is that all branches of revenue increased in the course of his reign, and that by his last five years the total royal income seems to have averaged £110,000 to £120,000 a year. That probably beats any peacetime figure from the late fifteenth century, and was about three times that of the 1450s. Henry definitely accumulated a significant surplus, though we can't say how big a one. It was still a third less than the royal revenue of the 1350s, but much more of it derived from the Crown's own resources. In particular, Henry built up the biggest landed estate of any king since William the Conqueror, giving him £40,000 a year. Once again, however, being successful did not make Henry popular. The ideal king of his time was supposed to be generous as well as efficient, and to be remembered as a conqueror of foreign foes and a peace-giver to his people; not as an accountant. Too much of Henry's way of ruling seemed to be about money: his policy of demanding bonds from the nobility and of fining rebels en masse were two such aspects of it. His notorious agents, Richard Empson and Edmund Dudley, hunted down even quite humble people who could be held to owe sums to the Crown, stretching the law to make such claims and imprisoning the victims until they paid. Henry sold government offices on a scale unique in English history, and once effectively tried to auction his mother off in marriage to the highest bidder. This was a regime to which grabbing cash consistently seemed to mean more than winning hearts.

It is easy to suggest why Henry behaved like this: he had, after all, spent his formative years as a penniless exile. The classic rich skinflint is somebody who knew poverty and insecurity as a child, and cannot lose the habit of going after money and stockpiling it even after making the first million. The fact remains, however, that this was not the image that either medieval or early modern Europe held of how a king should be. Henry's enduring reputation for rapacity and meanness remains thoroughly deserved.

Foreign Policy

Henry's dealings with foreign powers are best set in a long-term context, which reveals the scale of the difficulties that he faced. Back in 1400 the strongest power in north-western Europe had been France, which was flanked by two lesser states, England and the Duchy of Burgundy. Burgundy controlled most of what are now the Netherlands and Belgium, and therefore the European coast to the east of England. Any state that is personally controlled by a hereditary ruler – as all these were – is going to be subject to a lottery of sperms, germs and brain cells, generated by the accidents that individuals and families can suffer. In the early fifteenth century, England and Burgundy did very well out of this lottery: to use the metaphor of a dice game, each threw a double six. England did so by getting two royal brothers, Henry V and John, Duke of Bedford, who had exceptional military ability, while Burgundy had a duke, Philip the Good, who was not only equally able, but exceptionally long lived. France, however, suddenly threw a one, when its own king, Charles VI, went mad. This meant that the kingdom fell to pieces, enabling both England and Burgundy to grow much more powerful at its expense; England in particular established itself as the new superpower of the region, conquering some of the richest French provinces and taking Paris. After this, however, England threw a one, three times running, as both Henry V and Bedford died prematurely and the new king, Henry VI, proved completely incapable of ruling. France however now threw a double six, producing two clever and aggressive kings in succession.

As a result of these dynastic accidents, between 1435 and 1453 the French were able to drive the English off the Continent, leaving them with the single port of Calais. Things got worse when some of the English nobility, despairing of Henry VI, tried to grab and fix the dice for themselves, by putting in a better king. The result was a collapse into thirty years of intermittent civil conflict, to which the nineteenth-century novelist, Sir Walter Scott, gave the name the 'Wars of the Roses'. The breaking of English power left France and Burgundy to square up to each other in a fight for supremacy, but this made England's problems infinitely worse. The French and Burgundians repeatedly intervened in its civil wars by supporting opposite sides in them. Henry was himself the last beneficiary of this process, because Richard III had been friendly with Burgundy and so the French had given him the means to invade England and win the Battle of Bosworth.

This success itself left him with chronic problems. The most obvious was that the Dowager Duchess of Burgundy, Margaret, immediately began trying to remove him, both because he was a French candidate and because she was the sister of Richard III. She proceeded to sponsor first Lambert Simnel and then Perkin Warbeck to claim his throne. The second problem was that France was still regarded by most English people as their natural enemy, so that if he were to be accepted by them he had to shed an image as a French puppet. He had also to come to some understanding with Burgundy, which was England's main trading partner. France, moreover, had a specific objective in putting Henry on to the English throne: to neutralize England while it conquered the semi-independent Duchy of Brittany. To do this would give it a firm grip on the entire southern shore of the English Channel, for the first time in history, enabling it to strike at any part of the south British coastline. This was something which no conscientious English monarch could ever permit, and so Henry could not pay the price that the French expected for their support of him. In opposing them, however, he had to reckon with the new weakness of his kingdom, both absolutely and relative to the huge new size and power of France. In the 1430s the disposable income of the English monarchy had at times actually exceeded that of the French. By the time that he won at Bosworth, the French royal revenue was six times the size of his, and by the time that he died it was seven times larger and France had over three times the manpower of England. This terrific handicap would only be reduced if the French got another unlucky throw of the dynastic dice, but they did not. Between 1429 and 1560 every French monarch was a strong and able ruler.

Another problem was Scotland. For 200 years its rulers had been locked into almost constant hostility with England, which meant that if Henry went to war with a continental superpower he was likely to find himself fighting the Scots as well; and they were the only state that had a land frontier with England. Furthermore, he had to reckon with the specific issue of Berwick on Tweed, which had been medieval Scotland's most important port. During the long wars with England it had repeatedly changed hands, and possession of it became a point of honour to both nations. Henry found it on his hands, as the future Richard III had recaptured it in 1482, and so he automatically faced a resentful Scottish nation.

Another part of Henry's jigsaw of difficulties was Ireland. Under the Yorkists this had not been a problem. The kings of England were supposed to be its overlords, and nobles of English or Norman origin owned about half the island. The Yorkist policy had been simply to subcontract royal power to the strongest Anglo-Norman family, the Fitzgeralds. Their resources could not be matched by any other Irish magnates, and they kept Ireland from being a problem for the English kings. Henry was now faced with the stark choice of keeping the Fitzgeralds in charge of Irish government, which they might use against him because of their Yorkist loyalties, or replacing them and so ensuring their hostility. Within two years they had almost got rid of him, by joining with Margaret of Burgundy to support the invasion of Lambert Simnel.

Had these been the only factors providing the context for Henry's foreign policies, then he would probably not have survived, but he had others working in his favour. The greatest was that although France kept throwing high scores with the dynastic dice, Burgundy and Scotland did not. In Burgundy, Duke Philip the Good had been succeeded by the aptly named Charles the Reckless, who got himself killed in battle in 1477, leaving only a daughter who married the future Holy Roman Emperor, Maximilian of Habsburg. His realm was divided between Maximilian and the French. Maximilian got most of the Netherlands, but was not especially interested in them, and only prepared to make trouble for Henry if the latter became inconvenient. The Yorkist princess Margaret was left dependent on her personal wealth to fund attempts to unseat the Tudors. Likewise, the Scottish king who was ruling when Henry won England was James III, who succeeded three years

later in provoking some of his nobles into a rebellion in which
he got killed. He left a son, James IV, who was too young to
rule, and so during the crucial years in which Henry was establishing himself the Scots were not inclined to attack. England
was also lucky in that the main ambitions of the new powerful
French state lay not in northern Europe but in Italy, the richest
and most sophisticated part of the Continent. In 1494 they
invaded it, turning their backs on the English for the first time
in over two centuries, and once there they became involved in a
long and exhausting series of wars with another rising superpower, Spain. The Spanish proved a much more effective
balance to French power than Burgundy.

Henry's best policy, in such a situation, was to woo as many
foreign friends as possible, and avoid prolonged warfare, while
still posing as a credible fighting force. Between 1489 and 1492
he worked hard to keep the French from gaining Brittany, only
to find himself let down by all his allies and left to invade
France alone. He therefore withdrew his invasion force in
return for a handsome payment from the French, and after that
he avoided outright confrontation with them while encouraging other powers to fight them instead. He slowly bribed
and bullied both Maximilian and the Scots into cooperation,
and in 1503 made the first formal treaty between Scotland and
England since 1328, in which James IV married his daughter
Margaret. In Ireland he used similar tactics to bring the
Fitzgeralds to heel, imposing restraints on the ability of the
Irish Parliament to make laws without English approval which
were to last until the late eighteenth century. He then restored
the leading Fitzgerald to act as his deputy, and the whole family
remained loyal for the rest of his reign. All these achievements
were made by waging diplomacy with the intensity that other
rulers brought to war. During Henry's reign, payments for
ambassadors became a recurrent item of state expenditure for
the first time in English history.

The one thing that Henry failed utterly to accomplish was to
re-establish England as a great power and as an ally undoubtedly

worth having. France did swallow up Brittany, making itself even more powerful, and England more vulnerable, than before. Henry's reign marks a transition between his nation's medieval image as an aggressive monarchy, seizing pieces of Europe, and its modern one as a fortress island, closed off from the Continent. On the one occasion on which he prepared for a sustained foreign war – against Scotland in 1496 – he bungled it. He went for overkill, by preparing a huge army and fleet with the biggest siege train ever assembled by an English king, and the taxation needed for this just drove the West Country into rebellion. All the resources assembled for the war had to be spent on crushing Henry's own subjects, and his peace treaty with the Scots in 1503 represented a huge climb-down. By marrying Margaret to their king he implicitly treated them as equals in a way that previous English kings had scorned, and added a new risk to the game of dynastic dicing by giving them a claim to the throne of England. It could fairly be said that Henry made the best possible job of a very difficult and vulnerable position, and showed flexibility and common sense. His policies are, however, much easier to understand and justify from a modern perspective than from that of his own age, which preferred flamboyant and aggressive kings who enlarged their realms and enriched their nobility. In the judgement of his time, Henry was the second-rate ruler of a second-rate nation.

2

HENRY VIII (1509–47)

The regime of the second Tudor monarch was one of the most effective governments that England has ever had. It accomplished things that at first sight might have been considered impossible, and emerged from each process of change richer and stronger than before. It was genuinely revolutionary, on a scale unique for an early modern monarchy. It marked the beginning of the Church of England, the Irish Question, the English Bible, the Privy Council and the power of Parliament over all issues. It ended English monasticism and produced the largest redistribution of land in recorded English history, surpassing that at the Norman Conquest. It incorporated Wales into the English system of government on equal terms, produced an efficient new means of war taxation, and gave English sovereigns, ever since, the title of Defender of the Faith. Not for 100 years, since Henry V, had England produced a king with such an appetite for greatness, and the eighth Henry had ambitions beyond those of the fifth. Not for 200 years, since Edward I, had there been a ruler who combined such comprehensive egotism with such a readiness to demolish the traditional boundaries of political life. It is perfectly permissible, and indeed natural, to regret or deplore many aspects of the reign's achievements, and to question the value of some. None the less, there is still no denying the scale and importance of them; nor would they ever have been attempted, let alone achieved, by a ruler without Henry's peculiar combination of qualities.

The Ministry of Cardinal Wolsey

Thomas Wolsey, Henry's first great minister, has traditionally received a bad press from historians. To Protestants – and Protestant history was dominant in England from the mid-sixteenth to the mid-twentieth century – he represented everything that was wrong with the early Tudor Church. For Catholics, he was a useful person to blame for the attack on their religion which immediately followed his downfall. In the key school textbook of the 1950s and 1960s, written by Sir Geoffrey Elton, he was summed up as 'the most disappointing man who ever held great power in England'. These attitudes began to alter after 1970, commencing with the work of Jack Scarisbrick, who suggested that Wolsey deserved, if not three cheers, at least two. In 1990 Peter Gwyn published a biography which defended Wolsey against every charge made against him. Most specialists have stopped short of the high-tide mark of admiration set by Gwyn, but there is no doubt that the twenty-first-century Wolsey is the most attractive to be seen since his death.

His was a sensational rags to riches story. The age of the Renaissance and Reformation was notable in that European states tended to be run by cardinals who were also royal ministers. Wolsey still stands out for the lowness of his birth, the rapidity of his rise to fame, and the length of his service as a minister. His father was a Suffolk grazier, fattening livestock for a living. Young Thomas entered the Church, the single great contemporary career open to a talented poor boy, and got into royal service through the classic staircase of grammar school, Oxford University and a bishop's household. His big break came in 1513, when he revealed his exceptional abilities to understand finance and administration by keeping the royal armies supplied in Henry's first war. This shot him into the prime government post of Lord Chancellor. The skill most needed to run royal government was management, and this was probably the last time in history it could be managed by one person. Henry VII had been such a person, but his son was not, preferring to hand over the day-to-day work to the first individual to show the right mixture of ability and enthusiasm for it; and that was Wolsey. He brought to the job an enormous appetite for work – occasionally staying at his desk for eight hours at a stretch – and huge self-confidence. One of his key tasks was to filter state papers through to Henry, annotating documents and sending extracts of news.

The trouble with this system was that Henry was erratic. Not only did he demand to be in ultimate control of all policy, at least in his own mind, but he would take a sudden interest in the details of administration, without warning. On these occasions he would often overrule Wolsey. This was not just a reflection of the king's inherent instability but of his desire to keep his servants insecure, reminding them of his power to resume control at any time. Wolsey's role, moreover, was not just that of a patient workhorse; he needed to find ways of glorifying the king and making the latter's ambitions come to pass. In this sense, the Chancellor's natural extroversion was part of his appeal to Henry: they were kindred spirits in megalomania. In the actions and attitudes of government, Wolsey's job was to obtain whatever the king felt that he wanted at any particular time. As Henry's wishes, and the context of them, kept changing, his chief minister had to be an opportunist. At home and abroad, his general aim was to win honour and status for Henry, by any means which the moment offered.

Abroad, Henry was the third ruler in the Western European pecking order, after the kings of France and Spain, and so

Wolsey needed to seize any chance to make him look equal to the other two. The great problem here was that England wasn't equal. Like his father, Henry VIII faced a much richer and larger kingdom of France. Unlike his father, by 1517 he was also facing a union between the newly united kingdom of Spain, the Netherlands, and the German territories of the Holy Roman Empire, in the person of the Emperor Charles V – a superstate larger than anything known since ancient Rome. Both these combinations were bigger, wealthier and more efficiently taxed than England. In this situation, a foreign policy that made Henry look glorious – and this was what Henry himself absolutely demanded – had to rest on a large element of bluff. The remarkable thing is that it came as close to success as it did for as long as it did.

Wolsey's first task was to produce the logistics needed to win the war of 1513, and he did, enabling a terrific humiliation of both the traditional enemies, the French and Scots. Of these, the victory over the French was the one which impressed Europe. It involved no large battles and the territorial gains were meagre and temporary, but it made England look like a great power for the first time since the 1440s. It also, however, cost almost £1 million, when the annual income of the state was a little over £100,000. The money had been found by spending Henry VII's accumulated surplus, and now the national coffers were empty. Wolsey therefore had to make peace look more glorious than war, and rhetoric take the place of military muscle. He did so by dressing both up in vast international conferences, hugely ambitious treaties, and royal meetings such as the Field of Cloth of Gold, where Henry met the current King of France. These events combined the political weight and dignity of the modern United Nations with the excitement of the Olympic Games, giving peace-making both the glamour and the drama of war-mongering. Furthermore, England could just about afford them.

Ultimately, they were bound to fail, because nobody except Wolsey wanted peace: Henry, Charles V and the two successive

French kings, Louis XII and Francis I, were all natural warlords. When everyone went back to war in the early 1520s, Wolsey still thought big, aiming at capturing Paris, and at reconquering the medieval French territory of the English Crown. This time, however, the cash resources were not sufficient, and the French resisted effectively. The resulting string of failures marked the true end of the Hundred Years War, with the final writing off of the lost English possessions. There is no doubt that Wolsey's foreign policy ended in absolute failure. By the end of the 1520s England was left completely isolated, lacking any allies or gains for all the fighting and talking of the past sixteen years. England's true weakness had been revealed, and Wolsey himself had acquired a reputation as a braggart, a bully and a deceiver, who told lies, broke verbal promises and added sly small print to treaties. His foreign policy had been unique in its brilliance, flamboyance, ambition and imagination; but it had rested on pretence.

The results of his domestic policies were more mixed. There, as abroad, Wolsey found that the royal financial system was not adequate to support the kind of king that Henry wanted to be. He therefore had either to improve it or to make everybody think that it was better than it was. Being Wolsey, he did both. His great triumph was to implement the first realistic assessment of England's taxable wealth to be made for centuries, on which was based a new form of war taxation called the 'subsidy', which became standard for 100 years. But not only could it not produce enough to match the superpowers, it had to be voted by Parliaments, and Wolsey's combination of arrogance, ostentation and bullying made him unusually ill-suited to managing those. The result was that by the 1520s he could only finance Henry's wars by levying loans forced from propertied people, as well as subsidies, which proved too unpopular to be sustainable. In the end, he and Henry had to scrap their plans for war because their people were not prepared to pay for them, leaving the king helpless in Europe.

By contrast, there is no doubt that Wolsey scored a lasting and tremendous success in the provision of justice. The traditional royal law courts were becoming clogged up with serious overcrowding and delay. Wolsey therefore built up the courts maintained directly by the royal council and ministers to an all-time peak of efficiency. He increased the authority of his own Court of Chancery, and extended the powers of the Court of Star Chamber, staffed by royal councillors, to cover perjury and libel, as well as peace-keeping. He also gave the Star Chamber the role of supervising the whole common law system, and established four new committees of the council to hear cases, which grew into the Court of Requests. All these were lasting improvements to the system, which especially helped relatively poor people. It gave Wolsey a huge extra workload for almost no additional political power or influence.

In addition, he acted with equal energy to remedy the greatest single popular grievance of the age, the appropriation of common lands by the wealthier inhabitants of local communities. In 1517 he launched an initiative never attempted before by any government, a fact-finding commission to discover the true extent of the problem. The result was over 400 prosecutions of rich and powerful individuals, carried on by the state on behalf of the commoners whose rights they had violated. Most of these were successful. It was a stunning display of the willingness of the Crown to defend its weaker subjects, but made Wolsey some dangerous enemies among the stronger. Driven by his interest, towns began to make better provision for their inhabitants in general, helping the poor, laying up stocks of grain for times of famine and cleaning their streets. Thus he made a genuine contribution to the quality of life of the ordinary English.

His final problem was to build up a stronger structure of government without either strengthening his political rivals or outstripping the monarchy's regular resources. Here his trump card was his position in the Church, where the king helped him to obtain the offices of Archbishop of York and

Abbot of St Albans, the nation's richest monastery. Their revenues enabled him to maintain a gigantic household of bright young men, whom he used to carry on the extra work generated by more dynamic government activity. This was to be the Tudor pattern of government, by which top ministers paid staff from their own pockets to avoid increasing the salary bill of the state. Nobody, however, did it on such a scale as Wolsey. What is more contentious is whether he was good for the Church itself, and for the general quality of English religion. He led it, after all, at a time when, from the early 1520s, it was starting to face the challenge of the European Reformation, launched from Germany by Martin Luther. Wolsey's own direct response to that challenge was remarkable for its mildness. He ensured the burning of large quantities of heretical books, but not a single human being, even when under pressure from other churchmen to do so. He himself never undertook any of his personal responsibilities as archbishop and abbot, an unusual neglect of duty at the time. On the other hand, he appointed very able officials to govern them in his place. In his leadership of the Church, it needs to be appreciated that he had limited room for action. Henry's own priorities were to increase royal control of the Church and taxation of it, and it was hard for Wolsey to ask his fellow churchmen to reform the nature of the institution as well, without pushing them into complete opposition. When he tried to inspect the houses of friars in England, with a view to improving them into a defence against Lutheranism, he found that he had no right to do so. What he did do was to alert the Church's leaders to the need for reform and to draw up plans for it. Some of these were to be implemented during the next two decades; but all that Wolsey could do was produce blue-prints and train reformers.

In all these tasks Wolsey's own virtues and vices were of crucial importance. He genuinely enjoyed inflicting humili-ation on people, as one aspect of the relish with which he wielded power over others. People who stood up to him were likely to find themselves bullied, sometimes with petty malice. As a churchman he was less scandalous in his personal life than many European contemporaries, having fewer illegitimate children and accumulating smaller numbers of offices. He was also sincere in the performance of his religious duties. The problem here was that the leaders of the English Church were exceptionally well behaved, so that Wolsey's violation of the official rule of celibacy and his acquisition of wealth were shocking by national standards. His personal flamboyance made his pursuit of worldly pleasures look even more glaring. He pushed Popes into granting him lucrative offices, squabbled with bishops over profits, and thrust his way to the greatest prizes.

In general, Thomas Wolsey was no more greedy, ambitious and corrupt than most high royal servants and most churchmen of his age. What magnified these qualities in him were the ruthless energy, verve and self-promotion with which he set about gratifying them, and the spectacular success with which he did so. Every action that he took to benefit church or state looked like a demonstration of his own authority. Display was expected of a great cleric or minister, but he went over the top. As a politician, he was both more adroit and less ruthless than most. He never forgot that his vital lifeline in office was the trust of the king. When Henry thought that he had made a mistake, which was rare, Wolsey always grovelled shamelessly until he was forgiven. He was constantly challenged by rivals bidding for royal favour, and constantly manipulating or reforming the royal household and council to get rid of them. In the process, however, only one of them actually died, and this was the greatest noble of the realm, the Duke of Buckingham, who was beheaded in 1521 when Henry himself took murderously against him. As in his dealings with heretics, Wolsey was a good deal gentler than the general standards of his time. This still doesn't make him a nice man. To admire Wolsey, it is necessary to value efficiency, intelligence, cunning and ostentation over all other qualities. It is only fair, however, to point out that anybody in whom these other qualities were more in evidence could never have been chief minister to Henry VIII.

One final reflection may help to set Wolsey in perspective. In the early fifteenth century, England was also ruled on behalf of a young king called Henry by a brilliant, hard-working, arrogant, greedy and sensual man who was both a cardinal and a royal minister. This was Cardinal Beaufort. Yet he has always been remembered with general admiration as a great statesman. Could it be that Beaufort was lucky enough to live in a less demanding age, with no Reformation swelling up behind him? Or could it be that he was a member of the royal family, and so everybody expected him to lead and to show off? It may be worth wondering how much of the traditional animosity towards Wolsey has been bound up with the English class system.

The Royal Marriage Crisis

In addition to his failures as a warlord and conqueror, by the late 1520s Henry VIII had failed in another respect that referred directly to his manhood – in the production of an heir. On becoming king, he had impulsively married the widow of his elder brother Arthur, the Spanish princess Catherine of Aragon. The union at first seemed extremely happy, despite the fact that Henry soon displayed a lax sense of marital fidelity, but resulted in only one child which survived infancy, and that was a daughter, Mary. In 1527 he decided at last to get rid of Catherine and marry a new, fertile, queen. He could actually have done so through Wolsey himself, who had accumulated enough delegated authority to settle the whole matter in England. One of the great unanswered questions concerning the whole affair is why he did not, but chose instead to seek an annulment from the highest authority, the Pope himself. It is possible that he believed that only such a ruling would carry complete legal security. It is also possible, however, that to make the supreme head of the Church do his will, in front of the leaders of Europe, suited the ostentation which was the stylistic trademark of both Henry and Wolsey. This view is supported by the grounds on which Henry chose to make his case. Wolsey had told him that he could get what he wanted on a legal technicality, an apparent error in the original papal order allowing the king to marry Catherine. Instead, Henry decided to fight over the interpretation of Scripture, and to prove his superiority in it. Back in 1521 he had written a book to defend the traditional teachings of the Church against those of Martin Luther. It had been Wolsey's suggestion that he do so, and it duly netted the king another title, of Defender of the Faith, conferred by a grateful papacy at a time when war and diplomacy were bringing Henry little glory. The exercise seems to have given him a taste for proving his prowess in theology. Wolsey said that the decision to fight for annulment mainly on scriptural grounds was Henry's own, and its essential idiocy surely confirms this judgement; for in theological terms it was too shaky to win easily unless the court concerned were blatantly in its favour.

For a while it seemed as though a papal court actually would be, because just as Henry decided on his suit, the Emperor Charles V quarrelled with the reigning Pope, Clement VII, and sacked Rome. The Pope was now the emperor's prisoner, and likely to do anything that the English king wanted if Henry would rescue him. Henry and Wolsey, however, did not have the resources to attack Charles directly, and so tried instead to exploit Clement's misfortune by declaring that the papal authority was now suspended. Wolsey attempted to take over the Church himself, summoning the other cardinals to a meeting under his leadership, which would annul Henry's marriage as one item on its agenda. Clement scotched that plan by forbidding it, and Henry and Wolsey tried instead to get other European nations to rescue the Pope by force, with English encouragement but not English participation. Over the following two years, as Charles V defeated these attempts, Clement slowly concluded that he could best regain freedom and influence by befriending his captor Charles; and Charles, as the nephew of Catherine of Aragon, was determined to prevent Henry's annulment. Wolsey strove hard, instead, to get the French to take up its cause, by getting Henry to promise to marry a French princess once he was free to do so. This was indeed the one price which could have bought French support, and it failed because, at this point, Wolsey found out that his monarch was determined to marry one of his own courtiers, a nobody called Anne Boleyn.

There was now no real hope of obtaining the annulment, and any alternative easy resolution to the crisis was forfeited when all the men concerned in it, at home and abroad, found themselves trapped between two extraordinary women. On one side was Catherine, who surprised most people with the courage and tenacity with which she strove to remain queen. Clement's great hope was that she would agree to enter a nunnery, which would automatically dissolve her union with the king and let everybody off the hook; but she refused point-blank to do so. On the other was Anne, proving herself to be a powerful and determined politician and steeling the king's will to marry her at virtually any cost. By 1529, Wolsey's complete failure to obtain the annulment was clear. Given Henry's nature, the only thing that could have saved Wolsey's position as chief minister after that would have been the intervention of powerful friends on his behalf, and he had never made any. This was partly because of his own bossy nature, and partly because one of his chief attractions, in Henry's eyes, was his utter dependence on royal favour. It was his final misfortune that his failure had made a lasting enemy of Anne, the one person capable of a more intimate and potent relationship with Henry than Wolsey could ever form himself. None the less, although the cardinal was stripped off his political office and his palaces, he retained his dignity and wealth as Archbishop of York, which carried the status of a rich noble. He could probably have enjoyed them in peace until the end of his days. Instead, old, tired and ill as he was, he intrigued relentlessly to

regain political power. By the summer of 1530 he had decided
that he could never do so as long as Anne was around, and
began trying to ally with Catherine and the emperor to ruin
her. Instead, it was probably Anne who ruined him, by
revealing his plotting to Henry and playing on the king's
ingrained hostility to any servant who attempted to undermine
declared royal policy. Wolsey was arrested, and collapsed and
died of natural causes on his way to trial. Had he faced
condemnation and execution instead, he would have died as a
failed politician, and not as a martyr. He had always used the
Church as a motor for secular ends, even though he tried to do
it good on the way. In 1530, at last given the chance to devote
himself to it, and to his soul, he still reached out instinctively
for the state – and the state destroyed him.

By the time of Wolsey's death, Henry had been left with a
straight choice: to give up hope of escaping his marriage in the
near future or to follow the example of the Lutherans and the
other Protestant movements now appearing on the Continent,
and cast off papal authority. He might have played a waiting
game, for a new Pope or a change of relations between the
current one and emperor, but this suited neither his nature nor
his desire to wed Anne and sire an heir. Instead, the situation
held out the temptation to compensate for his humiliations on
the European scene during the past decade and become the first
monarch in Western or Central Europe to renounce papal
authority and set himself up as the direct mediator between his
people and their deity. This would at once pay back Clement and
give himself a power and sanctity sought by neither of his rivals
abroad and none of his English predecessors. To somebody of
Henry's personality, it was an irresistible temptation.

The Henrician Reformation

Between the mid-nineteenth and the mid-twentieth centuries,
there was a remarkable consensus among historians concerning
the pre-Reformation Church in England. It was that the once
vibrant and dynamic Christianity of the Middle Ages had run

down into a complex of lax and depopulating monasteries, worldly and absentee bishops, ignorant parish clergy and a popular religion bogged down in superstition and fear, focused on the cult of material objects and on buying a way out of the terrors of Purgatory, a place of torment where sins were purged away, which was presumed to await most people on death. These views were based on contemporary criticisms, by educated laity and prominent churchmen who were to produce both Protestant and Catholic leaders in the struggle that followed. The division among historians was over the remedy. Most scholars followed the dominant English tradition, of declaring that Protestantism had been an effective and appropriate one; modern Catholics, of course, argued that an overhaul within the existing doctrinal and structural framework would have been more appropriate. At least both sides had the same starting point.

That point vanished during the 1970s, because of a practical development in research techniques. A proliferation of county record offices made huge quantities of local sources easily available to scholars, drawing their attention to categories of material – the records of church courts, visitations, parish finances and wills – that had been relatively neglected before. At the same time, the expansion of the British university system, and the establishment of the doctoral thesis as the main qualification for a post in it, propelled an unprecedented number of historians onto them. By the 1980s, enough local studies had been published to support broader surveys of the results. They were undertaken first by Christopher Haigh and then by Jack Scarisbrick and Eamon Duffy, and revealed the early Tudor Church to have been one of the most successful and popular branches of Western Christendom. The monasteries were in slight trouble, hit by a general slump in population and agriculture and by a relative decline in support from the laity. They were still, however, almost all viable institutions. The friars were in worse financial trouble, but remained popular and dynamic. One of the reasons for the relative subtraction of support for these regular clergy was a boom in the popularity of new institutions. In the case of the rich, these were chantries, chapels where prayers were offered for the founder's soul, and in the case of commoners, parish guilds. The latter could be joined by all but the poorest people, and were open to most age groups and both sexes. Each member paid a small subscription per year to retain a priest to pray for the souls of its members. They afforded the joint comforts of a club and an insurance policy.

The parish was another institution flourishing in this period, its church being the main building of the local community. Parish accounts prove that churches were being constantly rebuilt and embellished at this time, with money provided by individual and collective efforts. The parish was also increasingly the centre of communal festivity and celebration. By 1520 it was the dominant custom in villages and provincial towns to meet the expenses of keeping up the liturgy and fabric by holding regular parties, dances and games. Another great focus of religious enthusiasm and loyalty was the cult of saints, who were thought to operate as powerful intercessors on behalf of their devotees. They seemed to provide ordinary people with personal friends and patrons in heaven. Many had special responsibility for curing particular illnesses or looking after particular occupations or age groups. There were almost as many female as male saints, and each parish church had not only a patron saint but side-chapels for the cults of up to twenty more. Shrines containing their relics or images were targets for pilgrimage, an activity which combined the pleasure of religious reassurance and a summer holiday. For those who wanted their help outside the formal parish structure, there were wayside chapels and holy wells. The church courts were cheap and fast compared with the royal courts and accordingly more popular. They were heavily used by ordinary people to deal with neighbourhood quarrels and slander and to enforce communal codes of good behaviour. Parish priests were generally commoners drawn from the district in which they served, so that they understood their neighbours. They were not expected to be very learned, because their job was to offer up ritual on behalf of their parish, especially in the regular enactment of the mass. Some were personally unpopular, but there was little overall tension between clergy and laity at the local level. Preaching was provided by the friars. The Church also remained, as spectacularly illustrated in the case of Wolsey, the surest means for a talented commoner to rise to wealth and power.

If the true picture of pre-Reformation English religion was so rosy, then the obvious problem is how to explain the need for the Reformation at all. Here four other factors have to be taken into account. The first was that, since the fourteenth century, England had harboured its own brand of radical heresy, known to the orthodox by the insulting general name of Lollardy (i.e. gabbling). To some extent these Lollards do matter as ancestors to English Protestantism, as some of their ideas, especially their hatred of the mass and the cult of saints, were to correspond to particular features of England's Reformation. They were not, however, a serious menace to the pre-Reformation Church. They were a small minority of the population, concentrated in a few areas of the south-east and often in a few families there. They were remarkably, and courageously, tenacious, but isolated and unpopular. Their main priority was not evangelism but survival.

In addition, the early Tudor Church did have clashes of interest with particular groups of laity. In general, lay people were becoming better educated in the later Middle Ages, more inclined to think about religion for themselves and more inclined to push for top administrative jobs, traditionally held by clerics. Common lawyers in particular were fighting a range war with the clergy over jurisdiction. Nobles were inclined to get touchy about the political power of bishops every time that the latter attempted to call the tune of policy-making as well as shouldering the tasks of government. Both could get a hearing from kings at moments when the latter were getting on badly with the papacy. More generally, the educated laity were starting to express some concern, and contempt, for aspects of popular piety, such as pilgrimage and the cult of saints, which they felt to be peripheral to true religion.

It is also quite true that some prominent churchmen complained about the failings of the Church in England. It is important to note, however, that they generally recognized that it was in need of further improvement, rather than essentially rotten, and that it was an unusually successful part of the Church as a whole. They deplored the very characteristics of it that recent historians have found so impressive: its localism, diversity and popular dynamism. What they wanted was something more structurally uniform and cohesive, better supervised and more focused on the Trinity and the essential doctrines of Christian salvation. They worried deeply that it was getting out of control, and becoming too diluted by popular wishes and local traditions and too preoccupied with externals.

The fourth factor followed on from this, and was the most important: that what was to become known as Protestantism presented the English with a wholly different way of approaching worship and the problem of salvation. To simplify this, it taught that all that was needed to reach heaven was to avoid and repent sin, and to have a genuine faith in Christ, as defined, in the last analysis, by the Bible. Purgatory did not exist, the intercession of saints was unnecessary, and most of the ceremonies of the medieval Church were either superfluous or dangerous. To the credit of the Reformation, it did not push over a decayed and tottering edifice, but seized, gutted and totally refurbished a strong and viable one. It did not convert, in the main, those who were lukewarm about the old church or in personal dispute with its members. It won over people who had formerly been enthusiastic about traditional religion: to adopt Diarmaid MacCulloch's phrase, white-hot Catholics became white-hot Protestants, and the most dynamic geographical centres of the old Church (such as East Anglia) became powerhouses of the new one. This is why the story and the study of the English Reformation are now even more exciting than before.

This is part of the context for Henry VIII's treatment of the Church, but another is provided by previous royal policy towards it. The Yorkist kings had, on the whole, bought the support of churchmen for their seizure of the throne by confirming and extending many of the Church's privileges within English society. Henry VII set about restricting these as part of his work of restoring the traditional strength of the monarchy. In particular, he increasingly sought to extend the power of the royal courts of justice over clergy. Henry VIII carried on this policy, and began to provoke protests that he was taking it too far. In 1510 the national assembly of English churchmen, Convocation, protested that its members were being threatened by 'wicked men'. Two years later a council of high clerics sitting at Rome angrily discussed the encroachment of English royal power on ecclesiastical privileges, and in 1514 two papal declarations called on the church in general to defend itself against secular rulers. In the next year there was almost a full-scale showdown. The flashpoint was the latest Act of Parliament restricting the legal privileges of clergy. The Abbot of Winchcombe, in Gloucestershire, denounced it, and with it the power of all royal courts over people in holy orders. Henry set up the warden of the English Franciscan friars, Henry Standish, to argue against him. The current House of Commons demanded that the abbot retract his words, whereupon Convocation insisted that Standish do the same. The royal judges declared that Convocation was breaking the law of the land.

An explosion was prevented by Wolsey's elevation to the office of Cardinal Legate of the Pope, in stages between 1515 and 1518. This managed to preserve all the outward forms of papal authority while laying the Church in England open to royal taxation and management as never before. In ceremonial and theoretical terms, it made Wolsey the equal of Henry. Each time that they appeared together on state occasions, the banners of the papacy, representing Wolsey's authority, were placed alongside those of the king. In practice, Wolsey never forgot that he was the king's servant. There is no doubt, likewise, that Wolsey's legatine office represented a major concession by the papacy rather than a compromise, granted at a moment when the current Pope needed English help against the French. The Pope concerned, and those who immediately followed, soon realized that it had not earned them much in return, as both Henry and Wolsey paid little regard or honour to them and neglected to build up a party at the papal court. This of course cost them both very dear when they needed papal goodwill to annul Henry's marriage, and the resulting removal of Wolsey destroyed the existing solution to the problem of the relationship between Church and Crown. It is not surprising that, under these circumstances, Henry felt that he had a straight choice between a humiliating submission to the papal will and a direct takeover of the Church in England. Given his personality, there was only one course to take.

In some respect, the Henrician Reformation resembled not so much a programme as a series of toppling dominoes. Between 1531 and 1535 Henry obtained a series of Acts of Parliament, replacing the Pope's power over the Church in England with his own, and declaring it treason to oppose this step. Examples were then made of individuals who had emerged as the most prominent defenders of papal authority, and who were now tried and executed: the most famous, finally canonized as Catholic saints, were the Bishop of Rochester, John Fisher, and the statesman and political philosopher, Sir Thomas More. Having taken over the Church, Henry had to justify his new authority by reforming it to take account of some of the most vehement criticisms made during the previous three decades. In 1536, accordingly, he obtained a parliamentary statute dissolving the smaller monasteries, with the declared aim of improving and preserving those which survived. Convocation issued a statement of belief concerning salvation, the sacraments and Purgatory which mixed ideas from the traditional Church and different kinds of continental reformer. The Crown followed by abolishing the feasts of

minor saints. Though very limited, these measures were sufficient to provoke both considerable popular resentment and
fear of much more drastic changes to follow. The result was the
biggest English rebellion of the entire sixteenth century, the
Pilgrimage of Grace, which covered the northern third of the
realm and had to be talked away rather than repressed directly.

Once this work was done, and the leaders executed, Henry
pushed forward with further reforms. Between 1538 and 1540
the remaining monasteries and the friaries were all dissolved,
pilgrimage abolished and the cults of saints' relics, shrines and
images suppressed. In part, these measures suited Henry's own
inclinations, for he had never been personally enthusiastic
about any of these features of traditional religion. They had
also been among the aspects of it which had drawn most criticism from proponents of reform. There may also, however,
have been contingent factors behind the new moves. Monks
and friars had proved to be the most determined opponents of
the royal takeover of the Church and the subsequent reforms,
and northern abbeys were prominent in the Pilgrimage of
Grace. Henry's savagery against them smacked of retaliation,
but there was also something of fear in it.

The surrender of the monasteries brought the Crown huge
amounts of lucrative land, at a time when it was acutely
vulnerable to enemies at home and abroad. Indeed, at the end of
1538 the worst-case situation came about in foreign affairs, as
Charles V and the French made friends at the plea of the Pope,
in order to prepare a joint campaign against heretical England.
This moment of rapprochement was short-lived, but its impact
on Henry's nerves is visible along the English sea coast to this
day. A hugely expensive building programme was commenced,
which sealed off the approaches to most harbours and
anchorages between East Anglia and the toe of Cornwall with
forts of the latest design, built to mount heavy guns and with-
stand their fire. Their construction and the ruin of the abbeys
were twin royal initiatives. In the same manner, it is possible
that the assault on the cult of saints, and especially of their

relics, was motivated in part by the fear that Henry himself, in executing defenders of the old Church, might be creating future candidates for canonization and veneration. The reforms were enforced by a powerful machinery of interrogation and supervision. A series of commissions and visitations, instituted by the Crown, bishops and archdeacons, summoned representatives of each parish and interrogated them to ensure that they had received the directions and were enacting them in full. At the height of the process of Reformation, an average parish could expect to face two or three of these in every year. Their effects are visible in the parish accounts. In 1538, it was officially directed that each parish should purchase a Bible translated into English, but few did so. Three years later, a penalty was imposed for failure to do so, and most rapidly complied.

Why did Henry's Reformation not provoke either a war of religion or an uprising so powerful and determined that it turned back the tide of reform? In part this was because of its idiosyncratic and half-baked nature. It offered enough to those who wanted a reformation of the continental sort to make them support Henry in the hope of more and better from them. At the same time, it could plausibly be represented as an improved form of Catholicism, for Henry upheld key aspects of traditional devotion such as clerical celibacy and the performance of the mass, with the bread and wine transformed into the body and blood of Christ. If anything is needed to establish that Henry himself was the driving force behind his Reformation, as George Bernard has pointed out, it is the adoption of his unique, crazily mixed and deeply personal theology. But there were also structural reasons for its success. The Church in England was led by its bishops, who were by this period all either hand-picked or approved by the monarchs. Both Henry VII and Henry VIII generally favoured conscientious administrators with a good record of loyalty to the Crown. As a group they were typified by the dutiful mediocrity of the reigning head of the English Church under the Pope at the time of the annulment controversy, the Archbishop of Canterbury, William Warham. Furthermore, bishops were generally relatively elderly at the time of appointment, and tended to die swiftly. This meant that, during the seven years in which Henry's breach with the papacy ripened, gaps regularly opened in their ranks, which the king could fill with supporters of his cause. In 1532, when Warham seemed at last to be nerving himself up to resist Henry, he dropped dead, allowing the king to put in a new archbishop, Thomas Cranmer, who was personally devoted to him and a keen supporter of the royal supremacy over the Church and of progressive reform of it. The unity of the bishops was thus broken up, a solid proponent of reformation was put at their head, and the single prelate who made a determined stand against it, Fisher, was put to death.

If the bishops were the people who might have taken a stand against the king's ambitions, then those whose support was needed to make this militarily effective were the nobility and gentry. To them the king could offer a massive bribe: a share in the land taken from the monasteries and friaries, which Henry proceeded to sell off or grant away at a great pace. The most powerful nobleman in the land by this stage was the Duke of Norfolk, who virtually doubled his property as a result. Those aristocrats with doubts about the process had no obvious leaders: the bishops, as said, could not function effectively as an opposition, and the lack of other male Tudors removed the chance that it might rally around a prince. At parish level, the core religious ceremonies, doctrines and decorations remained intact, as did the chantries and guilds. Some acquired the trappings of local monastery churches, while individual parishioners sometimes helped themselves (illegally) to the fabric of the dissolved houses. It counted for a great deal that Henry and his supporters ensured that his takeover of the Church was sanctioned by Parliament, as the representative community of the whole realm. This was a long and difficult process, requiring careful management by the government, which it applied with great skill. The resulting statutes were given preambles which justified each measure in terms of the common good and represented it as an improvement of the existing, and familiar, religion. On the whole, the process was over by 1540, but thereafter the king continued to nibble away at further aspects of the old Church, removing or reforming minor rites, casting doubt on the existence of Purgatory and taking an ominous interest in the wealth of guilds. Parish accounts and wills suggest a steep decline in the willingness of people to give money to support a traditional religion which could be under further threat.

Two further factors can be suggested for the success of the royal takeover. One is that the laity was not supposed, at this date, to be expert in theology. When the reforming statutes touched on matters of property or law, they were vigorously contested in Parliament. Few, if any, nobles or MPs could have felt qualified to dispute the need for religious reform, however, with the king and most bishops apparently set upon it. Another element in Henry's success was summed up famously in a letter from the head of an Oxford college, John London, in 1536: that what had occurred had essentially been a quarrel between the king and the Pope, and that none of the royal actions could be construed as heresy, of the kind preached by Luther and his followers.

Monarchs and Popes had long been falling out, and then usually composed their differences, and there was still a chance that this dispute might in time be healed; indeed, at this period, this remained true of the European Reformation as a whole. The least tangible of the forces that worked in Henry's favour was the sheer novelty of what he was attempting. As nobody had ever known of a similar situation before in Western Christendom, and as the government was careful to represent itself as producing a better version of the old religion, the sheer enormity of what was happening could not be appreciated by most of the English people.

The Henrician Reform of Government
During the 1530s and early 1540s, in addition, Henry's government carried out an extensive overhaul of its own structures. Four new departments were established to handle the

increased royal revenue, turning financial administration into a
series of well-defined packages; though in practice their duties
overlapped and much cash was still creamed off to private
royal coffers. The king's Council was streamlined into a
smaller 'Privy Council' of ministers and politicians, which
acted as an increasingly important and formalized executive
agent as well as a panel of advisers to the monarch. The royal
secretary became the chief executive agent of government,
though his political importance varied according to his personality. Wales, which had emerged from the Middle Ages as a
patchwork of estates owned and governed by the Crown and a
set of noble families, was divided into counties on the English
model. With these came the English apparatus of local
government and parliamentary seats; the reform was probably
propelled by the injustice of applying the statutes which
enforced the Reformation to a region which had no representation in the Parliaments which made them. A new approach
was also taken to the government of Ireland, which like Wales
had entered the Tudor period as a mosaic of different medieval
lordships. About half of these owed direct allegiance to the
English Crown, being owned by families of English or
Norman descent. The rest were in the hands of native
dynasties, some of which owed allegiance to the Tudors. An
added complication was that the rulers of England did not in
theory own Ireland; instead, they had conquered much of it
during the Middle Ages on behalf of the papacy, which
remained the notional overlord.

Henrician policy towards Ireland evolved in two phases. In
the 1530s, a royal army finally broke the power of the main
branch of the Fitzgeralds, the Earls of Kildare, who had ruled
the island on behalf of the Yorkists and Henry VII. Most of
the family's adult males were beheaded and its supporters
massacred, bringing a new level of atrocity to Irish warfare.
The religious houses in the regions within reach of the
Crown's officials were dissolved, and the proceeds shared
with the main surviving Anglo-Irish families, bringing them

into the new system. In the 1540s, Henry was proclaimed King of Ireland, evicting the papal overlordship, and the new kingdom was given a set of governmental institutions to parallel those of England. A policy was pursued, with considerable initial success, of persuading the main native lords to recognize Henry as their ruler in exchange for confirmation of their lands and powers with the titles of barons and earls on the English pattern. It seemed for a time that the whole land might be brought under Tudor rule, while retaining most of its traditional local leaders.

Meanwhile Henry struggled with the problem of the royal succession. Anne Boleyn had failed to produce the expected male heir, instead delivering a daughter, Elizabeth, and in 1536 he executed her on a charge of infidelity. Catherine died naturally in the same year, leaving Henry completely and legally free to remarry another lady from his court, Jane Seymour, who did produce a healthy boy, named Edward. She died of an infection resulting from the birth. Henry then married again, successively to a German princess, Anne of Cleves, and two more Englishwomen, Catherine Howard and Catherine Parr. The first was divorced because the king disliked her, and the second beheaded, like Anne, for alleged adultery; the third survived him and was personally the most impressive, becoming a successful author of devotional books. Not one became pregnant, however, and it seems that by this time the ageing king's virility was failing. He repeatedly redefined the line of succession in conformity with his current wishes. Everybody agreed that Edward was the obvious heir, but all Henry's matrimonial adventures had failed to produce a son in reserve. Instead he had Parliament rule that his daughters Mary and Elizabeth were next in line, even though he had previously declared both illegitimate. If all three died, then in common law the next heir should be the current ruler of Scotland, as the descendant of the king's sister, but Henry had this line disinherited by Parliament in favour of the Grey family, who came from his younger sister. It was a situation with a very dangerous potential for conflict and confusion.

In the 1540s Henry felt secure enough to turn back from domestic to foreign affairs as the main focus for his quest for glory. The fortification of the southern English coast and the proclamation of the Kingdom of Ireland were two aspects of his attempt to bequeath to his son a realm which was more secure and more extensive than that which Henry himself had inherited. Another was a further increase in the permanent royal navy. This had started near the opening of the reign, but was now accelerated: nineteen warships were built in 1544–6 alone. It was Henry who turned the English fleet from an occasional event into an institution. Most important, the sales of the monastery lands, combined with heavy taxation, had renewed the king's capacity to wage war. He accordingly tried to unite Scotland and England by a marriage alliance, using first diplomacy and then military pressure, and then attacked France once more. The Scottish war was indecisive, but the French one gained a port on the English Channel, Boulogne, to add to England's surviving French town, Calais. This conquest marked a new policy, of forgetting the former English possessions in France and attempting instead to acquire and hold strongholds on the coast opposite England. It was to have a history even longer than the Hundred Years War itself, not being abandoned until the 1660s. It was also hugely popular: in fact, to judge by signs of public rejoicing, the capture of Boulogne accompanied his siring of a healthy male heir as one of his two most acclaimed achievements. In reality, it was of little practical use and hugely expensive: the total cost of its reduction and maintenance was to exceed a million pounds.

Whether all the administrative changes added up to a 'Tudor Revolution in government', as Sir Geoffrey Elton once thought, is open to doubt. Those in Wales and Ireland were revolutionary in their scale and impact, and the creation of the Church of England was as important a shift. The reforms in English secular government, on the other hand, are better viewed as one stage in a process that spanned the first two-thirds of the century. Nor is it possible, in most cases, to determine how policy was made. At particular places and times, certain individuals feature as pivotally important: for example, Thomas Cromwell was undoubtedly the king's main executive agent and source of ideas in England during the 1530s and Sir Anthony St Leger was responsible for the reconciliation of Irish chiefs to the new Kingdom of Ireland in the 1540s. In many ways, Cromwell, who had been trained by Wolsey, represented his true successor, taking over the Church and reforming it directly, and using parliamentary legislation to drive home the improvements in urban life that the cardinal had encouraged. Never again, however, did a royal minister wield as much power as Wolsey had done, and how Henry reached specific decisions, and under whose influence, if any, is probably for the most part impossible to determine: we shall probably never know, for example, whether Anne Boleyn and Catherine Howard were innocent of the charges of infidelity for which they were executed. The evidence for Henrician court politics consists of inadequate and competing accounts left by courtiers and foreign ambassadors, and so a choice really consists of privileging one piece of gossip over another. What seems certain is that the overall thrust of government continued to reflect Henry's own dreams and desires, and that his personal involvement in government increased notably in his last ten years as his appetite for pleasure waned.

The Kingship of Henry VIII

In popular memory, Henry seems to rank as the most colourful English king of all time. He has appeared in films and on television more than any other, and is the only one commemorated in an enduring music-hall song ('I'm 'enery the Eighth I am'). This achievement, and the fact that he has been played on screen by (apparent) Cockneys such as Sid James and Ray Winstone, indicates part of his appeal – a sense of accessibility and laddishness. His image is one of the best-known of all English kings, largely thanks to one painting, by the German artist Hans Holbein, showing him standing, hands on hips, his massive frame and square-cut beard giving an impression of solidity and confidence. This persona, of inherent majesty and physical and moral bulk, is exactly the one that Henry himself set out to convey, to overshadow his predecessors and match or surpass the most powerful of his fellow rulers.

Why he did so is open to question. Clearly the answer must lie partly in his father's lack of willingness (for whatever reason) to entrust him with power and wealth. What is certain is that Henry's relentless quest for glory began as soon as he became king. In reaching for it he initially had two role models: King Arthur, the greatest legendary monarch of Britain, and Henry V, the victor of the battle of Agincourt and the most flamboyantly successful of England's medieval rulers. Our Henry identified with both. He had his own portrait painted in the royal seat on what was then believed to be King Arthur's Round Table, and was actually a medieval fake, displayed at Winchester Castle. Before launching his first war against France, he commissioned a new biography of Henry V, and during the war he imitated some of that king's actions. Later he reached beyond these British prototypes to identify instead with the godly kings of the Old Testament, such as David.

As a physical presence, Henry VIII was certainly massive. He stood over six feet in height, with superb muscles in his youth, and possessed a huge appetite for both food and sport: in his twenties he wore out eight horses in a day while hunting, and was a notable jouster, wrestler and dancer. At the age of forty-four, however, a falling horse rolled over him, permanently injuring one leg and his head. After that he was never wholly well, and his love of eating, no longer balanced by exercise, made him run to fat so much that in his last few years he measured four feet and six inches around the waist. His growing physical monstrosity, and discomfort, reinforced his increasingly savage temper.

He could be remarkably industrious. When writing his book against Martin Luther, he put in four hours a day until it was finished. He was the last English sovereign until Charles II to attend the debates of the English House of Lords, and chose to receive foreign ambassadors in person, giving 108 audiences to them in his last seven years. He told his secretaries to submit drafts of all state documents to him with wide margins and spaces between lines so that he could scribble corrections, and he underlined and annotated key passages in despatches from his diplomats abroad. He also had an amazing, encyclopaedic memory, for names, salaries, offices, pensions and grants. On the other hand, he did not attend his Council regularly, hated reading long letters and despatches, and disliked writing documents himself; we can tell how much he loved Anne Boleyn, not merely because of the fervour of his love letters to her, but because he put himself to the labour of penning them. Altogether, he was a chronic annotator, editor and commentator. He loved the detail of government but disliked its main business; he was a monarch obsessed with marginalia.

He has some claims to be remembered as both intelligent and cultured. He was quite a good musician, composing motets, a mass and songs. He collected a library of almost 1,000 volumes, mostly on theology but also on science and classical literature; and he certainly read them, because he scribbled over them. He loved clocks, amassing a huge collection, and had a real understanding of fortification, gunnery, archery, shipping, falconry, geometry, mathematics and astronomy. The most celebrated intellectual in contemporary Europe, Erasmus, visited Henry and was impressed by his appetite for knowledge. The English court was a model of decorum compared with some abroad; no duelling or brawling was allowed there, and its young men were expected to keep their mistresses tucked out of sight, as indeed Henry himself did. The king's only visible vices were gluttony, gambling and ostentation. In just one two-year period he spent £11,000 on jewels and lost £3,250 on cards, while by his death he owned fifty-five royal residences – an English royal record. None the less, he had a grosser side; his favourite recorded joke was about breaking wind. Furthermore, his zeal for information did not compensate for the fact that he couldn't really think. His reply to Luther consisted of a collection of 170 quotations from the Bible and the Church Fathers relating to the matter at issue (the sacraments); at no point did he notice that he wasn't actually answering Luther's arguments. He would have made an absolutely brilliant player of Trivial Pursuit or solver of crossword puzzles, but he was not an intellectual.

Henry could, beyond doubt, be delightful and charming company. He was boisterously affectionate, often hugging and patting his companions. He had a desperate desire to please: a French ambassador, Charles de Marillac, noted that he wanted 'to be in favour with everyone'. As part of this, he showed a real interest in other people; William Roper, the son-in-law of Sir (or St) Thomas More, commented on the king's ability to make everyone feel especially in favour with him. Erasmus found him sweet-natured and reasonable. He could be tremendously generous, loving to pardon criminals and to present his followers with titles, money and land. His drawbacks were all the other faces of this demonstrative, outgoing, flamboyant nature. When angry, he hit courtiers physically and abused them verbally. He threw emotional scenes which embarrassed all observers, the worst being after he executed his fifth wife, Catherine Howard, when he blubbered in public for weeks. His courtiers must often have felt that they were dealing with a huge child – but a lethally dangerous one. Because he so wanted to please and to be admired, he could not cope with either opposition or failure. Towards opponents and critics, he showed vindictive cruelty, and his reign probably had more political executions than any other. There were 330 in the years 1532 to 1540 alone, seventy of these merely for speaking against royal policy, an offence which Henry's regime added to the category of treason, which formerly had been reserved for actions alone. Those condemned for treachery, heresy or sedition were beheaded, hanged, disembowelled, burned or mutilated, sometimes with calculated brutality. A carpenter, John Wyot, was condemned to stand in the pillory for criticizing the government. He was made to do so in a dunce's cap, with one ear nailed to the wood, and at the end was given the choice of tearing himself loose or cutting off the ear. Those who served Henry loyally, but whom he held responsible for policies that turned out badly, were treated with little more mercy. Of his closest ministers and advisers, only one, Archbishop Cranmer, made it to the end of the reign without suffering either death or disgrace. It is notable that Henry seems to have enjoyed hunting not for the thrill of the chase so much for as the joy of killing.

For a king who read so much theology, and set himself up as God's leading representative in his realm, Henry displayed little real piety. The annotations he made on his books were concerned obsessively with the details of ceremony and with royal power. The damage which he did to the national historical heritage is clear, involving the destruction of hundreds of beautiful buildings and thousands of works of art, and incalculable losses of books, especially of theology and devotion. The end product of all this vandalism was neither a Protestant Church nor a reformed Catholic one, but a mutilated Catholic one in decay, being picked away piecemeal. As a soldier and a statesman he had little personal ability. He never displayed any capacity as a general, and his foreign policy consisted of moments of transitory success amid a basic pattern of failure and waste. The real successes of his reforms in government, in Wales, Ireland and the structure of central administration, were initiatives in which he himself took little interest.

As a monarch, Henry was determined to rule strongly and in person, and it is a further mark of his basic insecurity that he kept telling people that he did. He was, however, not clever, stable, industrious or self-disciplined enough to do so by facing up to problems and ministers directly. Instead, he relied on taking ideas from different people in turn and punishing them if they failed: once he was set on a course, the nature of his advisers was irrelevant, but it was crucial when, as so often, he was uncertain how to proceed. In his last ten years, as his physical powers weakened, he encouraged court factions to watch and plot against each other. He accepted complaints against his leading servants, and would then take the decision whether to arrest or vindicate the person concerned, keeping everybody insecure. He loved secrecy and intrigue. Cranmer noted that when he wanted an opinion on a particular book, he would hand it to a succession of people, telling each one that he was seeking that person's opinion alone, and that the latter should not discuss it with anyone else. At times he would issue an official royal order, with the support of his councillors, and then send the recipient a private and personal command to disregard it. One reason why it is difficult to account for the fall of most of his closest companions and advisers is that he generally showed them special kindness before moving against them, to put them off-guard. His favourite political dictum was 'fear makes men obey'; which is true, but does not make for good advice and coherent and stable government.

None the less, Henry had a long reign, accomplished enormous changes in his realm, and died still in power. In large part this was because he fitted both the medieval and the contemporary ideals of what a king should be. He suited the former model by being aggressive, audacious, generous, proud, flamboyant and sociable. He fitted the latter, formulated in the more sophisticated world of the Renaissance, by being a combination of the lion and the fox: at once majestic, charismatic, ruthless and devious. His peculiar mixture of showiness and insecurity proved particularly effective in dealing with three key political groups. One was the nobility. On the face of things Henry cherished it, showering its members with praises, offices, estates, cash and titles, leading them in their pastimes and welcoming them to a brilliant court. He tended, however, to entrust the old-established families only sparingly with power, and destroyed some at regular intervals, elevating new men in their place. By the end of the reign, half of the total existing peerage, and all those sitting on the Privy Council, had been created by him. The second group consisted of talented men from humbler social backgrounds, to whom Henry gave high office in both Church and state. He was extremely good at recognizing and harnessing real ability in people, and rewarded it lavishly, as long as it brought him good results. The third grouping consisted of an institution, Parliament, which he raised to a new level of importance in English government and law by taking it into partnership in effecting the changes that he wrought in his kingdom. It supplied him with a further stage on which he could parade his majesty, but also the security of endorsement of his key policies by the community of the realm. As a result, the statutes of the realm enacted under Henry VIII take up as many pages as those that had been passed during the previous 400 years. Tricky questions about the true extent of royal power were mostly avoided by confronting objectors with the combined power of king, Lords and Commons.

His reputation among modern historians has been low, his last unequivocal admirer among them having been A. F. Pollard, near the beginning of the twentieth century. This is partly because Henry's combination of qualities is one which is particularly unattractive to hard-working and responsible intellectuals, and partly because detailed research shows up Henry at his worst; he was definitely a king who looked better at a distance. None the less, there is no doubt that he had star quality, that he remained both feared and admired by his subjects until the end of his life, and that his achievements, positive and negative, were tremendous. It is significant that we do not remember him as 'Henry the Great', which is what he undoubtedly would have wanted, and that popular memory does not credit him with a single accomplishment which is regarded as glorious without controversy or qualification. What he has done is to impress himself on posterity – indelibly and supremely – as a physical and spiritual personality; and that is remarkable enough.

3

THE MID-TUDOR REGIMES

The Basic Problems

Between 1546 and 1570 the Tudor monarchy underwent a renewed period of relative insecurity and instability. In the late twentieth century historians often termed this 'the mid-Tudor Crisis'. The consensus now is that none of the problems experienced by government at this time were severe and long lasting enough to justify this label, but there was certainly an unusual amount of turbulence during these years. There were seven points at which prominent politicians fell from power, shaking or destroying the regimes of which they had been part. The late 1540s brought severe inflation and harvest failure, while the 1550s brought more bad harvests and the worst epidemic of the century, probably a strain of influenza. There were five major rebellions, five wars with foreign powers, four of which could be considered failures, and five official changes of the national religion. It is important to balance all this data by noting what did not happen during these years. There were no successful invasions by foreign powers, and no monarch, once crowned, was overthrown. The structure of government never broke down, and four out of the five big rebellions were crushed. The extent of the instability was therefore strictly limited, but it was none the less still significant.

At the root of it lay the continuing problems of the Tudor dynasty. At the end of 1546 the dying Henry VIII carried out his last purge of advisers, which included the imprisonment of England's premier nobleman, the Duke of Norfolk, and the execution of his heir. In January 1547 Henry's young son succeeded him as Edward VI. He seems to have been a lively and self-confident boy, with a reckless taste for gambling (he would bet on almost anything) and a personal dedication to the Protestant reform of religion. Had he lived to manhood he would certainly have been an ambitious, aggressive and evangelical king, who might either have led England to glory or ruined it in rash adventures. Instead he died in 1553 of a lung disease. As he was never old enough to rule personally, his realm was managed for him by regimes led by two successive noblemen. The first was his uncle Edward, the brother of Jane Seymour, who took the title of Duke of Somerset; the second, who seized power in 1549, was John Dudley, the son of Henry VII's most notorious financial agent, who became Duke of Northumberland. As Edward lay dying, he and Northumberland decided to safeguard the Reformation by excluding the next heir in blood, the king's Catholic sister, Mary. In her place, they installed Edward's second cousin, through Henry VIII's younger sister, Lady Jane Grey. This ploy was foiled by Mary, who immediately took the throne at the head of a rebellion, beheading first Northumberland and then Lady Jane. Mary married the heir to Spain, Philip, but failed to become pregnant before dying herself of stomach cancer in 1558. That left the last Tudor, Henry VIII's younger daughter Elizabeth, to succeed unopposed, and her remarkably long reign enabled her to stabilize the realm; although it needed more than ten years for political affairs to settle down.

The three monarchs who reigned in this time, therefore, consisted of a boy, followed by two successive women, who were respectively the first and second queens ever to rule England in their own right. None of them possessed a male heir, of their own body, to secure the line of succession, and two of them died after reigning for much less than a decade. To an age which believed that the norm of monarchy should be an adult king, with one or two male children to carry on the dynasty, the situation during these years was very disturbing indeed, and accounts in itself for the difficulties of government. It remains to be seen how each of the four regimes, those of Somerset, Northumberland, Mary and the young Elizabeth, fared in each of the traditional areas of government activity.

Central Politics and Government
Somerset seized supreme power by a coup which overturned the will of Henry VIII, by which he would have been one of a board of governors. He turned the Privy Council into a rubber stamp for his wishes and pushed Northumberland into deposing him in self-defence. He then tried to make a comeback and so left Northumberland no real option than to cut his head off. Northumberland proved a much more able politician, both in removing his enemies from office and in working with the Council, which he turned into a genuinely efficient governing team and source of advice. He would probably have retained power had not Edward died and Mary overthrown him. Mary ran a much bigger and more unwieldy Privy Council, but ran it well. She balanced various different political groups on it and chose an inner circle from all. When a politician tried to dictate policy to her, as Lord Paget once did by stirring up his supporters in Parliament to block legislation of which he disapproved, she gave him a verbal roasting that made him submit immediately. She did not, however, disgrace, let alone destroy her advisers as her father had done, and so gave her ministers a safety unknown in government circles for three decades. Elizabeth worked with a smaller Council, but

tried to give her leading servants the same security in the face of political rivalry and temporary failures. She was at first less successful than Mary, provoking three of her leading nobles, the current Duke of Norfolk and Earls of Northumberland and Westmorland, to conspiracy or rebellion. She defeated them, however, and in doing so gave high political life a genuine stability. She, Mary and Northumberland may be accounted an equally impressive trio of managers.

Public Finance

The royal finances were already in difficulty by the end of Henry's reign. Despite the huge sums raised by squandering the monastery lands and by taxation, the combined costs of forts, warships and armies had pushed the government to take the desperate step of devaluing the currency. This was in itself enough to produce an immediate inflation in the price of all commodities, and thus an incipient economic crisis. Somerset continued all these policies, intensifying the cycle of ruinously expensive warfare, taxation, debasement and debt, and might well have pushed the Crown into bankruptcy had he not been removed. Northumberland carried out a wholesale series of economies, pulling back the state from fiscal collapse, and left Mary the work of building up the royal income. This was a much harder task, not least because, unlike her father and brother, as a Catholic she could not plunder the Church to bring in extra resources; on the contrary, she needed to shed assets in order to re-endow it.

What she did was to streamline the fiscal machinery by amalgamating or reorganizing the administrative departments set up under her father. She then gave the Exchequer back its medieval role as the office which supervised most royal finance, placing the majority of the other departments under its control. In this manner she finally ended the emergency system of channelling cash through the royal household which had lasted ever since the Wars of the Roses. She then raised the yield of the customs, the dues imposed on trade in and out of the kingdom, by 75 per cent, and, even more impressively, got a Parliament to endorse this reform. She established a good relationship with the London merchant companies that enabled her to raise huge loans from them, and handed on to Elizabeth a larger debt, but also a bigger income and good credit. Elizabeth was able to build on her sister's achievement, and on the economic boom of the 1560s, by reducing the debt and producing a new and stable coinage. In this matter she completed the process of recovery from the disastrous policies of the 1540s.

Warfare and Foreign Policy

The Duke of Somerset wreaked such havoc with the public finances in pursuit of a particularly ambitious military adventure: no less than the conquest of Scotland. He broke its armed strength and then wore down resistance by planting English garrisons all across the south-eastern part of the kingdom. At the same time, he pushed forward the frontier of direct royal rule in Ireland. The idea was a personal obsession of his, which even Henry VIII had rejected as too expensive; and Henry had been correct. By 1549 almost £2.5 million had been spent on the venture, and England had 37,000 soldiers in its employ. Somerset crushed the Scottish army and planted his garrisons, but the Scots refused to surrender and the French came to their aid. He therefore found himself fighting a war on three fronts – in Scotland, Ireland and along the English Channel – and rapidly reached stalemate on each. He was unable to disengage, while the money on which his military effort relied was fast running out. Catastrophe was only averted by Northumberland, who overthrew Somerset and bought peace all round by surrendering almost everything for which England had been fighting. He withdrew completely from Scotland and gave back Boulogne to the French; only the Irish war spluttered on.

Mary was faced by an entirely different problem of foreign policy. To secure her dynasty and her Catholic religion, she

needed to produce a son as swiftly as possible. There were no
plausible domestic candidates for her to marry, and so she had
to find a foreign Catholic prince who was from a great royal
house, was free and willing to be her husband, and was not
French and so a traditional enemy of England. That list of
requirements was fitted by only one man: Philip, the son of
Charles V and heir through him to Spain and a range of other
territories in Italy and the Netherlands. In many ways, Philip
was a perfect match, being an experienced and able ruler, who
had a kingly appetite for both business and social life and
already had a son from a previous marriage to whom he could
leave his Spanish realms. Through him, England would gain an
heir, acquire a loyal foreign ally, and retain its independence. In
the event, however, many of the English felt that the power and
aggression that the Spanish had now manifested, especially in
their conquests in the Americas, made them too dangerous for
such an alliance. The proposal was seriously unpopular, and
when Mary insisted upon it, a rebellion immediately erupted.
Mary, however, showed the same tremendous courage that she
had displayed when seizing the throne. She stood firm, rallied
her supporters to defeat the rebels, and then married Philip,
but on terms almost outrageously favourable to England. He
was forced to keep a separate, Spanish, household, remained
uncrowned (thereby being denied an honour given to royal
wives), was barred from any part in English government, and
was denied any claim to succeed Mary as ruler. Mary had thus
pulled off a rapid series of amazing successes, through her own
audacity and determination, and all that remained now was for
her to produce a son.

It was at this point that everything began to go wrong. Not
only did the queen prove incapable of conceiving, but her
health began to decline instead, towards the death which
overcame her when she was still in her early forties and had
reigned for just five years. Meanwhile, England found itself
dragged into the latest war between France and Spain. It had at
first no intention of allowing this, but the French forced the

issue by finding an idiot with a thimbleful of English royal blood called Thomas Stafford, and sending him to overthrow Mary and so destroy the Anglo-Spanish entente. His invasion was easily foiled, but England and France were now effectively at war. The immediate result was a stunning success at St Quentin, when an Anglo-Spanish army routed the French royal forces. The French, thus humiliated, needed an equally resounding success, and got it by attacking Calais in midwinter 1558. The English there were taken completely by surprise, and the town fell. Hindsight permits the conclusion that it was no great loss, the place being of minimal military and commercial value to England and very expensive to defend. None the less, it represented the very last portion of the medieval English possessions in France, which had been gained with a huge effort and held against French attacks for more than two centuries. Its fall was a tremendous blow to English prestige, and made a dismal conclusion to the reign of Mary, who died in the same year. Elizabeth commenced her reign with a piece of luck as strikingly good as Mary's had been bad. Scotland collapsed into a civil war between a Protestant party hostile to the French forces still in the land, and a rival one more inclined to the French and Catholicism. Elizabeth sent an army in 1560 which tipped the balance in favour of the former, kicking the French out of the land and leaving a regime in power there which was grateful and friendly to England. However, she then pushed her luck by intervening in a civil war in France itself, to occupy another French Channel port, Le Havre. Her aim was to trade it for Calais, but her garrison was forced to surrender and its retreat made the loss of Calais final.

Superficially, therefore, the period contained a mighty English victory under Edward, over Scotland in 1548, an even more mighty defeat under Mary, at Calais, and a balance of success under Elizabeth. A second perspective would emphasize that the record of all three monarchs was in fact quite balanced. The two governments that acted for Edward failed to make a single lasting territorial gain, but neither did they lose any of the land that Henry VIII had inherited. It could even be argued that there was a genuine equality of profit and loss under Mary, the fall of Calais being offset by a further offensive in Ireland, which carved two new counties out of the native lordships of the Midlands. Yet another way of looking at things would be to say that in all three reigns the English lost a French port (Boulogne, Calais, Le Havre) and that the consequences of a disastrous intervention in Scotland, in 1547, were eventually healed by a more sensible one in 1560. In reality, a deeper process was at work. The reign of Henry VIII had proved that the English state was no longer strong enough to fight a sustained land war in Europe; that of Edward demonstrated that it could not even do so in Scotland, and by the 1560s it could not maintain even a foothold on the far side of the Channel. If it were to preserve any claim to being a front-rank European power, something would have to change: its own strength, that of its rivals, its approach to war and diplomacy, or its sphere of operation.

Social Policy

The Duke of Somerset used to have a very good press from historians as a statesman who, unlike most at his time, made a valiant effort to rule in the interests of ordinary people. As such, he fought encroachments on common rights, with more vigour than Wolsey had done, tried to aid towns in economic trouble, and patronized intellectuals who denounced the rich for their greed and spoke of the need to protect the interests of ordinary people. In the 1970s Michael Bush punctured this image of 'the Good Duke' by revealing him to have been an obsessive warlord who did far more harm to the welfare of his realm by taxation and currency devaluation than he did by proclamations concerning the common good. Recently Ethan Shagan has emphasized once more the novel extent to which Somerset invited commoners to present their economic grievances to the royal government and implied that they would be dealt with sympathetically. What cannot be denied are the consequences: that a combination of bad harvests, bad currency, heavy taxes, religious change, and the apparent willingness of the government to encourage discontent with landlords, provoked the bloodiest English rebellions of the century. Somerset's own government had to put them down, at a cost of £37,000 and about 8,500 lives, out of a population of just three million. As a percentage, that is larger than the proportion of the Japanese population killed by the attacks on Hiroshima and Nagasaki in 1945; the 'Good Duke of Somerset' was in effect more lethal to his people than two atomic bombs.

After that, Northumberland, wisely, just let things settle. Mary instituted a series of low-level and effective policies which were continued under Elizabeth. Facing the highest bread prices of the century, her councillors got the local justices, checked by a royal commission, to lay up stocks of grain and stop it being exported. She also passed laws to improve agriculture and cattle-breeding. Both queens, it must be admitted, also put through legislation of a well-intentioned but daft kind: to foster towns by crippling rural industry and putting the apprenticeship of young people to trades within a legal straitjacket. In practice, however, these did little harm because the English were sensible enough to ignore them. Furthermore, Mary's government made a decisive contribution to domestic defence, by passing the most significant among a series of Tudor statutes which replaced the old-style noble retinues with county-based militias, armed from public magazines, as a home guard for English territory. In the long term this was going to have a much greater impact on military history than the loss of Calais, although it has been less noticed both at the time and ever since.

Religion
Traditional-minded readers will have noticed that thus far this chapter has been remarkably favourable to Mary Tudor, who has been portrayed at best as a courageous and effective ruler

and at worst as a very unlucky one. This characterization is, of course, directly counter to the one which has obtained in most English history books until the late twentieth century, and all films and television dramas until the present. This is summed up by her popular nickname of 'Bloody Mary', delineating a monarch who was cruel, obsessive and misguided and whose reign represented a mercifully brief interlude of bigotry and repression before the long golden age created by her sister Elizabeth. Such an image is based, more or less completely, upon just one aspect of her rule: her dedication to the Roman Catholic religion and the persecution of English Protestants which accompanied it. It is also, more or less entirely, a deliberate creation of the Elizabethan regime that followed.

The three children of Henry VIII were not fond of each other. Edward attempted to disinherit both his sisters in order to put his cousin Jane on the throne. Mary refused to be crowned on the usual coronation chair because it had been polluted by her brother's former presence. She also wanted to behead Elizabeth, who survived only because there was no alternative successor to the throne remaining who was remotely acceptable to most of the English. Elizabeth naturally returned the compliment by encouraging a systematic denigration of her sister's reputation, which began almost as soon as Mary died. It is that denigration which became built into mainstream national culture, as Protestantism was made a central part of the English, and then British, identity and Mary was remembered as its most bitter and brutal enemy. As religious enthusiasm waned in modern times, liberalism simply stepped into its place, and the established reputation of Mary as the greatest religious persecutor in English history set her up as the prime villainess of those who celebrated England as the world's principal birthplace of liberalism and tolerance. Towards the end of the twentieth century, however, the revisionist movement in English Reformation studies, which emphasized the health and viability of the pre-Reformation Church, brought a new perspective on the reign. It made early

Protestantism look a great deal less popular, and its triumph much less easy and inevitable, than had traditionally been thought. In proportion with this, Mary's Catholicism came to seem more acceptable and understandable in the context of her time. This shift of opinion has intersected with an enhanced appreciation of the effectiveness of her regime in political and financial affairs to produce a much more positive recent assessment of the reign. It is time now, therefore, to compare the four governments once more, in an assessment of their religious policies, and suggest how successful revisionism has been in rehabilitating Mary's reputation.

Edward's reign produced the true implementation of a Protestant Reformation in England, as power was held by the surviving advisers of Henry VIII who had favoured reform, such as Archbishop Cranmer and the Duke of Somerset. Under Somerset's leadership, Catholic rites and the images of saints were cleared away from churches, and religious guilds, chantries and the doctrine of Purgatory were all abolished. The government seized and sold off the lands of the guilds and chantries, just as those of religious houses had been taken before. Under Northumberland, the medieval stone altars were removed and replaced with wooden communion tables, clergy forbidden to wear the traditional robes for services, and a completely Protestant liturgy prescribed. These changes were pushed forward by the whole system of inspection and visitation employed for the Henrician Reformation, and by a proportionate determination at the top. In 1548 the bishops rejected the abolition of the mass by one vote, whereupon Somerset arrested the leading conservatives among them and the future Duke of Northumberland shouted down those still at liberty who protested against the reform. Peter Marshall has suggested that the Edwardian Reformation was more like the Chinese Cultural Revolution of the 1960s than anything else in the modern world. It was a traumatic cataclysm, which connected England much more directly to continental Protestantism than ever before or after.

What is most significant about Peter Marshall's comparison is that the Cultural Revolution of Mao's China is now generally seen as a terrible mistake, having inflicted tremendous destruction for very little gain.

There is indeed this aspect to Edward's Reformation, but also another which has been emphasized recently by Diarmaid MacCulloch. He has reminded us that to the minority who advocated and secured it, these changes were extremely exciting. As contemporaries noted, it was very much a movement of angry young men, who embraced to the full its appeal as a movement of liberation from the chains of superstition. To many people, the discovery that they did not need to spend lots of money on church fittings and extended rituals, that the dead had no need for prayers, that meat could be eaten in Lent, that images of saints could be smashed rather than adored, and that it was possible to divorce a marital partner, was wonderfully cathartic. Even Diarmaid MacCulloch has acknowledged, however, that the Edwardian Reformation was turning sour by 1553. Clergy were complaining of the new disrespect of the laity, especially for ecclesiastical courts. The rebellions of 1549 destroyed the government's rhetoric of social justice, while two years later a serious epidemic, the 'sweating sickness', struck England, and seemed to be a sign of divine anger. Churchmen were starting to resent the plundering of the Church's wealth by royal ministers, and becoming aware of how much lay people at all levels were manipulating religious reform to make money, enhance local power and do down neighbours whom they disliked. None the less, this Reformation was viable in itself, and had Edward lived as long as his father or grandfather, we would have an Edwardian Church today.

Instead, Mary restored Catholic worship, using the same methods of enforcement, plus the burning alive of Cranmer and the other leading Protestant bishops. By the end of her reign every parish which has left accounts or a presence in visitation reports possessed the basic trappings of Catholicism once again: an image of its patron saint, a stone altar, a rood loft bearing an image of the crucified Christ, candlesticks, a censer for incense, a chalice to contain the wine that was transformed into Christ's blood in the mass, a crucifix, an altar cloth, robes for the priest and a mass book. Many had more books and ornaments than these.

This process of restoration was the more remarkable in that it was expensive. The work of reformation was relatively cheap, as all that was required were the wages of builders to demolish images and altars, and these could be covered by selling off the wood, cloth and metal yielded by the removal of Catholic decorations. To replace the latter, however, required a large effort of purchase and reconstruction; and the fact that every parish on record had managed it within a few years is especially noteworthy. Under Elizabeth, Protestantism was established once more, and so all the restored Catholic objects were taken away once again. The process was slower than under Edward, almost certainly because the new queen had no clearly recognized Protestant heir and there was a real risk that Catholic worship would return yet again when she died. The local records show that the removal of its trappings took up to ten years, instead of two or three as it had under Edward. The heavier and more expensive items, such as the rood lofts, were left in place longest. None the less, Elizabeth turned out to have a reign of extraordinary length, with a Protestant successor at the end of it, and so this time the removal of Catholicism from the parish churches was permanent.

Did this outward conformity to the successive regimes reflect genuine conversion of the bulk of the English to the views of each monarch? There are two crude tests that can be applied to answer this question. The first is the incidence of rebellion. If people were prepared to risk their lives in taking up arms against an official religious policy, this is the clearest possible indication of opposition to it. The Edwardian Reformation certainly faced it, in the shape of a full-scale rising in Devon and Cornwall in 1549, explicitly aimed at reversing the reforms, which was accompanied by further unrest in the rest of the West Country, the Midlands and the north. On the other hand, the uprisings in the south and east of England during the same summer, provoked by economic and social grievances, seem to have been generally approving of government policy. In 1553, however, the short-lived regime of Lady Jane Grey based its appeal explicitly on a Protestant identity, and was overthrown by Mary's rebellion, originating mainly in East Anglia, which appealed to a sense of hereditary right and avoided religious labelling. Mary did, however, rapidly make Catholicism the official faith, and it is notable that hers was the only reign in which nobody took arms against the government in the name of religion. It did survive a major upheaval – Wyatt's rebellion – which was led by people of Protestant sympathies; but the public aim of this was to prevent the queen's marriage to Philip, not to restore Protestantism. Elizabeth, by contrast, did face and defeat a Catholic rising, that of the northern earls (Northumberland and Westmorland) in 1569, and a series of Catholic conspiracies to depose or kill her after that. None of these threats, however, were as formidable to her as the western rebellion of 1549 had been to the government of the Duke of Somerset.

The other test is provided by wills. In the sixteenth century, the last will and testament made by an English person normally commenced by bequeathing her or his soul to heavenly powers. The formulae used for this could be highly significant, as by the mid-sixteenth century there were some forms of words which would only be used by Catholics, and others which were distinctively Protestant. It is also true that yet other forms could be employed by both and that some wills mixed aspects from both kinds of religion. In addition, many wills reflected the beliefs of those who drew them up – friends, relatives, priests or clerks – rather than those of the people whom they represented. None the less, they show clear and very significant patterns over time. By the end of the reign of Edward, use of Catholic formulae was in a minority almost everywhere in the kingdom, and was reduced to a mere 6–8 per cent in the south-east. Clearly Protestant wills, however, never made up more than a quarter of the total, even in London, so that most had adopted mixed or neutral forms. The fact that many of these wills were left by Catholics in disguise is suggested by the change that occurred with the accession of Mary, when Catholic formulae reappeared in large quantities. On the other hand, they only rose to a clear majority in the north of England, running at about half of the total in the south-east and so still leaving plenty of ground to the neutral kind. Under Elizabeth, Catholic forms dwindled rapidly again, reaching their Edwardian low point by the late 1560s, but clearly Protestant formulae only became a majority in most regions in the 1570s and 1580s. The total import of the evidence of both rebellion and will-making is that Mary's Catholicism attracted more spontaneous support from the English than Edwardian Protestantism or that of the early reign of Elizabeth.

To say this, however, is to skirt the central issue which has damned Mary's reputation, that of persecution. In just three years her regime probably burned 285 Protestants, an intensity of religious repression unique in English history. Some extenuations can be made for her action. The regimes of Henry VIII, Edward VI, Elizabeth and James I all put Protestants to death as well, for beliefs that were more radical than those permitted by the established Church of the time. In addition, Elizabeth executed almost 200 Catholics, in theory for treason but actually just for attempting to practise their religion. The executions that followed the rebellion of the northern earls add another couple of hundred to that figure. In the following century, the government of Charles II engaged in spurts of persecution in which anybody who met to worship outside the Church of England could be imprisoned. Over 400 Quakers, let alone Presbyterians, Baptists, Independents and other kinds of Protestant dissenter died in confinement, most because of the conditions in which they were held. It is a matter for personal taste whether readers would prefer this squalid and lingering end to a few minutes of agony in the middle of a bonfire; to those who do, it is Charles, the so-called Merry Monarch, who should perhaps be remembered as the greatest religious persecutor in English history.

On first seizing the throne, Mary declared a genuine freedom of worship, of a kind unique in Tudor history. This was a legal necessity, to enable Catholics to practise their religion again immediately while she set in train the legal measures to re-establish it officially. The measure did, however, also allow English Protestants an opportunity to display their own readiness to tolerate other beliefs, and some clearly had none. In London alone during this interim period, a cat was hanged in one church where Catholic worship had been restored, and ornaments wrecked in another. A priest was stabbed while celebrating mass, a Catholic procession attacked in the street and (most imaginatively) a Protestant ventriloquist counterfeited heavenly voices, denouncing the evils of Catholicism. Such incidents, given wide publicity, certainly strengthened Mary's case for persecution. To become a victim of it required some effort. Protestants who wished to leave the realm to live with co-religionists abroad were given ample time to do so. No inquisition was ever instigated in England, so that people were only troubled by the authorities if they identified themselves noisily as Protestants or were denounced as such. Those who had made no enemies amongst their neighbours, and kept their heads down, were safe; the ruling class closed ranks to protect its members, and there were no gentry among the martyrs. Once arrested and convicted of heretical opinions, people could save their lives by recanting those beliefs. There is no overall evidence that the burnings were unpopular. Some sympathy was displayed for victims who were unusually young, or were women, or suffered a prolonged death; but not in general.

Alongside its suppression of heresy, Mary's Church also had an impressive positive programme. Its bishops were mostly of academic distinction, and often of international status, and notably energetic. Most were good preachers, and put in three visitations of their dioceses, a level of performance only reached under Edward by one. Their integrity was shown at Mary's death, when, in sharp contrast to the large-scale changes of allegiance shown by bishops during every previous alteration of religious policy, only one was willing to accept the Protestant church of Elizabeth. Plans were drawn up for a seminary for priests to be founded in each diocese, three new Oxford colleges were founded, and the university course was streamlined to produce graduates more rapidly. Preachers were sent to tour dioceses and model sermons were printed for clergy who could not compose their own. The sale of ecclesiastical offices was discouraged, and land worth £29,000 restored to the Church by the Crown. All this was achieved despite the great blow – to add to Mary's other experiences of misfortune – that a Pope was elected, Paul IV, who was bitterly hostile to Spain, and therefore to England because Mary had married its ruler.

None of this quite diminishes the horror of what Mary's government did. This was an exceptionally brutal religious persecution even by the standards of early modern Europe. The Marian regime burned more people for heresy than the Spanish Inquisition and the French government put together, in any comparable period. All recent research has compelled the conclusions that ultimately it was Mary herself who drove it on, and that it was her own devotion to the mass that caused the questioning of suspects to focus on this particularly lethal issue; otherwise investigations might have concentrated on less sensitive areas of dogma incurring lesser penalties. The essential tragedy of the slaughter was its lack of effect: there is no evidence that it either damaged English Protestantism significantly or encouraged observers to convert to it. What it did do was to hand a powerful propaganda weapon to the Protestants who took over as soon as Mary died and Elizabeth succeeded. If it has functioned, ever since, as the great stain upon Mary's reputation, then she must incur most of the blame for that. In her own way, she was as impressive and as unpleasant as her father.

None the less, the overall conclusion must still be that it was Mary's Catholic Church that was the most popular among the English as a whole, and that had she reigned for even half as long as Elizabeth did – let alone had she ruled for as long, and produced a Catholic heir – then England would have been a Roman Catholic nation ever since. The strongly Protestant identity that it achieved instead really was the product of amazing luck; or, as some would say, of providence.

What emerges overall from a consideration of England between 1546 and 1570 is how limited the amount of instability that it experienced was, in view of the military, religious and dynastic strains to which it was subjected. It avoided any loss of its core territories, bankruptcy and outright civil war. This achievement can be put down to three main factors: to the lack of intervention by any foreign powers; to the inherent strength of the system of government inherited from the Middle Ages and nurtured by the first two Tudors; and to the royal personalities concerned. Of those who ruled during this period, only Somerset possessed the potential to wreck the nation completely, and as he was not a monarch he could be removed with the minimum of disruption. Among the monarchs themselves, Edward at least displayed real potential as a king, while both Mary and Elizabeth faced up to the challenges of introducing the English to female rule and proved to be sovereigns with abilities far above the average for early modern Europe. Once again, the Tudors had proved themselves – although always so different in personality and policy – to be a remarkably talented family.

4

INTERLUDE:
REBELLION IN TUDOR ENGLAND

Some aspects of the past, such as reigns or great events, form historical topics in themselves; others are the creation of historians. This second feature is certainly true of Tudor rebellions, which were turned into a 'subject' by a textbook published by Anthony Fletcher in 1968 – not coincidentally the year of uprisings across the Western world – which has been through four more editions since. What was so remarkable about the series of revolts discussed in the book was their apparent futility; all were crushed by the central government. Since the book first appeared, historians have added two major risings which were clear successes – one against taxation in 1525 and the one which put Mary on the throne – but these still left rebels against the Tudor state with an apparent one in six chance of achieving their aims. As well as being generally ineffectual, those who rebelled seem to have possessed a touching faith in the same government which ruthlessly suppressed and punished them. Only under Mary did an uprising set out with the professed aim of toppling the current monarch. Most displayed a genuine loyalty to the regime currently in power and expected it to pay attention to their grievances. In having this touching faith in hostile central powers, as in rebelling at all, they appear doubly misguided.

Since 1968 a large body of research has deepened understanding of the context of Tudor rebellions. It has reinforced the point that Tudor England was better organized than most states of the age to render direct political action by commoners unnecessary. The nation possessed, by sixteenth-century standards, an unusually uniform system of government and language, and an unusually representative central legislative body, Parliament. The realm had no major internal barriers, and was protected on the three sides by sea, with a weaker and less aggressive neighbour, Scotland, across its only land frontier. It was remarkable in retaining a system of taxation in which the rich (in theory) paid most, the poor none, and those between in proportion to their wealth, as assessed by their neighbours. Another of its archaic features, which likewise took some sting out of social and political inequalities, was the jury system, whereby the question of guilt in serious criminal cases was decided not by the judge but by a panel of amateurs chosen from the middle ranks of county society. Overwhelmingly, the Tudor English sought law rather than feared it, and showed a great and growing faith in the power of government to control crime, poverty and disease. Their common enemies, at local level, were not magistrates or tax-gatherers, but thieves, vagrants, hoarders of grain and sellers of adulterated goods. Their faith in the virtues of being governed would have been strengthened by the occasions on which, as in the case of Cardinal Wolsey's campaign against harmful enclosure, the royal administration actually seemed to punish the rich for oppressing the poor. The leaders of rebellions were indeed usually the men who normally functioned as government themselves at county or parish level: if not actually nobles or gentry, they were constables, churchwardens and the tithing men who assessed taxes. Despite all this, rebellion was not only relatively frequent, for most of the Tudor period, but very widespread in both geography and society. Far from being a marginal phenomenon, it involved towns, seaports and the countryside alike.

All this poses yet more starkly the question of why such a comparatively well-governed society rebelled with such apparent enthusiasm. The great turning point in the solution of it came in 1979, with the publication of an article by Diarmaid MacCulloch on Robert Kett's rebellion, which had occurred in Norfolk in 1549. This had been viewed as a classic, tragic and futile, Tudor uprising, in which commoners had taken up arms against their mistreatment by their landlords, and been bloodily crushed by the central government. What MacCulloch proved was that Kett's rising had been just one corner of a whole series which had covered the south-eastern quarter of England during the same summer. Each had followed the form taken by Kett's followers, of getting together in an armed camp and opening negotiations with the central government of the Duke of Somerset. All the other risings, however, had succeeded, to the extent that the government had sent out negotiators who had persuaded the rebels to disband, with assurances that their grievances would be dealt with or action taken to deal with them. An excellent snapshot of this process at its most effective survives from Sussex, where it was in the hands of the county's most powerful aristocrat, who was also a member of the royal government: the Earl of Arundel. He set up headquarters at Arundel Castle and summoned both the rebels and the gentry there. Having dispensed lavish hospitality to both, he heard the rebels' complaints about economic mistreatment case by case. As he proceeded, he punished both gentry who were proved to have mistreated the commoners and the agitators who had used the most extreme language against the existing social system when stirring up rebellion. Everybody accepted his judgements as fair and final. What went wrong in Norfolk was that there the government lacked a trusted negotiator, because the traditional one, the Duke of Norfolk, had been thrown from power by Henry VIII and was locked up in the Tower of London. Instead, it sent the Marquis of Northampton, who was both unfamiliar to the locals and bungled the job. Kett's men lost patience and stormed the city of Norwich, in doing so crossing the line into outright warfare and provoking a savage military retaliation from Somerset's regime. All the other risings, covering at least eight other counties, had not been noticed by historians because they had apparently succeeded in their objectives.

It is now necessary, therefore, to ask why Tudor rebellions did not break out, at particular times and places, as well as why they did. The sequence of the rebellions between 1525 and 1549 is particularly instructive in this regard. In 1525, Henry VIII's government needed a large sum of money in a hurry, to attack France during a spectacularly opportune moment when its king had just been captured by Charles V. It attempted to raise it by levying what was effectively a non-parliamentary tax from the kingdom, called the Amicable Grant, which saved the time needed to obtain a parliamentary one. This was, of course, of doubtful legality and came on the heels of heavy regular taxation, and East Anglia rose in rebellion against it. Henry sent nobles who knew the region best, the Dukes of Norfolk and Suffolk, to report on the situation, and they declared that the rebels were too numerous to crush and could not be persuaded to submit. As a result, the government scrapped both the plan for the Amicable Grant and the war that it was to fund, but saved its face by having the leaders of the revolt beg for royal mercy before they were pardoned for their actions. In view of this it is not surprising that the Pilgrimage of Grace, eleven years later, should have been similarly prepared to bargain, and that its leaders disbanded their armies when the king promised a series of measures to oblige their requests. What they did not realize was that religious policy was not as negotiable as fiscal, and that the king was far more deeply offended by their opposition. As a result, the most prominent were arrested after placing their trust in Henry, who used the excuse of further local unrest to declare that they had broken the terms of their pardon. The Henrician Reformation rolled forward; but on the other hand, a package of government measures was implemented to satisfy the rebels' economic and political demands, and to safeguard explicitly the core aspects of traditional religion.

Formidable as the Pilgrimage was, it covered only the northern third of the nation, while the Midlands and the south remained quiet. Almost certainly this was because the king had his trusted magnates busy in these areas, pre-eminently the Dukes of Norfolk and Suffolk in East Anglia, and the Courtenay family, led by his second cousin the Marquis of Exeter, in the West Country. These and their clients would have acted to reassure local people that royal policy was both more limited and more benevolent in its nature than rumour was making it seem to be. Why, then, did the same mechanism fail in the north? In Lincolnshire, where the first revolt broke out, there was no resident noble to do the work. In the north-east, the dominant local family, the Percies, was led by the current Earl of Northumberland. He was, however, incompetent and chronically ill, and the government had pushed him aside in favour of new men, and with him his younger brothers who, resenting this exclusion, were willing to join the Pilgrimage. In the north-west, the common people had unusually bitter economic grievances against the nobility, and were less disposed to listen to them, while in Yorkshire the local barons, Hussey and Darcy, belonged to the court faction which had supported Catherine of Aragon. They were now completely out of power and willing to gamble on joining the rebels as a way of forcing a passage back into it. After the suppression of the rebellion, the royal government installed a new regional council to run the North, on which local lay and clerical leaders joined forces to monitor and address popular concerns. The vacuum in Lincolnshire was ruthlessly filled when the king transplanted the Duke of Suffolk there from East Anglia, where he had a capable negotiator already in the form of the Duke of Norfolk.

Over ten years later, in 1549, another wave of sustained religious reformation was launched. In the south-eastern counties, where reformed religion had made the greatest impact, the rebels of that summer concentrated on economic problems, and seemed supportive of the religious reforms. Most of the North remained quiet, cowed by the executions in 1537 and also well managed by its Council. It was the West Country which rebelled now, in the name of traditional religion, because there circumstances had altered dramatically. In 1538 Henry had turned savagely against the Courtenays and destroyed their power, beheading the Marquis of Exeter. The key government man in the region in 1549 was a newcomer, Lord Russell, who did not command local respect and trust; and former retainers of the dead marquis were among the local leaders who led the people in arms. These western rebels seemed to have learned, furthermore, from the fate of the Pilgrims of Grace, and realized that their religious demands were not likely to be negotiable. Their statement of grievances, submitted to the royal government, was far more peremptory and forceful than those formulated by the Pilgrims. Instead of sitting still and talking, as the Pilgrims had done and the south-eastern rebels did, they laid siege to Exeter as a first step to clearing the road to London, and three pitched battles, which the government only won because of its superiority in cavalry and firepower, were needed to put the western rising down.

What is consistent throughout the whole history of Tudor popular rebellions, from those against Henry VIII to those against Elizabeth I, is the manner in which they sought to preserve the existing legal and social system, as one which their participants felt generally worked in their interests as well as those of the powerful and rich. This is signalled by the readiness with which they took as leaders the people prepared to support their cause who were nearest to the top of society as normally constituted. The monarch was, of course, the best of all, if he or she could be persuaded to agree to and embrace the rebels' wishes. Below the level of the Crown, rebels made the best of whom they could get, taking on nobles and greater or lesser gentry, as they were willing to serve. What is just as important is that when not even a gentleman was initially willing to join, rebels were quite capable of proceeding in any case, in formidable strength, led only by their parish priests and wealthier farmers or craftsmen, as happened when the Amicable Grant was thrown off or the West rose in 1549. Furthermore, rebels were also perfectly capable of putting irresistible pressure on their social superiors to follow their wishes, as happened at times during the Pilgrimage of Grace, or using a violent language of hostility and contempt towards the greedier members of the gentry, as occurred in the southeastern risings of 1549. It remains true, though, that even risings that began entirely as movements of the common people, and employed a language of social confrontation, depended on upper-class acceptance to succeed in the end. Those that opposed the Amicable Grant won out because they convinced the local aristocracy to urge the king to agree with their complaints. The Pilgrims were content to be led by nobles once they had recruited them, and the armed camps of 1549 believed, with some reason, that they were dealing with a government that would hear their grievances. In addition, a coherent and common language of popular politics, embodying a claimed right to protest, demonstrate and march against threats to the well-being of ordinary people, covered a wide range of different religious, social and political attitudes specific to times and places.

One further problem needs to be resolved. The succession of rebellions listed by Anthony Fletcher, stretching between 1489 and 1570, forms a natural and indivisible continuation of those of the late Middle Ages, which had included such famous episodes as the Peasants' Revolt of 1381 and Jack Cade's rebellion in 1450. After 1570, however, we are in a new world, for there was not a single further large uprising until the outbreak of full-scale civil war in 1642. A very significant shift clearly occurred in mid-Elizabethan England and, once more, it is Diarmaid MacCulloch who has suggested what it was, supported by Andy Wood. They have drawn attention to the social consequences of the twin great economic developments of the Tudor period: a steady and increasing rise in the population, and an associated (and partly resulting) increase in the price of all commodities, and especially of food. This meant that anybody who owned or leased land that produced a surplus of foodstuffs above the level needed to sustain the owner's household was likely to get richer and richer. Anybody who controlled less land than this, or none, was likely to become more and more impoverished. As a result, English communities which had entered the sixteenth century consisting of a number of landholders of fairly similar wealth left it comprised of a few very wealthy families and a large number of landless labourers and craftspeople.

This economic polarization split them politically. Villages and small towns which had collectively risen to defend common interests against royal policies which seemed to menace them were now run by newly formed parish elites who identified more readily with government in general, from the Crown downwards, to maintain their position as rulers of a mass of poorer neighbours. Furthermore, those elites now had new weapons with which to pursue their own causes at a national level, provided by their greater wealth and the sophistication – increasingly including literacy – which came with it. They could sue opponents and oppressors in courts of law or find sympathetic Members of Parliament or even royal courtiers to further their causes. Cavalry, men-at-arms and artillery, promises, statutes and betrayals, and the executioner's ropes and knives, had all failed to undermine seriously the readiness of English commoners to muster and march against the central government in defence of their own material and spiritual wellbeing, ever since the fourteenth century. It was instead the anonymous, fundamental and impersonal forces, embodied in registers of births and in price indices, which brought that tradition to an end.

5

SCOTLAND (1485–1560)

Scotland in the early modern period was a considerably smaller and poorer nation than England. It had a fifth of the population of its neighbour, and the royal income was equivalent to that of an English earl. These disadvantages merely helped to propel the Scots into becoming one of the most inventive and adventurous peoples in history. In the sixteenth century they had their own distinctive language; not Gaelic, the Irish tongue spoken across the Highlands and Western Isles, nor Norn, the dialect of Norse that survived in the Northern Isles, but Scots itself, the official language of the kingdom. A variant of German, like English, it had 50,000 words unique to itself, of which it has given one, 'glamour', to the English-speaking peoples. The kingdom was older than that of England, having been unified in 843 when the English were still divided between half a dozen realms. It was also proud to note that the area that became England had been conquered successively by the Romans, the Anglo-Saxons, the Vikings and the Normans, whereas Scotland had resisted the lot, and then beaten off the

English in turn. The first Scotsman known to history, a tribal king called Calgacus, who appears in the work of the Roman historian Tacitus, was characterized by his determination to preserve his people's freedom, as their most valuable possession of all.

By the early sixteenth century Scotland represented a paradox, at least in the eyes of outsiders. It had no external enemies save the English, who mostly left it alone, which meant that it had no need for sustained warfare. As a result, taxes were light, Parliaments harmonious, the government stayed out of debt and justice was simple and efficient. The realm was in many ways very cultured: it had three universities (and added a fourth before 1600) when the much more numerous English only had two, while its rulers spent heavily on magnificence, owning the largest cannon, the largest ship and some of the most beautiful palaces in Europe, and being surrounded by some of the best poets. It was also, in many ways, more stable than England: between 1399 and 1499 two Scottish kings were killed by their subjects, without much effect on the state itself, but six English rulers were deposed in the same period and the resulting instability altered basic patterns of government. Scottish civil wars were tiny compared with those in England with no challenges to the dynasty and few confiscations of noble land. There was little poverty and no popular uprisings. On the other hand, if Scottish political violence was much more muted then it was also more ingrained, with blood feud, murder and kidnapping all featuring in it and the government being disputed for years on end between different factions of nobles.

The key to the paradox lay in the nature of the dynasty in charge, the Stewarts, who were probably the most accident-prone royal family in late medieval or early modern Europe. The monarchs they produced had an unnerving habit of dying prematurely, so that every one of them to rule between 1400 and 1625 came to the throne a child, allowing the magnates to fight among themselves, on and off, until he or she grew up.

Five kings called James held the throne in succession, father to son, between 1406 and 1542. The first was murdered by rebels, the second was killed by an exploding cannon, and the third fell in battle against discontented nobles. That left the fourth, who succeeded in 1488, to make an absolutely marvellous job of putting the kingdom back together. He was almost the ideal medieval and Renaissance king: charismatic, brave, muscular, highly sexed, compulsively extrovert, and dedicated both to staging lavish court pageants and to ensuring the proper dispensation of justice by his courts. He was soon wildly popular. To consolidate this, and to ensure that he was respected by foreign potentates, he felt it necessary to inflict a crushing humiliation on the traditional national enemy, the English. In this he was probably correct, but he underestimated his own lack of military experience. In 1513 he launched his attack and was completely outmanoeuvred by a smaller English force in the hills near Flodden. The result was the last battle in Britain to be fought with medieval weapons, probably the largest ever fought between English and Scots, and certainly the most destructive to the Scottish state. James was boxed in on difficult terrain, and responded by leading a headlong charge against the centre of his opponents, much as Richard III had done; the Tudors were fortunate in facing royal enemies with a taste for suicidal courage. The king was killed along with twenty-nine noblemen or high churchmen and about 10,000 commoners.

That left his son, James V, to come of age in 1528 and pick up the pieces again. He was as able as his father, but somehow lacked his gift for popularity, seeming meaner and more calculating, and more inclined to let his court favourites enrich themselves at the expense of established noble families. In 1542 he too succumbed to the urge to fight England. He avoided battle in person but forgot that an army camp at that time was a dangerous place in itself. It was probably there that he caught either cholera or dysentery and died in the prime of life, leaving only a baby daughter, Mary. The fourth and the fifth James had governed in a similar way. Like the early Tudors, they worked hard to maximize profits from traditional sources of royal income, and topped those up with money gained from the Church. In the Scottish case, the latter was even more important, because the kings were relatively and absolutely poorer: Scottish churchmen had collectively ten times the annual revenue of their king. The solution was much less drastic than that adopted by Henry VIII and Edward VI but just as effective, the rulers remaining faithful and pampered adherents of the papacy while gaining ever more access to ecclesiastical wealth and patronage. By 1540 they controlled the appointment of bishops, could tax churchmen to an unprecedented level, and use church revenues to pay their own servants and church appointments to reward their followers and provide for their illegitimate children. It seemed that they had managed to obtain most of the practical benefits of a doctrinal Reformation without the need to implement one.

After the sudden death of James V, the Scots were faced with another long royal minority, of a more traumatic kind than those before. This was entirely the fault of Henry VIII, who seized the opportunity to unite the two kingdoms, with England as the senior partner, by marrying his young son Edward to the little Scottish queen. When the Scots proved reluctant to accept this, Henry sent an army which killed 3,000 of them and laid waste the south of their country: long afterwards, the novelist Sir Walter Scott was to give this action the wonderfully ironic nickname of the 'Rough Wooing'. As soon as Henry died, the Duke of Somerset renewed the attempt, with a full-scale invasion of Scotland. At Pinkie, near Edinburgh, he destroyed the Scottish national army, killing 10,000. Although few members of the elite died, many more commoners subsequently perished of hunger and disease as a result of the ravaging of the land by Somerset's soldiers: for them it was a worse disaster than Flodden. In desperation, the Scots took the only course left to them which promised to preserve their independence. They sent little Mary to safety in

France, and welcomed in a French army which held back the English until Somerset's government ran out of money and he fell from power. The English withdrew, but the French remained, to keep the country secure and prop up the regency government of Mary's mother, herself a French princess called Mary of Guise.

The Scots thus found themselves locked into an international contest played for very high stakes. Powering it was the great rivalry between the kings of France and the House of Habsburg, led by the Emperor Charles V, and his son Philip who was inheriting his Spanish, Italian and Netherland territories. The implications of that rivalry for Britain became more dramatic as soon as Edward Tudor died and was succeeded by his sister Mary. Because Henry VIII had declared both of his surviving daughters illegitimate, their claim to the throne was doubtful even though Henry had eventually restated it by Act of Parliament. By contrast, James V and his daughter both had a legitimate claim to England, in common law, through James's Tudor mother. Henry had disqualified this by statute, but it was by no means clear that he had a legal right to do so. As a result, the child-queen Mary Stewart could quite feasibly be deemed the rightful heir to Edward VI, and the French encouraged her to make just this claim. They further raised the stakes by betrothing and then marrying Mary to the heir to the French throne, Francis, without any saving treaty clauses that prevented a subsequent union of France and Scotland. Mary Tudor, of course, intensified the conflict by marrying the archenemy of the French, Philip of Spain. In the mid-1550s it looked as if the most likely fate for the British Isles would be to become an extension of the French monarchy, or else to be contested between warring satellites of France and Spain.

A series of chance occurrences prevented either development. The first was the death of Mary Tudor, and the conversion of England into a Protestant state ruled by Elizabeth, snapping its firm alliance with Spain. This made an impact in turn upon Protestantism in Scotland itself. In contrast to those of England, the rulers of Scotland – whether monarchs, the great nobles who held power while the latter were minors, or the regent Mary of Guise in the 1550s – had remained more or less firmly Catholic. None the less, Protestants had appeared in the kingdom from the 1520s onwards, and the government had engaged in sporadic persecution of them, although never with consistency or determination; there seem to have been only twenty-one executions for heresy, spread over thirty years. Mary of Guise chose to adopt precisely the policy which Mary Tudor has always been condemned for rejecting: to kill the Reformation with kindness, ignoring Protestants while reforming the Catholic Church in Scotland. An effective religious toleration was accompanied by an impressively broad programme to improve the education, morality and preaching skills of the existing clergy and to grant or lease out church lands to the laity, to deprive them of any material incentive for a change of religion. If Mary Tudor has always been censured for her severity, however, then Mary of Guise has attracted condemnation for her leniency. Neither of the groups of national historians involved has noticed the contradictions in this double verdict, which should powerfully reinforce a sense of how difficult Protestantism was to eradicate by either policy. In Scotland, toleration left the Protestants intact, and self-confident, while the policy of Catholic renewal was neither given enough time nor enough central enforcement to make much effect.

Now befell the next accident that was to transform British political and religious affairs. For 130 years, the French had repeatedly thrown the dynastic dice and emerged as winners, every one of their monarchs being relatively able and taking the throne as an adult. The ruler who had foiled the English in Scotland, and taken Calais from them, was the last of this succession of charismatic, warlike and popular kings, Henry II. In 1559 he made peace with Philip of Spain, thereby freeing himself, if necessary, for further intervention in Scotland. Instead, as he competed in a tournament following the peace treaty, a lance blade ran into his head. It killed him in the prime of life, putting his son Francis on to the throne in his place. This, of course, made Mary, Queen of Scots, the Queen of France as well, but both she and her husband were a little too young to rule effectively. Effective power fell into the hands of the Italian Queen Mother, and rival groups of French nobles began to struggle amongst themselves to advise or displace her. Here the pressures of the Reformation, long building up within French society, greatly worsened the problem, as some of those politicians now polarized around Catholic and Protestant positions. The fabric of French politics, held together for so long by dynastic good fortune, began to unravel, as the nation lurched slowly but progressively towards civil war.

The transformation of England into a Protestant state, and the distraction of the French, gave the Scottish Protestants their opportunity to launch an attack on the Catholic Church and government. By the end of 1559 the country had crumbled into open conflict, in which the Catholic party, aided by the French soldiers still occupying the land, soon gained the upper hand. The Protestants were rescued in 1560 by Elizabeth of England, who sent a large army and navy to their aid. This, together with atrocities committed by the French, convinced many waverers that the Reformation was the better and more viable cause. At this critical moment, the dynastic dice rolled again, and Mary of Guise died of dropsy. Leaderless, her party surrendered and the French sailed home, after which the English army promptly withdrew, leaving a Protestant government in control of the land. All the damage that the 1540s had done to Anglo-Scottish relations had now been repaired, as the new Scottish regime looked on the English Crown as its greatest benefactor and ally.

Scottish Christianity was now submitted to a Reformation very different from that of England, being at once gentler and more thorough. There was no wholesale dissolution and dispossession of the old Church; instead, its sources of money were gradually diverted, and its institutions and personnel were left to die out naturally. Alongside it the reformers slowly built a new national Church, or Kirk to give it the proper Scots name, based on the Calvinist system of ecclesiastical government that had been developed in Switzerland and was spreading into France and Germany: a hierarchy of committees and assemblies on which ministers sat with laymen. They started with the 'kirk session' within the parish, then rose up through regional presbyteries and provincial synods to the full national assembly. Relics of medieval religion which had survived in England, such as bishops, cathedrals, choral music, organs, ceremonies and seasonal festivals such as Christmas and Easter, were swept away. There was one further contrast with the English experience, and an ominous one: the English changes of religion had all been led by the current monarch, while the Scottish one was first imposed by overthrowing the authority of the monarch. At the same time there was no legitimate Protestant rival to that sovereign, young Mary, who remained the theoretical ruler of Scotland while divided from it by geography and now by religion. It was not a situation which could endure indefinitely, but the Scots in 1560 could envisage no likely solution to it.

6

ELIZABETH I (1558–1603)

Elizabethan Government

The story of governmental processes in the reign of the last Tudor has two aspects: first, that of a well-reformed and efficient central administration which was allowed to run down, and secondly of a reform of local government which was just commencing when the reign began and was triumphantly completed in the course of it.

Henry VIII had bequeathed an efficient system of war taxation, the subsidy, and Mary an effective system of taxes on foreign trade, the customs. Neither served to match the resources of France or Spain, and the ruthlessness with which those were exploited by their rulers, but they made the best of what was customarily available in England. The Elizabethan government failed to maintain the regular updating that was needed to keep both systems working properly, and in an age of inflation, the subsidy remained based on assessments of wealth made under Henry VIII, while taxpayers became more and more expert at evading payment. The nobility proclaimed itself to be two-thirds poorer by the end of the reign, in the face of all economic evidence. William Cecil, Lord Burghley, who was responsible for state finance for most of the reign as Lord Treasurer, reported himself to be earning £133 a year when his own records show him to have been raking in about £4,000. As a result, the average yield of a subsidy had almost halved by 1600, and a vicious circle was set up whereby Parliament had to vote them more and more frequently to support warfare, whereupon the yield of each fell still further. The customs rates remained unrevised too, and new kinds of goods were not added. Initially this neglect may have been a calculated risk on the part of the regime: to buy the goodwill of taxpayers while it fully established itself and its Church. Later, however, the inertia became ingrained, and ultimately must be charged against Elizabeth herself, who showed no inclination to tackle the problem.

The result was real financial trouble: parliamentary subsidies covered less than half the cost of Elizabeth's wars. The shortfall was made up by selling assets, including almost £900,000 worth of Crown land, by borrowing; by failing to pay bills; and by making captains pay for their own ships and colonels for their own regiments. A vignette of the Elizabethan military system is provided by the siege of Edinburgh Castle in 1573, where the English soldiers were ordered to crawl after every cannonball fired at the fortress and try to retrieve it. A knock-on effect was parsimony in government. One muddy day, when the queen was riding back to London from her hunting lodge at Royston, she found that her pearl necklace had broken. Her attendants were sent back along the road to search for every lost pearl. She spent a tenth of what her father had done on building, and sold off six palaces. The pay of her servants was held at the level that it had attained under her father, which, in a time of inflation, reduced it far below that at which it could comfortably support them. To take its place, a host of patents and monopolies were granted to Crown officials, which they could exploit for personal gain. The results could be difficult for everybody. Conrad Russell has told the sad story of Mr Middlemore, a civil servant who was first given power to sell licences for the export of peas and beans. This was made illegal, whereupon he was empowered to search for former Crown land that had slipped into private hands. He provoked so many complaints that the queen gave him the right to sell licences to export long bows instead, only to find that somebody else had that already. Two more attempts to reward him backfired before he slips out of the records. As for consumers, these monopolies doubled the price of steel, trebled that of starch and put up that of salt eleven times over.

Just as in military affairs, civil government could only be run by sub-letting responsibilities. The great government ministers each had to employ up to five secretaries to get their jobs done. The Court of Chancery had six official clerks to transact its business, each of whom had to pay up to forty private assistants to cope with the flow of paperwork. The main financial department, the Exchequer, had ninety-four salaried posts, but up to 200 people actually at work there. Of those ninety-four official appointees, the government had sold to fifty-seven the right to choose their own successors, to compensate further for the low level of pay; in addition, the sale price of a post could effectively supply an old age pension. As a further incentive to take the Crown's offices, the latter were awarded for life, and the result was that the administration was clogged at several points by geriatrics: Elizabeth's first Lord Treasurer, the Marquis of Winchester, died at the age of ninety-seven. To run the government at all therefore, let alone to make any profit from it, officials had to embezzle public money or demand fees from members of the public with whom they dealt. The six Clerks of Chancery each earned salaries of £750 per year, but their actual annual take was estimated at around £3,000 each, the income of an earl. Without that income, supplied by litigants to get their suits accepted and speeded up, they could not have employed all those assistants to run the court.

The problem was that Crown servants who had got used to embezzlement and racketeering to make the system work would often go further, and loot it for their own profit. In 1571 the accounts of the Exchequer were checked, and it was found that three out of its four main officials, the Tellers, had diverted funds to their private uses. When old Winchester finally died, it was found that £46,000 of public money had slipped into his own coffers. Faced with the approach of a Spanish invasion force, the leading royal ministers went to check on the amount currently held in the Exchequer and found that one of the current Tellers had almost emptied it, by lending out the royal cash reserves to private clients and pocketing the interest. As the man concerned had been appointed by the same ministers, they dared not expose him for fear of the impact on their own reputations. Instead they arranged to borrow back the Crown's own money from those to whom it had been lent, paying the latter to keep their mouths shut. The Teller responsible for this situation remained in office for ten more years. Things got no better in the next decade. In 1593, the Treasurer at War, Sir Thomas Shirley, was investigated for alleged malpractice, and it was found that he was receiving an official salary of £365 per annum, while making about £16,000, most of which he was spending on himself. Clearly, by paying tiny salaries the government was encouraging a culture of profiteering which was costing it enormous sums.

What, then, of the main organs of policy-making? The principal instrument of government was the Privy Council, established by Henry VIII. Under Elizabeth it was small, with an average attendance of six to nine people, and ever more overworked. In the 1560s it was meeting three or four times a week; by the 1590s, every day. This was because of the list of duties that it had accumulated: to advise the queen on policy; to deal with crime, the militia, national defence and poor relief; to collect data on Catholics and monitor their persecution; to plan war efforts; to fix prices and wages, and supervise local government; to refer petitions and defective statutes to the law courts; and to supervise budgets and authorize all expenditure. As a body, it was dominated by Burghley, and in the last years of the reign by his younger son Robert. A common loyalty to the queen, and to the Protestant religion, kept it harmonious for most of the time.

The great law-making institution was, of course, Parliament, which consisted of the monarch, the hereditary aristocracy assembled in the House of Lords, and the elected representatives of the counties and towns gathered in the House of Commons. No legislation could be passed, or taxes authorized, without Parliament, and yet it only met for a total of 5.5 per cent of the whole reign. It was a curious phenomenon in another way, in that it managed to become both more and less efficient. Efficiency was improved by its acquisition, during the sixteenth century, of clerks and journals to keep a record of the Commons' business, through enhanced legal privileges for MPs to enable them to concentrate on their work, and by the establishment of a regular chamber at Westminster in which they could meet. No other European representative assembly allowed such a range and density of discussion. Under Mary, the average number of statues passed during a session was forty-eight; it rose to 126 under Elizabeth. The problem was that many more measures were now failing as well. Under Edward, over a third of the Bills submitted to Parliament became law, while under Elizabeth that proportion shrank to a fifth. This meant that by 1600 anybody trying to obtain an Act of Parliament had an 80 per cent chance of failure, and the lobbying needed for success was very expensive. The system was just getting clogged up by excessive demand, and in the later part of the reign the Crown was trying to take pressure off by making more law in royal proclamations, or granting individuals the right to ignore defective laws.

A Tudor Parliament was undoubtedly an institution, having regular arrangements for all meetings and the ability to carry over business between sessions. It was also, however, an event, with personnel, issues and moods that could differ dramatically between each session. Under Tudor rule the House of Commons grew from 292 to 462 Members, mostly under pressure from local gentry seeking seats, making it the largest representative body in Europe. Parliament's powers were weaker than the state assemblies of contemporary Aragon, Sicily, the Netherlands, Denmark, Sweden and Brandenburg, but rule without it was still inconceivable. Elizabeth insisted that it could only discuss state issues if she invited it to do so. She was on doubtful legal ground here, as Parliaments had breached this rule under each of her three predecessors; but as she generally ruled well there were seldom issues over which MPs felt inclined to challenge her. The great discovery of modern historians, above all Michael Graves, has been the importance of the so-called 'men of business', MPs who were informally recruited by members of the government to represent its views and help in the direction of the House of Commons. The combination of these techniques and popular and well-explained policies meant that relations between the Crown and the Houses of Parliament were usually harmonious unless the Privy Council itself was divided or fell out with the queen. None the less, the reign saw a series of disagreements between the queen and particular Parliaments over her claim to limit what the latter could discuss.

All these institutions were dependent on, and lubricated by, the royal court and the counties. Like her sister but unlike her father, Elizabeth minimized divisions among her courtiers as she did among her councillors. The two, indeed, overlapped: members of the Privy Council also staffed her household, while their womenfolk ran her Privy Chamber. This system broke down towards the end of her reign, as the two drew apart. Some leading courtiers, like Sir Walter Raleigh, were never on the Council, while others, like the Earl of Essex, were always outvoted there despite a powerful court following, and tension grew as a result. The main role of the court was to link government to the provinces. Prominent courtiers were also the most important of the queen's hosts when she went on progress through the counties, and the pageants and other entertainments that they staged there were thrown open to the general public. They often intervened passionately in relatively minor local affairs. When one rich heiress came on the marriage market in Glamorgan, she was wooed by two ambitious young courtiers, Herbert Croft and Robert Sidney. Favouring the former, she found a bloc of magnates led by Burghley and Raleigh; but in the end she was more impressed by the latter's patrons, who included the current royal favourite, the Earl of Leicester.

The classic best-case situation was to have a county led by a powerful and capable nobleman who was trusted by the queen. The result was smooth and harmonious government from both central and local points of view: and that was the case in Derbyshire, Durham, Cheshire, Lancashire, Sussex and Leicestershire. Where the local magnate was out of favour with the queen, the communications on which administration depended broke down, and local politics became acrimonious: such was, at times, the fate of Hampshire, Nottinghamshire and Glamorgan. One solution to that problem, for local gentry, was to encourage Elizabeth to destroy that nobleman completely, to clear the way for a more effective replacement. This tactic could, however, rebound if a local power vacuum resulted instead, in which different contenders fought for supremacy, and that occurred in Norfolk, Suffolk and Northumberland. The least fortunate counties were those in which no dominant figure had emerged, and which remained torn by opposed power blocs, such as Wiltshire, Herefordshire and Kent. Alternatively, there were others, such as Essex, which lacked a magnate but in which the gentry had learned to cooperate as a team, producing efficient government by a different route. There was therefore no one pattern of local politics, but in each case the links between county and court were vital. The records of town councils show much more effort being made to lobby courtiers to have activities authorized or privileges granted by the Crown than to get legislation through Parliament to the same end.

On to all this was being projected a Tudor revolution in local government, by which processes and powers were set up in all or many counties to deal with epidemic disease, poverty, defence, the regulation of the economy, religious non-conformity and political dissent. The burden of all these was carried by the wealthier gentry of each county, who acted as the justices of the peace who enforced law and the deputy-lieutenants who led the newly formed militia, and also staffed *ad hoc* commissions to enforce religious change, drain marshes, combat piracy and undertake a range of other tasks. The same people sat as MPs, representing themselves as local leaders and almost never consulting the constituents for whom they spoke: parliamentary seats were only put up for an actual election if the local notables fell out. All such posts were unpaid, office confirming instead the prestige of local leadership. As justices, they were the most hard-worked of all, being officially responsible for enacting 309 statutes, 176 of which had been added since 1485. The burden was shouldered in part by increasing their number, so that commissions for most counties more or less doubled under Elizabeth's rule and those on them had to work even harder. Some of this huge expansion of governance was driven by technological invention, such as the increasing importance of gunpowder in warfare which meant that responsibility for local defence was given to bodies of men trained in the use of standardized firearms, bought and stored by the county. Much was due to the corresponding rise in the population, and in prices, which will be discussed later, producing novel social strains. Underlying both the change in administration and the change in defence, however, was something more intangible. The English state had emerged in the early Middle Ages as one of the most comprehensively and intensely governed in Europe. In the sixteenth century, this basic and inherited trust in government was simply applied to more and more tasks, on the assumption that it could make existence better and better for all in the realm.

To take another perspective, this process was one aspect of a huge extension in the state which took place under the Tudors. It engulfed the Church, bringing it all under Crown control and eliminating its separate legal privileges and its links with a foreign potentate, the Pope, and international religious orders. It brought in the aristocracy, eliminating areas of separate jurisdiction by nobles and local power bases run by princes. It created a huge, and increasingly sophisticated, Parliament. All this was an extension of uniform and systematized government, and not of royal power as such, for at each point royal authority was checked or limited within its own machinery. The great landowners were still vital to politics and administration, but were incorporated within the new system, and rulers still depended on them for all enforcement and protection of their authority. The English monarchy therefore reached the end of the Tudor period with a curious double aspect. It possessed an increasingly ramshackle machinery of central government and warfare, suspended from a series of financial and administrative shoestrings. On the other hand, it had one of the strongest and most ambitious systems of local government in the world. The reconciliation of that paradox was to be one of the greatest problems for the next dynasty, and the following century.

The Elizabethan Church

Around 1965 the accepted picture of Elizabethan religion looked like a well-kept garden, with neatly tended flowerbeds and lawns. Thirty years later it resembled such a garden after a herd of cattle had trampled over it. During the first decade of the twenty-first century, some renewed access and order has been provided to the scene, and a fresh consensus seems to be emerging among the specialists who earlier created such wreckage in it. The traditional view had been built up over more than a century, by an Anglo-American alliance of historians, culminating in the 1950s with the interpretation of Sir John Neale on the British side and William Haller in the

United States. It portrayed the Church settlement of 1559 as a perfect compromise, Catholic in its hierarchy (with bishops, archdeacons and cathedrals) and the wearing of clerical robes during rituals, and Protestant in its service, its theology and the decorations of its churches. This was the result of the innate English genius for compromise, working through Elizabeth's skills as a ruler. In particular, it represented a creative tension between the queen's more conservative instincts and a brash lobby of radical Protestants, nicknamed 'Puritans', in her Parliaments. From the church as upheld by Elizabeth came the great tradition of the world's Anglican Communion. From the Elizabethan Puritans came ultimately the equally great tradition of English Protestant dissent: that of Cromwell, Milton and Bunyan, of the United Reformed Church, Baptists and Society of Friends, and of the Pilgrim Fathers and the American system of disestablished community churches. Marxist historians, in turn, took the Puritans and made them into symptoms and forces of social and economic change, breaking down establishment, hierarchy and monopoly in English life. They linked them to the rise of a middle class, of capitalism and individualism, to make them the religious expression of early modernity. It was all neat, plausible and comforting, a picture which had something for every kind of Protestant, and most atheists and agnostics, in the English-speaking world. So what went wrong?

First, in the 1970s, historians realized that they could not agree upon who the Puritans were. To some, they were members of a small movement which appeared in the 1570s and challenged the structure of the Elizabethan Church, campaigning for it to be given a Calvinist church like the newly reformed Scottish Kirk. To others, they were simply 'the hotter sort of Protestant', those members of the reformed Church who were most zealous for the new faith. In the 1560s, however, there were no 'cool' Protestants among genuine converts to the new religion. There was a large minority of would-be Catholics and a majority of people who were neutral, confused and grudgingly conformist. Genuine Protestants represented another minority, all inherently enthusiastic. By either definition, the Puritans became a non-event: by the former, they were too few to matter, and by the latter, indistinguishable from Protestants in general.

Then historians realized that they did not understand Elizabeth. It is clear that the settlement of 1559 was a rushed and unexpected compromise. Elizabeth had made it plain that she wanted a Protestant Church, led by her instead of the Pope and without monks or the mass. Beyond that her intentions and expectations are a matter of conjecture. She certainly expected most of Mary's clergy to defect to serve her, and was shocked when all but one bishop, and hundreds of parish clergy – a fifth of those of London – refused to do so. That threw her back on the services of hard-line Protestants whom she had not expected to need, so that seventeen of her first twenty-five bishops had been men who had gone into exile under Mary. We also have a shortage of information for what Elizabeth herself was actually doing in this period, and when she made recorded comments we find that, like a wily politician, she was saying different things to different people. Experts in these events therefore cannot agree over whether she basically wanted a reformed Catholic Church like her father's and was forced to have a more Protestant one, or whether she wanted a more Protestant kind of Church but was forced to settle for a more conservative one. The church that did result was certainly not Catholic, but represented a mixture of Lutheran and Calvinist elements imported from the Continent, of which the former had much more in common with Catholicism than the latter.

We do have some insight into the queen's religious attitudes. Susan Doran has studied her letters, and found that her most abiding commitment was to her own power over the Church, asserted against Catholic and Protestants alike. She certainly saw herself as a Protestant, serving a providential God, but was vague over matters of theological belief. That should have made her willing to accept further change and compromise in religious affairs; but here we hit another aspect of her nature, revealed in her actions rather than recorded statements of principle. This was her dislike of change, once a situation had become established and familiar. Whether or not she actually wanted the settlement of 1559, she obstinately refused to alter it after it had been established. This focuses attention on the settlement itself, and recent research has emphasized what a botched job it was. To judge from the reactions of contemporaries, it was the most imperfect Church which has ever existed. Everybody who supported it for the first century of its existence seems to have done so despite reservations concerning some aspect of it. The Elizabethan bishop, John Jewel, who wrote the first official defence of it, referred to it in private as a 'leaden mediocrity'.

Its core beliefs were supposedly defined by the legislation and Prayer Book of 1559 and the Thirty-Nine Articles of 1563. Among the points that these documents left confused or obscure were whether the Church of England was simply an improved version of the Church of Rome, or something completely different and opposed to it, associated instead with the continental Protestant Churches; whether human beings could save themselves from sin by their own efforts; whether the clergy had a sacred status which set them off from the laity; whether the royal supremacy over the Church was vested in the monarch alone or in the monarch as a part of Parliament; and whether bishops had either absolute power over the lesser clergy or any role in running the state.

The Elizabethan Church therefore represented an ideological and administrative fudge, a stop-gap arrangement which for twenty years was regarded by virtually everybody as destined for inevitable alteration. This was, after all, how the Henrician and Edwardian Reformations had indeed proceeded, in instalments designed to achieve what was practicable at each moment. Only Elizabeth's extraordinary personality prevented that from occurring, and committed English

Protestants in general were shocked to find that no more reformation was actually going to occur. Absolutely none of them,
with the exception of the queen herself, seems to have been
content with the Church as settled in 1559. When they realized
that the queen was going to stick with it, they were forced to
choose between putting up with the situation or declaring
open dissatisfaction. The term 'Puritan' is best applied under
Elizabeth to those who refused to accept the settlement,
however unwillingly, and campaigned for further reformation.
This is the original meaning of the word, and it is one which
has united recent historians. The distinction between the two
types of Protestant first emerged in 1566, when the clergy of
London found that the queen seriously expected them to wear
the vestments prescribed by the settlement: the special dress
for services which represented a vestige of that worn by
Catholic priests. There is no sign that Elizabeth was especially
fond of vestments themselves, but they were now in the rule
book and she was responsible for maintaining the rules. The
man caught between queen and clergy was the Bishop of
London, Edmund Grindal, who himself grumbled about
having to wear the vestments. Finding some of the best
preachers in London unwilling to put on what they regarded as
rags of popery, he relocated them to the provinces, where they
were further from the queen's eyes.

The second clash began in 1571, after the defeat of the reign's
big Catholic uprising, of the northern earls. Many Protestants
now felt that the time had come for a further purge of features
of the Church that reminded them of Catholicism; and among
them were most of the bishops and Privy Council, and a large
party – perhaps a majority – in Parliament. This should have
been an overwhelming combination, but Elizabeth simply
refused to budge. Her stance persuaded some clergy to lose
faith in the settlement altogether, and start campaigning for a
wholesale revision of it, including the abolition of bishops. The
outright battle between queen and Church came in 1577, over
the issue of prophesyings. These were informal gatherings of

clerical and lay Protestants in the provinces, to pray together and concert efforts to complete the conversion of their localities. As such, they compensated for the fact that the structure of the reformed Church, taken straight over from Catholicism, was simply not designed for evangelism. There was a yawning gap between the higher and lower clergy, and no provision for co-option of the laity: the prophesyings took care of both problems and, as such, they were supported by Grindal, now Archbishop of Canterbury, two-thirds of the other bishops, and most of the Privy Council. Elizabeth, however, detested them. Because of their informal nature, they were not under her control as the formal Church could be. Moreover, they encouraged people to think about religion for themselves instead of listening to what the regime had to say about it. Her instinctual hostility was turned implacable by two actually unrelated incidents, cases of physical assault by local religious fanatics which persuaded her that to encourage religious discussion led inevitably to disorder. Accordingly, she simply overruled the majority of her advisers and banned the prophesyings. Her action was too much for Grindal, who went into open mutiny and found himself suspended from his job for life. This had never happened to an Archbishop of Canterbury before, and was a stunning illustration of what the royal supremacy could actually mean.

The true strength of Elizabeth's position was that she was the only option that the Protestants had: there was no obvious Protestant contender for the throne, and the heir in blood was the Catholic Mary, Queen of Scots. From now on, moreover, things at last began to swing her way, for two reasons which both derived from the fact that she had now reigned, successfully, for almost twenty years. One was that the key objective of the English Reformation was at last being achieved, and the majority of the English converted into active support for Protestantism. This meant that those who privately preferred Catholicism now had no realistic prospect of it without a coup or an invasion. Some of them set to work actively to

prevent further reform and to support the queen in hanging
on to the existing Church. The key person here was probably
Sir Christopher Hatton, a prominent courtier who delib-
erated recruited young clergy prepared to defend the
settlement of 1559. He could do so because of the second
consequence of Elizabeth's survival: that after twenty years a
generation of English had grown up who were used to the
compromise of 1559 and did not regard it as ridiculous. They
were, on the contrary, inclined to regard it as normal.

The greatest of this generation was John Whitgift, whom
Elizabeth promoted to Archbishop of Canterbury as soon as
the wretched Grindal died. In 1583 he turned directly on the
Puritans and did exactly what Grindal would never have done:
demanded that the clergy accept the whole body of ceremonies
prescribed for the church in 1559. Until now a lot of them had
been getting along by ignoring those that they did not like, and
Whitgift, supported by Elizabeth, was determined to flush
them out. He did, so that in a short time almost 400 ministers
were suspended from office. This, however, provoked such an
outcry in both Parliament and the Privy Council that queen
and archbishop were forced to back down. Elizabeth banned
the further discussion of religion in Parliament, but Whitgift
restored most of the suspended ministers.

Royal policy now took three main forms. One was a persecution of Roman Catholics, which reinforced the regime's
Protestant credentials and delighted Puritans in particular,
coupled with the opening of war with Catholic Spain. The
second was a continued harassment of individual Puritans who
made a public fuss about conforming to the requirements of
the Church. The third was an encouragement of young
protégés of Whitgift who began to extol the structure of the
Church, with bishops and cathedrals, as one instituted by
divine command, rather than a practical convenience. The
government, and especially the queen, seemed to be vindicated
by its defeat of the Spanish Armada, apparently the strongest
possible indication that God approved of what it was doing.

Buoyed up by this success, she and Whitgift felt able to take their policy a stage further, by arresting the leaders of the movement for the abolition of bishops. This spelled the final defeat of the Elizabethan Puritan movement.

It was now the turn of Whitgift to receive a defeat, when he tried at last to tighten up the theology of the Church of England. What he aimed at, specifically, was a clarification of its doctrine of salvation. He came up with a formula designed to unite most or all English Protestants within the broad spectrum of belief held by continental Calvinist Churches. To his surprise, Elizabeth forbade him to publish it as orthodoxy. Typically, she did not made her reasons for doing so clear, but Whitgift's plan very obviously ran counter to two of her most consistent instincts, as expressed in her letters. The first was, of course, her desire to keep control of her Church. The one thing that she clearly could not do in it, as a laywoman, was to make doctrine. For her archbishop to do so, although he apparently did have the right, by impli- cation dismissed her authority. The other was her genuine confusion over what the rules of salvation really were. Her intellect and her knowledge of the Bible were both good enough to tell her that Scripture was imprecise in many matters of doctrine. Her main grudge against Catholicism, apart from the fact that it was led by somebody else, was that it attempted to specify what the Bible did not. She did not wish to fall into the same error.

Elizabeth therefore ended her reign with what was in many ways a stunning victory. Her determination and resilience had preserved the settlement of 1559 against all opponents and created the most flexible and broadly based Christian Church in the world. She had secured to it at least the outward alle- giance of 95 per cent of the population; but she had also left three potentially serious weaknesses in it. The first was that the Puritans were still there, and although they were a minority of clergy and laity they were quite a large and well-distributed one. Fortunately for the government it was divided. Some

Puritans objected to the vestments of the national Church, some to its ceremonies, some to its cathedrals, and some to the lot. In general they were not a menace to other sorts of Anglican, or to the Crown, as long as they were left in peace to ignore such aspects of liturgy and dress as they found offensive. They would only produce serious trouble if a ruler appeared who was determined to enforce the rules upon them. In that eventuality, the trouble would be the worse in that English Puritanism had turned not simply into set of wish-lists for reform but a remarkably uniform religious subculture. It was distinguished by an intense preoccupation with personal salvation, a reliance on the authority of Scripture as absolutely paramount, and a belief that the majority of humans were predestined to damnation.

The second weakness of the Church was that towards the end of Elizabeth's reign a rival tendency was appearing within it, of members who were certainly not Catholic but wanted a religion that was more Catholic in some respects than that which was the norm in England by 1600. The loose definition of the Church actually allowed for such a reinterpretation within the limits of the law. If this movement began seriously to pull at the nature of Anglicanism, it would provoke the Puritans to haul more determinedly in the opposite direction. Before Elizabeth's death, it had no collective name. In the early seventeenth century it acquired, from its opponents, that of 'Arminianism', after a Dutch Protestant heretic. Its roots in Elizabeth's reign lay in a series of independent and largely disconnected initiatives. One was an attack on the Calvinist theory, popular among the majority of committed Elizabethan Protestants, that the identities of that minority of humans who were going to get to heaven had been decided from the creation of the world. From the 1580s onwards, some English Protestants – especially at Cambridge University – began to suggest that humans might have a general potential for salvation, as Catholics preached. Another initiative, associated particularly with Richard Hooker, was to portray the Church of England as a home-grown improvement of the medieval church, rather than as one wing of a Continent-wide resistance movement to the evils of popery. Alongside these developments was a growing reaction at parish level, of people who wanted more physical beauty and ornamentation in their churches, and more emphasis on ceremony. Collectively, all these trends represented a growing challenge to mainstream Elizabethan Protestantism, from the opposite side to that of Puritanism. Together, they were turning the English Church into the most dynamic, internally variable and unstable in the world.

The third weakness was that the process of reformation had left the English provinces a patchwork of different types of Anglicanism. West Sussex was very resistant to Puritanism; East Sussex was very Puritan. The East Riding of Yorkshire was very conservative in its Protestantism; the West Riding very radical. York itself was a notable centre of conservatism, but the county's biggest port, Hull, a notable centre of Puritanism. Lancashire was the most Catholic county left in England, but had a Puritan corner around Manchester. Herefordshire was a very conservative county, but was developing a Puritan enclave in the north-west, around the Harley family. Even at village level, Puritans could represent a distinct group among parishioners. If religious tensions were seriously to increase in England, this would mean that the fracture lines would run not between regions, but within county, town and even village communities. The situation held the potential for a civil war much more dreadful than anything known before.

In 1600 such a catastrophe was still unlikely, and would remain so if English rulers behaved with sufficient wisdom. None the less, Elizabeth had created the situation from which it might develop. There have been in the history of human affairs few rulers who seem to have cared less than she did about what happened after her death. This is largely because there have been very few who, like she, had no children, no surviving siblings, distrusted their cousins and were also very dynamic, strong-willed and able. In the last analysis, the

Elizabethan Church Settlement was unique, and problematic, because so was the queen who presided over it.

Elizabethan Catholicism

Something upon which all recent historians of Elizabethan England have been agreed is the need to reintegrate Catholics into the mainstream of Tudor history. Until the 1970s, the study of them was carried on inside a ghetto, populated by Catholic historians, who cooperated little with other scholars and were largely ignored by the latter. They reproduced the characteristics of English Catholics in general, by being interested in what to them was a heroic story of resistance and survival on the part of that small percentage of the population which continued an open allegiance to the Church of Rome. As such it was a tale of martyrdom, stoicism and secrecy on the part of an embattled minority. Most English historians, working consciously or not in a Protestant tradition, tended to sideline the Catholics as either a lunatic fringe or a set of sentimental and unworldly reactionaries. As Peter Marshall has noted, the main textbook on the English Reformation between the 1960s and 1980s, by Geoffrey Dickens, relegated them to two pages, in a chapter dedicated to 'residual problems'.

Since the 1970s a succession of historians, starting with John Bossy and Christopher Haigh and joined more recently by Alexandra Walsham, Lucy Wooding and Peter Marshall, has constructed a new approach to the subject. This emphasizes that there was no such thing as 'Elizabethan Catholicism': instead there were different Catholicisms, some existing alongside each other and some developing out of each other over time. In the 1560s most English people who preferred the traditional religion seem to have decided that the Elizabethan Church was just about tolerable, especially as Elizabeth could die at any moment and had no obvious Protestant heir. The regime did impose a fine for persistent failure to attend church, representing a day's pay for a craftsman, and from 1563 such defaulters could not enter university or law school. There was no law, however, which said that people had to attend church enthusiastically. The Lancashire squire Thomas Leyland of Leigh brought a dog along to each service with bells on its collar. He played with it every time the minister spoke, and so drowned out the service; and this was perfectly legal. The prominent Elizabethan Catholic Robert Persons was later to recall, with only some exaggeration, that for the first ten years of the reign all Catholics went to the established Church. During that period they posed no risk to the regime. When a college to train priests for service in England was founded at Douai, in Spanish territory, it was not to launch a missionary effort but to have fresh clergy ready if Elizabeth died or reconverted. Visitation records from the 1560s reveal lots of Catholic practices and ornaments surviving in the national Church, but almost nobody staying away from it.

Attitudes began to change from the middle of that decade. In 1565, the reigning Pope ordered the English not to attend the Protestant worship, for the first time. After that the government began to put pressure on the gentry, at least, to keep attending. This in turn helped to provoke the rebellion of northern Catholics in 1569, and Elizabeth's excommunication by the Pope. The government struck back by making it treason to obey any papal directives, and the Catholic seminaries retaliated by starting to send over missionaries: 438 by the end of the reign. With so many of the English still uncommitted to either Catholicism or Protestantism even by 1570, there was a real chance that this missionary effort could pull the rug out from under the regime's feet. The pressure increased when the Jesuits began to arrive in 1580, and from the mid-1570s recusancy – deliberate absence from the national Church – was starting to become a serious problem for the first time. In 1578 there were eleven recusants recorded in and around Richmond, Yorkshire; by 1590 some 219 were present. So, in 1581 and 1585 the laws were tightened to make it treason to be a missionary priest or to protect one, and the fines for recusancy were raised to £20, crippling anybody except the rich. From 1577 priests were hunted down, and about half those sent from foreign seminaries were arrested, and about half of those in turn – a total of 124 – were executed, along with 59 lay supporters. To be a seminary priest in Elizabethan England was therefore a dangerous job, but as Peter Marshall has pointed out, the persecution of Catholic laity was thirty-eight times less intense than that of Protestant laity had been under Mary. This was a plank of the Elizabethan regime's public stance: that it was prosecuting people for treasonable activities, and not for religious beliefs. The assertion is given some support by the fact that most executions occurred during the most dangerous period of Elizabeth's war with Spain, when Catholics could most credibly be viewed as allies of a hostile power.

Clearly, the government won the contest: by 1600 identifiable Catholics were reduced to about 6 per cent of the population of England, and this proportion diminished further thereafter. The main reasons for this are the sheer length of Elizabeth's reign, the comparative unity and determination of her government, and its control of all the more obvious and accessible sources of education, information and patronage. In addition, Christopher Haigh has argued that the popes gave the missionaries no leader and no plan, so that their distribution and activities were haphazard: by 1580 the North of England had 40 per cent of recusants, but only 20 per cent of priests. Furthermore, persecution forced priests into the arms of the gentry, the only people who could provide the refuges in which they could celebrate mass. This, Haigh has argued, switched the energy of the Counter-Reformation effort from the populace to gentry households, and turned Catholicism into a domestic religion. A common analogy currently employed by historians is that of twenty-first century Britain's relationship with its Islamic population. The latter is clearly not a threat in itself, but contains a few extremists who represent a danger to the national community in general. The implication of this comparison is that the Elizabethan government should have behaved more towards Catholics as the modern British one did to Muslims: instead of attacking them in general, it should have picked off conspirators while trying to cultivate the goodwill of the majority. Left in peace, the argument runs, Catholics could be expected to diminish naturally; and the record of the seventeenth century was to show that most of them were instinctively loyal to the English Crown.

This orthodox case, however, also recognizes that to some extent the government actually did distinguish between loyal and disloyal Catholics. The queen bestowed knighthoods and state visits on some recusants, and allowed them to remain in local government. Her favourite in the 1590s, the Earl of Essex, had Catholics among his personal followers, and the first official list of recusants, issued in 1592, contained only 4,000 names, which was clearly a deliberate sampling of the true number. Moreover, while Elizabeth urged on the capture of priests sent from foreign seminaries, she and the law were always gentler towards those who had served in the Marian Church. What the recent orthodoxy suggests is that the government did not go far enough to protect the loyal majority, but succumbed to a sincere but misguided distrust of it. It is a view that unites the new scholarship with traditional Catholic history. During the past few years, none the less, it has been increasingly undermined by the work of Peter Lake and Michael Questier, and the results of this clash of opinion may now be summarized.

It is true that most publications by English Catholics, and most private letters between them, advocated submission to the regime, and even cooperation with it. On the other hand, they also attacked the regime as corrupt, illegal and evil, and regarded submission as a regrettable necessity; they undermined it even while rejecting direct resistance to it. It is also true that many remained servants of the state in practice as well as theory, giving it active support; but at least as many slid between loyalty and disloyalty according to circumstance. It is correct to argue that the number of recusants was always small, but equally true that Catholics who attended the national church were probably much more numerous. Elizabethan Catholicism should be regarded as consisting of both, and it is notable that recusants were concentrated among women, the rich and the aged, those groups who were least vulnerable to the law. This suggests that many Catholics were indeed concealed among those who came to church. Priests generally avoided direct involvement in politics, but their very presence acted as a rejection and criticism of the official religion. Finally, there is no doubt that the number of Catholics who actually conspired against the government was tiny and that none of their plots got near success: the closest to do so involved William Parry, who actually got into Elizabeth's presence with a knife at the ready, but then lost his nerve. On the other hand, this lack of success was in large part due to the exceptional care taken by the government to guard against them. Among contemporary European leaders, two successive French kings and the leader of the Dutch all died at the hands of Catholic assassins: the threat was patently a real one.

Above all, the fashionable simile, which compares Catholics to modern British Muslims, is fundamentally wrong. To make it work properly, there would need to exist a single world leader of Islam, openly devoted to the destruction of the British government and completely safe from British retaliation. Most of Europe, like Britain, would not have been Islamic, but the USA, Russia and China would all have been fundamentalist Muslim states, with the American president talking openly of intervention in Britain. Queen Elizabeth II would have been a devoted governor of the Church of England, but Prince Charles a dedicated Muslim who had been held in prison for many years and was associated with plots to overthrow his mother. Prince William would have been an Anglican, but said to have a soft spot for Muslims because of his father. Put into that situation, it is hard to imagine that the modern British government would have been any less frightened of British Muslims than the Elizabethan government was of Catholics.

It may be, however, that the whole discussion of Elizabethan Catholicism has been fundamentally misconceived, and that the true danger posed by Catholics to the Elizabethan Church Settlement was of a quite different kind, which is usually ignored because it is redefined. This consisted of the attempts within the Church – which have been mentioned earlier – to reform it to make it more Catholic than the one sought hitherto by the majority of English Protestants. They appeared even as the great majority of the English were at last converted to the new religion. If the growth of recusancy was one feature of that conversion experience, then the appearance of forms of Anglo-Catholicism, later nicknamed Arminianism, was another. They were, for reasons also suggested above, to pose a more dangerous problem for the established Church. Put like that, the Catholic threat from within the Church was more significant than the one outside it, even though it was one that had sacrificed both the Pope and the mass and so lacked the two defining characteristics of true Catholicism.

The sum of all these reflections is that it is just to fault Elizabethan Protestants for being too suspicious of individual Catholics, and for acting with too much brutality towards their priests. It is difficult, however, to conclude that their fear of Catholicism was itself misguided.

Foreign Policy

At the opening of Elizabeth's reign, the chief policy imperative abroad was that which had dominated English statecraft for most of the previous 400 years: hostility to France, and therefore friendship with anybody who posed a threat to the French. As the latter had just taken Calais, and had an army stationed in Scotland, they seemed even more dangerous to England than before. This made imperative a continuation of the Tudor tradition of friendship with Spain. The latter was strained slightly by Elizabeth's profession of Protestantism, which turned her realm automatically into the greatest Protestant power in the world and put the Spanish on the opposite side of the confessional divide. France, however, was also Catholic, and as long as Elizabeth did nothing to aid the international cause of religious reform, she and Philip still possessed more common interests than points of division.

The 1560s were to bring about a diplomatic revolution, which the 1570s were to complete. First the French descended into their own wars of religion, which were to last for the remainder of the century. This enabled the English to throw them out of Scotland, and install a friendly Protestant government there, but it also reversed the whole traditional balance of power, turning France from an aggressive superpower into a broken and paralysed state, vulnerable to invasion and manipulation by its neighbours. In 1567, by contrast, Philip decided to strengthen his grip on the Netherlands, which he had inherited, together with Spain and most of Italy, from his father Charles V. Hitherto they had been largely self-governing; now he resolved to bring them under firmer control as part of an intolerant Catholic monarchy centred on Spain itself. A huge Spanish army of occupation was sent to them, intended to crush local resistance to this scheme, and representing, in the process, a serious potential threat to England's control of the Channel and therefore to Elizabeth itself. As one of her councillors, the Earl of Sussex, put it, 'the case will be hard with the queen and with England if ever the French possess or the Spaniards tyrannise over the Low Countries'.

The aims of English foreign policy between 1570 and 1585 were therefore clear and consistent: a French royal government which was friendly to England and tolerant to its own Protestants, and the return of the Netherlands to their former practical self-government, preferably under a weak and notional Spanish rule or in the worst case as a newly independent Protestant state. Realizing those objectives was nightmarishly difficult, as the queen's government sought to find French politicians who were both willing and capable enough to fit the bill, and supplied financial and diplomatic aid to rebels in the Netherlands while trying to keep the peace with

Spain. By 1585 it was clearly failing in both objectives. Philip was slowly but surely regaining the Netherlands for strong and intolerant Spanish Catholic rule, reducing his opponents to Dutch Protestants holding out in a few northern seaboard towns. At the same time he had conquered Portugal and taken over its colonial empire, greatly strengthening his power in the Atlantic. A substantial faction of French Catholics had now become prepared to make their nation a Spanish client in order to eradicate Protestantism. In that year, therefore, Elizabeth at last made a formal alliance with the Dutch rebels to send an army to save them from reduction by Spain. Her aim was to force Philip to negotiate with them; instead she found herself at war with him.

Philip rapidly concluded that his objectives in France and the Netherlands could be secured most easily by eliminating England; and the result was the invasion force that he sent against it in 1588, known as the Spanish Armada and representing the largest combination of soldiers and sailors that had ever sailed from a European port. It represented a compromise between two very different plans: to launch a carefully prepared amphibious operation directly from Spain, or to send over the Spanish army of the Netherlands in a swift attack using the element of surprise. What Philip actually did was to send a large fleet from Spain to the English Channel, to collect the army of the Netherlands and ferry it over to England. Even though it still caught Elizabeth's government off guard, the plan was too complex and clumsy, and underestimated the superior power of the English fleet, which had larger and better armed ships. The queen had continued the build-up of sea power commenced by her father and sustained by her sister; she had spent more on her ships than any other ruler in peacetime, and produced the most heavily armed navy in the world. The result was history's first big fight between the new style of war fleet, dependent on cannon and sails. Her captains could not destroy the Armada in battle, but they harried it so relentlessly that it was unable to achieve its rendezvous with the army and was driven up into the North Sea instead. From there, its whole objective now lost, it had to make its way home around the British Isles, suffering heavy losses from storms and collisions with coastlines on the way. It was a colossal English victory, and arguably the greatest naval disaster in Spanish history.

Philip was now even more determined to prosecute the war with vigour, and it lasted beyond both his lifetime and that of Elizabeth, being waged until 1604. England found itself fighting on five different fronts, sometimes simultaneously: its armies continued to support the Dutch rebels, intervened in the French civil wars and had to deal with a major conflict in Ireland as well, while its fleets operated on the coasts of Spain and Portugal and among the Spanish colonies of the Caribbean. Perhaps 12 per cent of the young adult males of England saw military service during these years. Remarkably, in view of the comparatively limited nature of her resources and her increasing ramshackle financial system, Elizabeth achieved all of her military targets. She enabled the Dutch to establish an independent Protestant state in the northern half of the Netherlands, while the Spanish consolidated their control of the southern half: the opposite coast of the English Channel was taking on its enduring political shape, of being safely divided between France, Belgium and the Dutch Netherlands. She assisted a new royal family, the Bourbons, to take over France, which led the faction in the French wars that had been most amenable to England and hostile to Spain, and most willing to tolerate Protestantism. Ireland was thoroughly conquered, at last, and English naval supremacy established in the northern Atlantic. As part of the latter process, English trade links were dispersed around the Atlantic coasts of Europe instead of being concentrated on the Netherlands as before. The trick was to send out small expeditions with limited strategic objectives, paid for, as said above, partly by their officers. As a result, Elizabeth did not make a single foreign conquest, nor plant a single lasting colony, nor win a single major battle abroad; but she took on the strongest monarchy in the Christian world, with no other state to assist her, and won everything that she sought in doing so, without ever running out of money. In an age characterized by ruinously expensive warfare and religious division, in which France and Russia fell to pieces, the German states all temporarily ceased to function as great powers, and Spain repeatedly went bankrupt and lost the northern Netherlands, this was success indeed.

The British Isles

An English Protestant, contemplating the world around on New Year's Day 1560, would have found it a distinctly scary place. To the south were the Catholic French, who were also to the north as well, occupying Scotland and propping up its Catholic government. To the east were the Netherlands, ruled by the Catholic Philip of Spain, and to the west was Ireland, nominally ruled by Elizabeth but full of semi-independent Catholic lords, one of whom, Shane O'Neill, was currently in rebellion and seeking aid from the French. Forty-three years later, at the death of Elizabeth, the whole vista had changed. Scotland was held by a friendly Protestant regime, and the main ports of the Netherlands by independent Dutch Protestants. France was ruled by a new dynasty which tolerated Protestants and at least did not view the English as natural enemies, while Ireland had been brought under secure English Protestant control. It was a typical Elizabethan catalogue of successes, but won with huge difficulty and cost in human suffering, especially to the Irish.

The first hole in the ring of enemies was punched during 1560, when the French were ejected from Scotland and the Protestant government installed. The next year this achievement was already imperilled, as the Catholic Queen of Scots, Mary, returned to take charge of her realm. She was now nineteen years old and at the peak of her vigour and fertility – courageous, charismatic, charming, six feet tall and determined to rule the entire British Isles if she could. She had not wanted to come home, but at the end of 1560 the dynastic dice had rolled against France again: her young husband, the king, has died of an illness and the French had pushed her out. After a short, frantic search for a new husband, she reluctantly appeared in Scotland, and spent four years in a kind of political limbo. She confirmed the Protestant government in power, but balanced it with a Catholic royal household, and would neither convert to the reformed religion herself nor ratify its legal existence. While in France, she had explicitly claimed the thrones of England and Ireland, in opposition to Elizabeth. To make a working relationship with the latter, it was essential to give up this claim, which Mary was very willing to do if she were recognized formally as Elizabeth's heiress in return. Elizabeth, however, was not prepared to name any successor, for fear of diminishing her own authority, while her more fervently Protestant councillors, above all William Cecil, the future Lord Burghley, could not bear the prospect of another Catholic ruler. As a result, neither part of the deal was made.

Mary remains one of the most controversial figures of her age, and there is no agreement over either her character or her performance as monarch. Her detractors hold that her policy of inactivity amounted to dereliction of duty, and destabilized both Scottish politics and relations with England. Her admirers reply that it worked quite well in practice, giving her a firm grip on power. They point out how she then neatly trumped Elizabeth in the dynastic stakes, during 1565, by marrying Henry, Lord Darnley, an individual almost unique among the British nobility in having a hereditary claim to the Scottish, Irish and English thrones. This made Mary's own legal claim to all three almost unassailable, and she followed this coup by giving birth to a healthy boy, James, to secure her own line of succession, and strengthening the Catholic party in Scotland. Her critics reply that Darnley turned out to be stupid and unstable, plunging Scottish politics into a morass of conspiracy, assassination and blood feud. Her defenders answer that Mary handled this well, trapping him into a political isolation in which he was murdered by his enemies, possibly with her connivance.

All agree, however, that she now made two fatal mistakes. The first was to fail to have her husband's death investigated with apparent impartiality, and to get swiftly remarried to one of the men most suspected of the crime, the Earl of Bothwell. That made her so unpopular that she was deposed and replaced by her baby son. She escaped captivity in 1567, only to be defeated in battle and make her second serious error: she fled to England, trusting that Elizabeth would either give her aid or let her pass through to France. Instead, the English queen locked her up for twenty years, in which Mary, inevitably, began first to plot to escape and then to overthrow Elizabeth. Eventually the latter's councillors persuaded her that the only safety lay in cutting off Mary's head. Only two aspects of Mary's career as a queen seem beyond dispute. One was that she faced an appallingly difficult task on her return to Scotland, of working with a government and kirk divided from her in religion and supported by a strong and suspicious neighbouring kingdom. The other is that, although she possessed many political virtues, she was a poor judge of character and acted with too much haste in tense situations: and those two weaknesses destroyed her.

In the wake of its queen's flight, Scotland collapsed into six years of civil war between her personal friends and enemies, cutting across the religious division. It was only ended by another English army, sent in 1573 to tip the balance in favour of her opponents and of the succession of governments that they installed in the name of her son. The land was left chronically unstable and divided: of the four men who ruled Scotland as the young James VI grew up, two were murdered, one executed and one forced to flee abroad. James himself was to survive two alleged attempts to assassinate him and a successful one to kidnap him. What repaired the situation, in the end, was that he turned out to be one of the best kings in Scottish

history, judged simply by results: some of his Stewart predecessors may have been more talented, but he combined genuine
political skills with a successful evasion of the family
propensity for premature death.

From 1585 onwards he set about the stabilization of his
kingdom. He divided the new Protestant Kirk from the
nobility, and then against itself, putting up with harangues
from ministers who preached up its independence from royal
authority and detaching the moderates from them. Slowly he
persuaded it to accept his control, and eventually to accept
bishops back as the agents of it. He split the Scottish Catholics,
in turn, punishing the more turbulent and favouring the most
amenable. He took the nobility as partners in government,
married an intelligent Danish princess and produced a
succession of children with her, and kept Scotland out of the
war between England and Spain while maintaining good relations with the English. His one weakness was with money. The
Reformation had removed the great prop of the Church's
financial resources from the royal income, and so taxes had to
be substituted. This was a difficult situation in itself, but James
worsened it by showing no understanding of the need to
balance the books and the means to do so. On his wedding day
his purse was so empty that he had to borrow a pair of socks in
which to get married. None the less, his mismanagement of
money was overshadowed by his political achievements. The
greatest of all these was to show himself capable of the patience
and reserve that his mother had never achieved. Elizabeth
refused to name him as her heir until she was actually dying, so
he just waited for her to go, while making himself as agreeable
as possible to her leading followers. In 1603 the Crowns of
England and Ireland fell into his hands, in an ironic reversal of
the ambition of Henry VIII to unite the three realms.

The reign of James was also the one in which the Scottish
Reformation took root, as, coming to the throne so young, he
reigned for even longer than Elizabeth had done in England. It
made its greatest appeal in the Lowlands, and especially in the

towns and among the lesser landowners, or lairds, the equivalents of the English gentry; both groups who stood to gain by the new system of ecclesiastical government which put some power in the hands of local laity. The lairds, in addition, gained at a national level, because the process of religious reform gave them seats in Parliament for the first time. By 1578 all but 10 per cent of Lowland Scottish parishes already had either a minister, who could perform all religious duties, or a reader, who could recite the basic lessons of the new faith. By 1600 the majority had their own ministers, though there were hardly any, as yet, in the Western Highlands and Isles. About a quarter of the clergy of the old Church defected to the new Kirk, and this was many fewer than could have been the case, because the Protestant religious leaders were very selective in those whom they would allow to serve as ministers. Death was made the penalty for saying mass, but this law was slackly enforced, and claimed only one or two victims. It helped the situation that Scotland mattered so much less than England to international Catholicism that no sustained missionary effort was mounted there. By 1600 the old religion was confined to a few areas where great noble families, such as the Gordons in the north-east, and the Maxwells in the south-west, still professed and protected it. The combination of strong decentralized ecclesiastical government, in the parish committees known as kirk sessions, with a powerful national body, the General Assembly, in which local representatives met as in a Parliament, produced a much more cohesive Church than in England. Scottish Protestants suffered none of the divisive and centrifugal tendencies which vexed the Anglican Church almost from its establishment.

What, then, of Ireland? As has been emphasized, one of Elizabeth's achievements was to subdue it comprehensively. Ever since her time, doubts have been cast upon the necessity for this policy and the wisdom of it, and during the past thirty years they have been expressed most cogently by Steven Ellis. He has pointed out that Ireland ought to have posed no problem at all for the Tudors, unless they had chosen to make it into one. In 1541 about half of it was still in the hands of native, 'Old Irish' chieftains, who were riddled by traditional mutual hostilities and never going to unite against the English Crown unless it pushed them to do so. The other half was mostly owned by the descendants of medieval English and Norman settlers, the 'Old English', who held all the seaports and most other towns and could be relied on for a basic loyalty to the Crown, largely because of their inherited animosity towards the natives. A test case of this truth provided at the opening of Elizabeth's reign was that of the leading Ulster chief, Shane O'Neill. He had absolutely no natural hostility towards the English, and had only developed one because the Crown's governors had refused to recognize his right to succeed to his family lordship, which was valid under native Irish law but not English. As a result, the viceregal government in Dublin made expensive and fruitless efforts to destroy him for over a decade, until in 1567 he was killed by a rival local chief, of the MacDonnells, who sent his head to the English Lord Deputy as a goodwill gesture.

These realities, however, made little impact on English royal policy, which from the mid 1550s took a sustained new form: to impose direct rule on the entire island and convert or coerce the natives into adopting English administrative, legal and social customs. With the accession of Elizabeth, a religious dimension was added to this programme: to enforce Protestantism, on the English model, as well. In part this initiative stemmed from fear, that the growing strength of both France and Spain would make it increasingly likely that either power would land armies in Ireland, where they would find allies among discontented chiefs. It was therefore vital, so this argument ran, for the English Crown to close and bolt this strategic back door to Britain. In part the new policy derived from injured pride and thwarted ambition: with the final end of English dreams of a domain in France, ambitious men who wanted glory and land now had to turn westward for both, and Ireland seemed the

most promising source. It was also a product of fiscal calcu-
lation. As the English state found itself outclassed in money and
manpower by its European rivals, the attractions of an under-
developed land upon its far side, which might be turned into a
reservoir of both, became much more obvious. Finally, Ireland
succumbed to that Tudor English zeal for systematization and
improvement of all things, using the reforming power of
government, which was already having such an impact on the
Church, on Wales and on local administration.

The truly tragic aspect of Elizabeth's policy towards her
other kingdom was that she adopted this policy without being
able or prepared to give it consistent support. She resolved that
it should only be governed by English newcomers appointed
wholly because of her own favour and completely lacking any
local power base. With these royal deputies came swarms of
greedy Englishmen eager to take land and office away from
anybody who was there before them. The queen, however,
denied them the money and the instructions to enable them to
carry out a steady and well-directed programme of extending
royal power and English ways of life. Royal authority became
represented by a series of administrations which alienated both
the natives and the medieval English settlers, but had only
limited strength. The result was a stop–go process, in which the
New English who pushed into the island under Elizabeth's
rule provoked Old Irish chiefs and outlying Old English
nobles into rebellion, piecemeal. The queen was forced to send
over supplies of soldiers and money to put down the larger
uprisings, after which the lands of the rebels were, increasingly,
confiscated and divided among the New English and some Old
English and Old Irish allies. At the same time the Old English
would be taxed, with unprecedented severity, to pay for these
expeditions, from which they themselves gained relatively
little profit. After each was complete, Elizabeth would cut off
the funding, reduce the soldiers and order the New English
to behave better towards the traditional inhabitants; which
they would usually disregard, stirring up another round of

uprisings. The New English soldiers, regarding Ireland as a semi-savage land and having to deal with opponents who waged guerrilla warfare from woods and bogs, behaved with a viciousness unknown in British conflicts. They routinely killed civilians of both sexes, and devastated large areas with the specific intention – all too effectively achieved – of reducing the inhabitants to famine.

One episode from these operations may serve as exemplary. In 1575 the ruling Lord Deputy, the Earl of Essex, sent a naval expedition to terrorize the MacDonnells, the same clan which had done such good service to the government by eliminating Shane O'Neill. Essex, however, had obtained a royal grant of some of their land. The English found that they had sent their women and children, numbering several hundred, to apparent safety on the offshore isle of Rathlin, guarded by a few soldiers. On capturing it, the attackers lost a total of three men, and used this as an excuse to slaughter everybody on it, hunting down the last in caves and on cliffs. The commander of the English fleet was one Francis Drake, who was to become an enduring national hero as the greatest of all Elizabethan seamen: but this episode in his career never entered English popular memory.

By 1590 three-quarters of Ireland had been brought under direct royal control by these methods. Ominously, the advances in state and New English power had not been accompanied by a proportionate one in Protestantism. By this date the great majority of the British had genuinely embraced the reformed religion, but only a small minority of the Irish. In part the problem was structural, that the new Church of Ireland was much poorer and more decentralized that those of England and Scotland. Until now it had lacked any college to train ministers, and neither the Crown nor its representatives made the necessary money available for a missionary effort. There was also, however, a major political difficulty: that the new religion was associated so firmly with the New English, that not only the Old Irish but the Old English had very little incentive to identify with it. The Old English, who had until within living memory been the mainstay of English rule in Ireland, were starting to reinforce their commitment to Catholicism, as one sign of their resentment of the way in which they had been treated under Elizabeth. None the less, most of them were still loyal, if with increasing sullenness, and only one province still remained outside direct governmental control: the northern one, of Ulster.

The greatest native chief there was now Hugh O'Neill, a very able and intelligent politician, educated in English ways, using the English title of Earl of Tyrone, keeping an army trained and armed on the English model, and very willing to keep his region loyal to the queen if he were only placed officially in charge of it. For their own part, neither the English government nor its Irish deputy wanted trouble with him; but once again they were unable to control their New English men on the spot, who harassed and slighted O'Neill until he rose in revolt in 1594. The resulting war engulfed most of the island, as other Old Irish threw in their lot with him and he proclaimed a Catholic crusade and made a partnership with Spain. The decisive battle was fought at Kinsale in 1601, when only superior military skill enabled the reigning English governor to defeat the allied Hispano-Irish army. O'Neill made peace two years later, on terms that left his lands and political power in Ulster intact: the government had spent about £2 million and shed huge quantities of blood in order to get back to its original position.

In fact there had been a decisive change. O'Neill had lost his army, which made him still more vulnerable to the renewed bullying and threats of the encroaching New English. In 1607 he became convinced that they had persuaded the new monarch, James I, to arrest him, and fled to Europe with the other leading native chiefs of Ulster, an event known in Irish historical tradition as 'the Flight of the Earls'. His intention was to return with another Spanish army, but Spain was now at peace with England and he died in exile. The threat that he posed, none the less, seemed real enough and provoked King James to destroy his Irish power base by dividing his lands, and those of his companions in flight, among new owners who included some Old Irish but larger numbers of English and Scottish settlers. Ulster, which had been the most independent, Catholic and Old Irish of provinces, was transformed within a decade into the one most populated by Protestant newcomers.

Logically, James and his ministers should now have finished the job by launching a sustained missionary effort to convert the remainder of the island's population, but they still lacked the money, the mechanisms and the interest to do so. Instead, royal policy became one of toleration and attrition. Protestants were left in charge of the established church and the government, dominating central and local offices and (through the mass creation of new peers and boroughs) the Irish Parliament. The Catholics, both Old Irish and Old English, still owned most of the land. The two groups, now divided very starkly by religion, were left eyeing each other warily, with the New English occasionally grabbing more land from Old Irish chiefs or buying it up as the latter suffered from their lack of business experience and contacts and got into debt. Sporadically, the Dublin governments would launch campaigns to force the Old English into Protestantism by fines and threats, but these were never maintained. The official hope was that Irish society would slowly stabilize and reunite as more and more ambitious Catholics were prepared to convert in exchange for a hope of power. It was in reality a powder keg; but one which would not ignite as long as nobody threw in a flame.

Could things have turned out differently? The Steven Ellis argument suggests that they could, and points to the contrasting case of Wales. The Welsh had been conquered by the English Crown in the thirteenth century, and the best of the spoils allotted to New English newcomers much as those of Ireland were under Elizabeth. The native population retaliated with a succession of rebellions, each of which was followed by more savage laws to repress and discriminate against it in favour of English settlers. As a nation, Wales was saved by a complete accident of history: that the English king Henry V left a frisky French widow, Catherine, who fell in love with one of her household, a handsome young Welshman called Owain, son of Maredudd, son of Tudor. The English shortened this to Owen Tudor. They were married, and when the royal family discovered this it was disposed to tolerate it, first because Catherine was now too far from the throne to make her actions seem important, and then because of the outbreak of the Wars of the Roses, when the ruling dynasty became glad of all the loyal relatives it could find. The resulting self-destruction of the Plantagenet royal house left Henry Tudor as the only feasible contender for those who wanted to bring down Richard III, and so England duly found itself with a Welshman on its throne. The discriminatory laws against the Welsh were repealed, and they were allowed to come to England, and to the royal court, to make their fortunes. Some did exceptionally well: the Syssell family, Anglicized to Cecil, produced the chief minister of Elizabeth I, while that of Morgan Williams of Glamorgan, which changed its name to Cromwell, was to go on to still greater things in the next century.

Above all, the Welsh were given control of their own land. When it was incorporated into the English system of government, under Henry VIII, no New English were allowed to flood in to staff the new county offices or be returned for the new parliamentary seats: it was the native gentry who filled most of both. Under Elizabeth, almost all the bishops in Wales were local men, the Bible and Prayer Book were swiftly translated into Welsh, and Jesus College, Oxford, was founded to train Welsh ministers. Welsh religion had been exceptionally free of heresy and insulated from continental Protestant ideas, and the Reformation there was unusually slow in taking off. It was, however, entrusted to the native ruling class, who made it their own. By the end of Elizabeth's reign, Wales was both one of the most Protestant parts of the realm and one of the most loyal to the Crown, while still maintaining its own strongly marked national and cultural identity. It is hard to avoid the suspicion, at least, that if Catherine's love-match had been with somebody called Fitzgerald, or even (to stretch a possibility much further) O'Brien, then the whole history of the British Isles might have been different. By entrusting the Old English wholeheartedly with the Reformation and the spoils of office and of conquest, it seems arguable that the Tudors would have bequeathed a largely Protestant Ireland to posterity. It is, however, impossible to have things both ways in history: and had Catherine's lover not been a Tudor, then subsequent generations would probably have had to reckon with a rebellious, alienated and largely Catholic Wales.

Elizabeth's Reputation

In popular memory, Elizabeth narrowly beats Queen Victoria as the greatest queen that England has ever known, to judge both from the number of portrayals of her in novels and on the television and cinema screen, and the consistent admiration which she is accorded in them. Her iconic status is further illustrated by the fact that when a pub is called 'The Queen's Head', it is most commonly Elizabeth's face that is displayed on the board. In the Great Britons poll of 2002 she emerged as the favourite monarch in British history. She is one of those rulers who have left an image which is now pretty well proof against anything that historians may say.

The process of turning her into a legend commenced soon after her death, and took two different forms. One was to make her the embodiment of aggressive and committed Protestant religion. Elizabeth's actual record in this respect was shaky, but in comparative terms it was unrivalled. No other English monarch between 1500 and 1700 could match her support for international Protestantism, and her defeat of the Spanish Armada was the greatest English victory over a foreign foe between Agincourt in 1415 and Blenheim in 1704. A perfect blueprint for this portrait of her was left in the work which, next to the Bible, was to become the essential reading of zealous English Protestants: John Foxe's *Book of Martyrs*. Ironically, Foxe knew perfectly well that in reality she did not match his image of her as a godly crusader, and it was intended to rebuke her; but later generations took it for reality. As her immediate successors, the Stuart kings, failed much more completely to live up to the image, her apparent example became a stick with which to beat them, embodied in books, the theatre, sermons, stained-glass windows, prints, poems, monuments and the celebration of the anniversary of her accession as an unofficial national holiday.

The alternative portrait was one designed for those who wished to look more deeply into the nature of the reign. It was the work of the greatest English historian of the age, William Camden, and was more or less an official history, commissioned by Burghley and completed under the eye of the new king James I. What it showed was a queen with superlative political skills, who pursued moderation in religion and statecraft: admirable but a bit of a cold fish. As a contrast to her, he rehabilitated the king's mother Mary, Queen of Scots, as a less able ruler but a more human and endearing personality. All the problems of the reign were blamed on the intrigues of loyal but misguided court factions, and especially on the Puritans for trying to overturn the queen's policies of balance and conciliation. This was an image which perfectly fitted what the new king and court wanted to hear, but was also to some extent based on solid evidence. For almost 400 years it was the history of the reign that was accepted by virtually all intellectuals. It was assimilated neatly into the modern boom in the writing of history, which resulted in more than a hundred biographies of Elizabeth being published between the opening of 1890 and the end of 2002: most of these were based firmly on Camden's image. The same is true of the representations on film, save that they worry more about it. From Bette Davis in the 1930s to Glenda Jackson in the 1970s to Cate Blanchett and Helen Mirren in the 2000s: screen Elizabeths have consciously sacrificed true love and intimacy in order to make a better job of ruling. With Camden's Queen of England has also come his Queen of Scots: on film, in novels and in 'pop' biographies, Mary has emerged as the weaker ruler but the more human, deserving sympathy as Elizabeth merits admiration.

This great tradition came up for review by professionals in the years of revisionism after 1970, when an unprecedented number of academic historians began conducting research of a novel intensity and indifference to received opinions. The contemporary records were, inevitably, less favourable to Elizabeth than the accounts which had followed her death. They turned out to include the attacks of Catholics, the complaints of Puritans and a series of critiques of the regime, published by disgruntled courtiers between 1572 and 1592, which accused the queen of being the puppet of unscrupulous politicians. When historians worked through the surviving papers of her ministers, they found that most had referred to her at times with exasperation and disrespect. The same ministers were shown up as having some unpleasant traits of their own. Burghley, in particular, who had seemed the exemplary royal servant, loyal, self-effacing and sagacious, was revealed as a Protestant bigot and a master of dirty political tricks, who certainly tried to manipulate his royal mistress whether or not he succeeded. Sir Geoffrey Elton made the first telling assertion by a modern historian that Elizabeth was the instrument of her advisers. His pupil Christopher Haigh produced the first full-bloodedly revisionist biography in 1988, portraying her as somebody who possessed star quality at a distance but at close quarters turned out to be a bundle of hysterics and histrionics, growing into a bossy old bat trying desperately to cling to her youth: Whitehall Palace had become Sunset Boulevard.

In the same period, between 1970 and 1990, a number of other forces worked against her reputation. A new interest in political culture revealed the skilful way in which the regime had represented itself, in propaganda and image projection, giving historians the impression that by admiring it they were falling for a confidence trick four centuries old. The study of the financial records exposed the dreadful way in which she had allowed the revenue system to run down. Research into the Elizabethan Church turned what had seemed to be an ideal compromise into a constant precarious balancing act which encouraged divisive and disruptive tendencies. Analyses of her rule over Ireland identified her reign as the birthplace for all of the land's modern troubles. Patrick Collinson noticed that, in their desperate need to preserve a Protestant settlement, in the face of Elizabeth's failure to produce an heir or name a successor, the queen's ministers developed ideas which were to be very dangerous to the monarchy. They drew up a plan for an aristocratic republic in the event of the queen's death, with Parliament choosing the next monarch. They also ensured that Mary was legally tried and executed, whereas Elizabeth would have preferred her to be murdered, to prove that the English could destroy anointed monarchs whom they deemed to have become dangerous. Both set precedents which were to have fatal effects two generations later. Elizabeth appeared increasingly to be a ruler who had achieved short-term success at the expense of all who came after her: a sovereign almost criminally indifferent to a future which did not include her.

It seemed for a while therefore that she was becoming one of the main casualties of late-twentieth-century historical revisionism. At that point, however, a different ideological force of the period came to her rescue: feminism. She was, after all, an outstanding example of a strong and successful woman, operating in public life on what seemed to be her own terms. At the least this suggested that the new sensitivity to gender issues in history had to be applied to her reign. In its strongest form, it invited any emancipated woman to regard her as a sister. The result has been a general recognition that, however it is rated in relative terms, the issue of Elizabeth's womanhood has to be accorded considerable importance. A long-lived female monarch, ruling without a husband, was simply an unprecedented phenomenon in England and one that made most people nervous. The degree to which individual historians factor in the issue is, predictably, varied. Some, such as Anne McLaren, see it as fundamental, and make the reasonable point that Elizabeth's relations with her followers, characterized by their peculiar mixture of intimacy and detachment, stability and tension, were only possible to a single woman. Most subordinate it to religion and politics, arguing with equal cogency that a king who led a Protestant Reformation and then failed to marry or secure a Protestant succession would have called forth similar reactions to those produced by Elizabeth.

There is at present no consensual or coherent picture of the queen shared even by experts inside Britain. Four recent views seem to me to be particularly revealing. Richard Rex has published a textbook which sums up the revisionist case against her; significantly, it is dedicated to the hundreds of Catholics executed by her regime after the rising of 1569. Susan Doran has accumulated a succession of studies which make her a more straightforward person than others do: more willing to marry, more consistent and devout in her religion, and fairer in her treatment of courtiers. David Starkey has emerged as her greatest current admirer, making a full-blooded restatement of her image as a national heroine. Finally, John Guy, in his prize-winning biography of Mary, Queen of Scots, has given us an Elizabeth who is emotional, erratic, unreasonable, shifty and unpleasant, with Burghley functioning as her evil genius. What is really interesting to me is that each of these positions, bolstered by modern professional scholarship as they are, reproduces one from Elizabeth's own lifetime. Richard Rex is the ultimate heir of the Elizabethan Catholic view; Susan Doran expresses Elizabeth as the queen portrayed herself; David Starkey has restated Camden's history; and John Guy the arguments of Mary's supporters. It seems that professional historians are still as much the prisoners of the past as the servants of the present.

The Woman at the Centre

So what does my own Elizabeth look like? I would emphasize four aspects of her character in particular, in order to get as close as possible to the human being beneath the crown. The first is the frustrated spinster, the other face of the Virgin Queen. She seems to have had no objections to marriage as such: she certainly intended to keep control of her realm, but might have wed a husband who had carefully restricted powers. The problem here was one of opportunity. At the opening of her reign she seems to have been genuinely in love with Robert Dudley, but he was clearly unacceptable to her other supporters, and there was never a better domestic candidate. That left her to look abroad, and there no Protestant princes were available of sufficient status to make a match for an English queen. On the other hand, she could find no Catholic royal family which contained an eligible man prepared to forgo the public practice of his religion. In the end she just ran out of options.

She did, however, have both a passionate nature and a need for affection, and the strain of celibacy and isolation told upon her and those who served her. It certainly showed in her treatment of her maids of honour, who were expected not to marry as well, and were disgraced if they did. One, Mary Shelton, sought her permission to do so, and the queen beat her so hard that she broke a finger. It showed in her attitude towards the Church. As a Protestant, Elizabeth was supposed to favour married clergy, and she certainly permitted them; but she could never bring herself to receive her bishops' wives with enthusiasm. It also rebounded on the affairs of the nation. For an unusually shrewd and intelligent woman, she had a glaring weakness for handsome and dashing men who excelled in superficial glitter. Four in particular were indulged by her: the aforementioned Robert Dudley, whom she made Earl of Leicester; the French Duke of Anjou; Sir Walter Raleigh; and the second Earl of Essex (son of the butcher of the Irish). All proved to be liabilities when trusted with really important responsibilities, all to some extent disrupted national politics, and in the end she had to cut off Essex's head in order to save her government.

Starved of love in the straightforward sense, she compensated by demanding it from her followers and subjects as a whole. She had an insatiable appetite for compliment and adoration. One of her most successful courtiers, Sir Christopher Hatton, remarked that 'The queen did fish for men's souls'. She dressed to dazzle: in 1600 she owned 103 robes, 269 gowns, 96 cloaks and 26 fans. Like her father, she loved to gamble on cards; unlike him, she always insisted on winning, so that courtiers had to set up funds to pay their obligatory losses. The other side of this aspect of her nature was revealed in the pet names that she gave her courtiers and the solicitude with which she visited them when they were ill. Possessive and emotionally needy she may have been, but she did win the love or respect of those around her. She also made an impact on a wider public. Sara Mendelson has worked through the records of opinion, made by both government informers and local observers, and found that they testify to an overwhelming affection for her among her subjects. One of the most telling illustrations is found in the private papers of an astrologer called Simon Forman. He was no romantic, being an unscrupulous and hard-bitten lecher, but recorded with joy and pride a dream in which his queen had offered him a kiss.

The second aspect of her nature to be emphasized here is pathological conservatism. It should not be confused with caution: Elizabeth could and did take some serious risks, both at home and abroad, and it may be remembered that she ended up waging war on a geographical scale never attempted by any previous monarch. Nor was it a love of established ways as such, as she proved by systematically remodelling her predecessor's government and church. What she hated to do was to change any situation to which she had become accustomed as queen. This has already been illustrated in the major cases of state finance and religion. It also showed in high politics. She found it hard to get rid of familiar figures in the political land-scape, showing great reluctance to put to death the nation's premier peer, the current Duke of Norfolk, and the Queen of Scots, even when she was persuaded that both had been plotting against her. It was painful for her to acquire the new as well as to remove the old. Her Privy Council got smaller and smaller, and five of its members succeeded their fathers upon it; and none were great nobles who might expect to do so by birth. This all had the benefit of giving the politics of her reign a unique stability in Tudor and Stuart England, with ministers serving longer, and dying more often in office, than under any other ruler. It also narrowed political opportunity dangerously towards the end.

The same pattern shows up with regard to the bounds of her realm. She was determined to hang on to all territory which she thought as being her rightful inheritance. For a decade she destabilized relations with the French by trying to get back Calais, and her treatment of Ireland derived from her conviction that, as its theoretical queen, she should be able to govern every foot of it. She showed no interest, by contrast, in acquiring any new lands. At times the Dutch were willing to adopt her as their sovereign in return for large-scale and sustained military aid, and had she been inclined to agree, and fortunate enough to survive the consequences, she might have acquired a new domain in the Netherlands to replace the lost medieval one in France. In the event, she never gave the prospect serious consideration. Her interventions in Scotland were made after great hesitation, and only after she became convinced that the security of England depended on them.

Her use of patronage displayed identical traits. As her reign went on, she gave fewer and fewer titles and grants of land, preferring to reward servants with economic monopolies and licences which were lucrative but easily withdrawn. She cher-ished the existing peerage, giving them royal properties, using a personal touch in her letters to them, letting them run up arrears of taxation and evade it on an increasing scale, and caring for the education of young nobles. What she avoided was the creation of new titles. She made in fact just ten during her very long reign – the longest of any English monarch between 1377 and 1820 – and of these only one (Burghley) was not already of noble or royal blood. Under her rule, the total size of the peerage declined from fifty-seven to fifty-five titles. This all created a huge log-jam of people waiting for honours and gifts that they felt appropriate to their rank, which had to be breached as soon as the queen died.

The third aspect of Elizabeth now highlighted may tentatively be termed the feminist. There is no doubt that she did suffer from the contemporary convention that women should normally have no place in public life, and her chief ministers all referred at times (behind her back) to her womanly weaknesses and tried to make policy for her in a manner that would probably not have been dared under an adult king. Among the many delightful anecdotes dug up by Christopher Haigh to illustrate his own biography of her is that of a London woman in the 1590s who, on seeing her, exclaimed (too loudly) 'Oh Lord, the queen is a woman. How could it be?' Elizabeth squarely confronted this prejudice, at all social levels, by declaring herself to be the exception which proved the rule. Her line was that women were indeed generally unfit for political authority, but that she herself was not a woman: she was a goddess. To give this more nuance, she was set apart from the run of humanity by her royal blood, by the holy oil which consecrated her as a monarch, and by the will and favour of the Christian God, who had chosen her for the throne. This enabled her to transcend all the usual limitations of her sex. Her taste for power-dressing was not simply an expression of personal flamboyance but of this sense of herself as a living icon. She loved to parade herself before her people, and coupled a taste for visual display with a genius for gracious and memorable comments, served up to gratify different audience. When I myself went up to a Cambridge college, to commence my undergraduate studies there, I was informed proudly in the welcoming address to students that Queen Elizabeth had visited it, and praised it for its age and piety. When I took up my permanent academic post at Bristol University, I was informed proudly in the speech of welcome to new staff that Queen Elizabeth had visited the city and declared one of its parish churches to be the finest in England. In her lofty grace of public manner, as in her dazzling appearance, she made herself into a fitting representative of a deity.

Her womanhood ensured, however, that there was one traditional aspect of the royal role that she was completely unable to fulfil: this was still an age in which adult rulers were expected to posture, at least, as warlords, in a world in which men alone did the fighting. It was Elizabeth's bad luck that, with this disqualification, she had to preside over one of the most complex and ambitious war efforts that the English had ever launched. Military expeditions incurred her dislike for four reasons: they were risky, they were expensive, once launched they were out of her control, and they moved the limelight away from her. That is one reason why she liked to keep them as small and brief as possible, with limited objectives. For a court which was at the centre of such prolonged and extensive operations, it notably lacked a military atmosphere. War heroes were not showered with titles, lands and favours, and civilian councillors were more prominent and influential.

Finally, this portrait of Elizabeth would present her as a superlative performer, with an enormous personality and a proportionate talent for deploying it to maximum effect. She terrorized her courtiers with her moods, so that those arriving at court needed a warning of them: although not a dangerous employer as her father had been, she could be a nerve-racking one. She hated having her subjects serve anybody else: when one of her courtiers, Sir Nicholas Clifford, returned from abroad wearing the chain of a foreign decoration, she exclaimed that 'My dogs wear my collars'. Whereas other monarchs worried that their nobility spent too much time at court and not enough attending to their duties in the provinces,

Elizabeth liked to keep most of them dancing attendance on her. She boasted to the ambassadors of other states of her popularity, and expected elaborate compliments from them as the opening move in all diplomacy. She was expert at ruling with a combination of the stroke and the slap, charmingly and dazzlingly gracious at one moment and bossy and bullying at another. Secure in her position as the last Tudor and the only credible Protestant incumbent of her throne, she could treat opposition with all of her father's ruthlessness, though none of his bloodlust. Archbishop Grindal was one victim of this trait, while she dealt with attempts by Parliaments to persuade her into unwelcome policies first by trying to talk them away and then simply by vetoing the measures that they presented if they refused to take the hint.

She had fewer intellectual interests than Henry VIII but more of an intellect. Both, however, had a more or less equal tendency to enjoy the pomp and majesty of monarchy while avoiding the administrative grind. She preferred not to attend the Privy Council, and so never lost a suspicion that its members, or groups among them, were twisting evidence or telling lies in order to push her into actions which she was reluctant to take. This was in fact absolutely correct at times, and a number of such cases of deception are recorded, such as the bogus story that the French were to land another army in Scotland, which persuaded her to invade it in 1560; the luring of Mary, Queen of Scots, into plotting to assassinate Elizabeth, which provided the vital evidence needed to execute Mary; and the attempt to stop the queen learning about the coming of the Spanish Armada, until they had made better preparations to meet it and seemed less taken by surprise. Her response to such manipulation was to delay decisions until she felt more confident that she was not being hoodwinked into them. The result was a pattern of postponements, cancellations and contradictions in decision-making, which had a particularly serious impact on diplomatic and military affairs. During her last years, her government was starting to show signs of strain.

The Spanish war had reached stalemate, with the English more anxious to make peace than their opponents. Court politics had become unusually divisive and embittered, leading to the rebellion and execution of her final toy-boy, Essex, and then a monopoly of power by Burghley's son Robert Cecil. The last Parliament of the reign turned directly upon the queen over the issue of the economic monopolies that she was granting as rewards to her followers; and she was forced to surrender to its demands. Her splendid costumes made an ever more glaring contrast with her physical decay: one Venetian ambassador reported that she stank so much that it was wise to stand upwind of her.

None the less, nobody should lose sight of three basic truths: that she coped outstandingly well in a particularly difficult period for European monarchies; that the story of her reign is one of a string of major successes achieved with very limited resources; and that she possessed genuine intelligence, political shrewdness and strength of personality. Like her father, but with more stability, she had both an intense need for attention and affection and an ability to reward them. She was not merely charismatic, but a mistress of the art of outreach: she was loved and remembered by commoners largely because she noticed them. One such piece of consideration, noted by David Starkey, may be taken to exemplify this: on her pre-coronation entry into London, she was handed a sprig of rosemary by a humble woman, and when she reached Westminster, she displayed it prominently alongside the rich gifts made to her formally by the leading citizens. This is the sort of gesture, so simple and yet so remarkable, on which enduring reputations are based.

7

POST-REFORMATION BRITAIN
(1560–1640)

Introduction

The political history of Britain alters dramatically at the year 1603, with the union of the Crowns of Scotland and England under James VI and I. The social history does not, however, and instead forms a distinctive period in both realms which spans the eighty years between the downfall of Catholicism in both during 1559–60 and the collapse of effective royal control of them in 1640. It was characterized by the effects of religious reform and of an inflation of population and prices, producing between them a time of exceptional tension and excitement in both society and religion. One label for it used in recent years has been 'Jacobethan', after the two monarchs whose reigns straddle most of it, Elizabeth and James; but it is one which gives too much weight to rulers and ignores the fact that over a quarter of those years involved two more sovereigns, Mary, Queen of Scots, and Charles I. The term 'Post-Reformation' also poses difficulties, as the process of Reformation itself

certainly occupied the first two or three decades of the period
and arguably continued in some respects until the end of the
seventeenth century. None the less, it does highlight the
importance of religious reform in shaping social attitudes, and
avoids the worse shortcomings of alternative labels. As when
dealing with political history, both the records and the history
that has been written from them exist in much greater quantity
for England than for Scotland and Wales, so that this is only in
part a British study. None the less, for England at least, a great
deal of valuable research has now been carried out.

Popular Politics

Why did the common people of post Reformation England
put up with post-Reformation England? To put the question
with more precision, why did they continue to tolerate a
political system that denied most of them the franchise, and a
social system which ensured that most of the profits of their
labour went to others? This has always been a stark problem
for historians, and one that was only sharpened by the work of
social and economic specialists since 1970, which revealed how
distinctive and how brutal conditions in the period were.
Between 1500 and 1640 the number of people in Britain more
or less doubled, with the fastest growth occurring in England
between 1575 and 1600. The English were, in fact, increasing
by an average 0.6 per cent per year in an economy which could
absorb a growth of up to 0.5 per cent. The missing 0.1 per cent,
year on year, meant that the supply of food and goods was not
keeping pace with the supply of persons. The result was a huge
inflation of prices: overall, they seem to have risen six times
over in Britain between 1500 and 1630. Incomes failed to
increase in proportion: in England in general their real value
seems to have halved between 1500 and 1640, though in
London the fall was only a quarter. By 1600 it is possible that in
a normal year nine-tenths of the earnings of the lowest grade of
manual worker would have to be spent simply on food and
drink. Out of the one-tenth remaining would have to come all

the other necessities of life, including rent, which was going up along with every other expense. Even in the upland valleys of Glamorgan, poor grazing land for the most part, rents more than doubled between 1570 and 1631. On the richer farms of the Vale of Glamorgan to the south, they rose almost four times between 1559 and 1632, while in the North Welsh border country around Chirk, the increase was tenfold from just 1595 to 1631; and in this, as in other respects, the English economy led the way. On top of the basic population pressure came other stresses. The importation of huge quantities of silver into Europe from the new Spanish colonies in the Americas may have produced a currency inflation that reinforced the effect of population pressure on prices. At periods between 1550 and 1650 widespread war on the Continent disrupted the markets for English products and produced serious trade and industrial depressions. In addition, even the weather was going wrong: since 1300 the European climate had been cooling, and this reached its furthest point between 1580 and 1680, in a miniature Ice Age. Lowland English rivers now froze each winter, snow lay all the year round on the Scottish mountains, and the amount of time in which crops could be grown contracted by about thirty days.

The result was to polarize society between the minority who could make a profit from land, and the majority who could not. The rising price of food and level of rent meant that the former were steadily growing richer and the latter poorer. This turned most villages from communities of smallholders into collections of landless labourers employed by a few rich farmers. It sent the greatest landowners on a spending spree greater than anything they had enjoyed before. This was the age of the 'prodigy house', huge mansions like Longleat, Audley End and Burghley, which were built with so many rooms that some were left empty for lack of purpose. It was the time of the pre-feast, a sumptuous banquet laid before guests, which would be thrown away before they could tuck in, to be replaced by a yet finer one; some hosts provided a succession of these. Such conspicuous consumption by the elite coexisted with the increasing impoverishment and fear of the masses. It is easier to understand why Scotland and Wales came through this period intact: they had much smaller populations, living in more dispersed societies which handled subsistence economics well and had little actual poverty. The puzzle is how England survived, with its much denser concentrations of people, much more glaring social extremes, and long tradition of popular rebellion and of savage animosity between classes, voiced at moments of tension.

In the event, it did more than survive: it stabilized still further. The years between 1569 and 1642 became the longest period of internal peace that England had known since it had been a province of the Roman Empire. By the 1620s it was probably the least violent state in Europe. Its society was internalizing a new concept of law observance, as part of a duty to the nation. In 1550, a crime was still regarded, as it had been since prehistory, as an offence committed against an individual, which could be dealt with through negotiation and compensation. By 1650 it was commonly viewed more as a breach in a national code, demanding a fixed penalty. Local magistrates had begun to regulate the activities of commoners as never before, controlling alehouses, parish festivities and church attendance. In 1580, parish officers had committed much the same offences as anybody else, including drunkenness, violence and theft, and a third of their brides were pregnant at marriage. By 1680 they rarely appeared in court as defendants, and then mostly for 'middle-class' crimes such as embezzlement, while bridal pregnancy had become confined to the very poor. Most crimes were not committed as expressions of anger or desperation, but as short-cuts to greater wealth, and criminals were not admired or protected by the population in general.

At the same time, this was not a population which could be described as peaceful by modern standards. Brawling was a frequent accompaniment of merry-making, and in twenty-four out of the twenty-nine years of the early Stuart period, the

Shrove Tuesday holiday in London, the traditional venting of high spirits before the solemn season of Lent, led to criminal prosecutions for serious violence. Nor had the English become blindly deferential. To choose just one example of the many that prove this point, it is only necessary to visit Norwich Cathedral in 1640, when the seats allotted to the city corporation had been moved under the public galleries. The wealthy merchants concerned were subjected to a weekly rain of excrement, furniture and saliva, against which their only defence was to beg the cathedral chapter to shift them back out of range.

So how did the English manage to be so unruly and yet so self-controlled, and how did they come through such terrible economic pressure apparently more cohesive and closely regulated than before? The reasons were all rooted in their existing social and political system, with its tradition of protest and negotiation and of royal governments that paid some attention to the grievances of commoners, considered earlier when discussing Tudor rebellions. In the early Stuart period, social groups continued to be capable of uniting against economic problems. The most obvious of these was the supply of food, of which the mainstay was bread. The period contained two huge failures of the cereal crops, in 1629–31 and 1646–9. These affected most of Europe, producing widespread popular revolt; in England, by contrast, they provoked government action. In the first of these, ordinary people in certain areas took the law into their own hands, by seizing stocks of grain which were being hoarded until the price went still higher or were being loaded on to ships bound for parts of the Continent which were prepared to pay more. The royal government ordered the local Justices of the Peace to stop these, but also to stop the hoarding and the export of grain which had provoked them. The magistrates worked hard to do this until conditions improved.

In the late 1640s what happened was even more impressive, because there was no royal administration to give the orders: the king was now a prisoner, and the kingdom caught in prolonged political crisis tipping at times into civil war. In these circumstances the justices worked on unbidden, impounding stocks of grain and making sure that they were sold at reasonable prices. The greatest English industry of the time, and one especially vulnerable to the fluctuations of foreign markets, was cloth-making. The government reacted to its problems by sponsoring new Acts of Parliament, such as one in 1598 which directed employers to raise wages in times of high prices, and one in 1603 which imposed a statutory minimum wage, something not seen again until the end of the twentieth century. In the depression of the 1620s, underemployed workers did not turn to violence: instead they petitioned the justices, who informed the Privy Council, which looked at the national laws again while encouraging a string of local measures to address the problem.

The justices were, as before, only the top tier of local government, which now reached deep into the parish. Until the sixteenth century, a parish had been essentially a unit of the Church, functioning largely outside the state system. Under the Tudors it became the main local expression of state authority, but mediated through the parishioners who actually ran it. Central government worked with Parliaments to make laws, but it was county, city and parish officials who determined how the results were applied. By the late seventeenth century, about one in every twenty adult males was holding some local office at any one time, while in London the proportion was one in ten. Even by 1600, most parishes had no gentleman residing in them, so that the inhabitants had to run them for themselves. This pattern fitted the ancient ideal of citizenship, which consisted more of participating in government than voting for it.

Even so, parliamentary processes themselves were not wholly out of reach of ordinary people. Most often, the county and city elites would decide amongst themselves which of their number would occupy seats in any election: only in a minority of cases, before 1640, did they quarrel amongst themselves and put up rival candidates, thereby permitting an election. None the less, that minority could amount to scores of contests, and here the electors were decisive. There were a few boroughs in which all householders could vote, and in the counties anybody could do so who owned land worth at least £2 per annum. Inflation turned that into an increasingly easy qualification during the Tudor period, while the lack of an electoral register potentially enabled large numbers to vote who actually failed to achieve it. Although social mobility was limited, there were genuine opportunities for people to better themselves: London apprentices had a seven to one chance in favour of becoming householders in their own right, while a third of them went on to join the elite companies which dominated the trades of the city. Government in post-Reformation England was expanding and deepening, rather than centralizing: the state represented a growing reservoir of authority on which people drew for their own needs. The early modern English were both subjects and citizens.

During the reign of Elizabeth, the Privy Council, Parliaments, justices and parish officers worked together to apply the old principle of progressive taxation to the growing problems of poverty, hunger and social polarization. The impetus came from the council, drawing on local models, to produce a system by which the richer members of each parish paid a rate to keep the poor and helpless in it from starving. It was completed in law by 1600, and slowly put into action during the following century, being mostly in place by 1660. Inefficient and corrupt it could certainly be, but it was the best national provision of relief in its age, and must have done much to take the social tension out of economic hardship. From the 1600s onwards, there was also an ever-widening escape route from poverty in England, not available to most Europeans: to go overseas, to Ireland or to the English colonies in North America, where better conditions might obtain.

At the same time, society continued to be bonded together by the fact that the royal government would at times apparently

act against the rich on behalf of their social inferiors. Once
more, a test issue was enclosure. Almost 100 years after Wolsey
had first set the example of going after landlords who took
away common rights, royal government was still acting upon it.
In 1607, rioting against new enclosures of common land
affected three Midland counties. The Crown responded exactly
as Wolsey had done, with a commission of enquiry, which
reported back that in many cases the grievances of the rioters
had been just. The guilty landowners were duly prosecuted by
royal officials, and the Earl of Lincoln was the most eminent of
a succession of them to suffer heavy fines. The harvest failures
of 1629–31 produced another spate of protests, which the
government followed up once again. This time it was Lord
Brudenell who was the most prominent of a series of gentry
punished by the state after popular complaints. He had
enclosed common land with a view to converting it to sheep
pasture, a form of farming which required little labour and
would therefore tend automatically to reduce employment and
increase poverty. When fining him in the royal Court of Star
Chamber, the reigning Archbishop of Canterbury accused him
of having 'devoured the people with a shepherd and a dog'.

The government always ordered the suppression of rioting as
well, and the arrest of those who had instigated it. Those ring-
leaders were by definition few; after a particularly serious riot at
Malden in Essex, during 1629, eight people were indicted out of
300 involved. Their treatment followed a highly significant
pattern. If, on investigation, they were shown to have confined
themselves to urging others to break down harmful enclosures,
or stop grain from being hoarded or exported, then they were
rebuked and bound over to keep the peace; and the bonds spec-
ified were usually small and not always actually demanded. If,
on the other hand, they had incited others to steal grain, or
denounced landowners in general, and the society and governmental systems with which they were associated, then they
were put to death. In 1596 two young men in Oxfordshire
decided to lead a popular rebellion that would overthrow the

local gentry, and then move on London. After just two others turned up to support them, they called off the plan; but news of it leaked, and all involved were arrested. The two leaders died in prison, apparently of the treatment that they received there, and two of their friends were hanged, drawn and quartered as traitors. As John Walter has pointed out, having thus turned a farcical episode into a horrific example, the central government went on to fine the local gentry whose treatment of commoners had provoked such local hatred, and to put a new law against enclosure through the next Parliament, to address one of the grievances concerned.

When all this is said, there remain some spectacular cases in which the Crown united with landowners in actions which were contrary to the interests of commoners, and provoked violent reactions. These tended to be in areas marginal to the main economic centres of the nation, which were subordinated to what was perceived to be the national good. One consisted of the Fens, the marshes dividing East Anglia from the Midlands, and represented underused land which, during a time of population growth and food shortage, could be drained and converted into rich arable land. During the 1620s and 1630s many of the landowners there, including the king, commenced this work. It ran counter to the interests of the Fenlanders themselves, from middle-rank landowners downwards, who relied on the marshland for grazing, and its vegetable and animal products. They responded by destroying the new works and by taking the developers to court, only to be punished for the riots and defeated in the legal actions. They merely bided their time, however, and on each occasion on which the central government became distracted by war or rebellion thereafter, they demolished the drainage works again, and the farms erected on the reclaimed land. Gradually, as the century wore on, they were given a share in the profits of the improvement projects, or compensation for loss of rights. Where they were not, the cost of maintaining the schemes in the face of local hostility eventually rendered them no longer viable.

Even more striking are the events that occurred simultaneously in the royal forests of Wiltshire, Somerset and Dorset. There the Crown likewise attempted to combine its own enrichment with that of the nation by having the land enclosed and divided up for agricultural exploitation. It took care to reconcile local opinion by giving all who owned land, including smallholders, a cut of the proceeds. What it did not take into account was that the forests also contained a large population of landless people who lived by cottage industry partly dependent on forest products. They could find nobody except a few very minor gentry to take up their cause, but when enclosure began they resisted it ferociously. The combined forces of central and local government needed years to quell the initial outbreak of rioting and, just as in the Fens, local people proceeded to attack the 'improvements' again at every point during the next three decades at which the attention of the authorities was distracted. They also eventually won their cause, either by forcing the abandonment of the schemes or by being awarded compensation.

Even as they fought every institution and body to which they had been accustomed to defer, the commoners, like earlier rebels, still sought to preserve the fabric of the normal political and social order. Where they could find no leaders who had any inherent status, they awarded fictional titles, usually military, to those who came forward. The chief coordinator of the 1607 Midland riots was called 'Captain Pouch', while those who performed the same function in the western forests were nicknamed 'Lady Skimmington'. This expression was normally applied to the mock processions and pieces of street theatre used to mock and humiliate individuals who offended the morality of their local communities: wife-beaters, husband-naggers, petty thieves and so forth. The men to whom it was applied were seen as reminding the Crown of its misdeeds in a similar fashion. The symbols and rituals adopted by those involved in such resistance reveal an intense preoccupation with spurious legality. By copying the trappings of normal authority, they felt able to take actions which, in a just world, ought to have been taken by their social superiors on their behalf. Thus the forms of law and order could be observed while the reality was suspended.

At the Wiltshire village of Great Wishford, the rioters drilled like militiamen, with red feathers and badges as insignia, before destroying the local enclosures. In another part of that county, having learned that the legal definition of riot consisted of an action committed by three or more persons, they formed into couples for the same work. In the Fens, locals started a fund to pay for lawyers to plead their case in London. At one community in that region, the village men kicked a football across a recently drained land, calling it their customary pitch, and demolished all the works that they found in the way of their game. In the Forest of Dean, Gloucestershire, commoners paraded and burned effigies of the enclosing gentry before attacking their hedges and fences. Those of Feckenham Forest, Worcestershire, donned masks for the act of demolition, not to conceal their identities, which were obvious, but to become impersonal agents of justice even as public executioners masked their faces before performing their duties. In Braydon Forest, Wiltshire, men put on women's clothes before proceeding to the work of destruction, again as part of a process of distancing themselves from their normal roles. Enclosure rioters in the Welsh valley of Ystrad Marchell, Montgomeryshire, did exactly the same thing, without any sign of communication between the two; these were a symbolic action that ran deep enough to be instinctive. Both forms of response, the giving of spurious titles to leaders and the donning of ritual dress for riot, were to last far into the nineteenth century, when Captain Swing led southern English labourers against the new farm machinery and the Rebecca rioters donned frocks to attack turnpike gates on Welsh highways. They have, indeed, not wholly disappeared, as anybody who witnessed one of the protests against road-building schemes in the 1990s will be aware.

Thus, as the great age of popular rebellion passed away during the Elizabethan period, the same mechanisms of protest, resistance and negotiation remained in action, but at the level of riot rather than of revolt. They served a social order that was certainly unequal and unjust by modern standards, but was by those of early modern Europe remarkably tough and flexible, with relatively responsible social elites and responsive central government, and normally dutiful commoners who were prepared to defend their own interests by both legal means and direct physical action when threatened. It saw its people through some of the worst economic conditions that Europe has ever experienced.

Crime and Poverty

By the European standards of the age, Wales and Scotland had only an average level of violence, while England was remarkably peaceful. Travellers did not seem to worry greatly about being robbed or killed on English roads or streets. In Essex, a county with perfect legal records for the period, twenty-five parishes never experienced any accusations of felony at all between 1560 and 1640, while very few suffered a rate of them greater than one every two years. This was partly because of good policing, constables and magistrates being both local and numerous in every district. At the remote hill town of Kirkby Lonsdale, in Westmorland, they represented 35 individuals out of a total adult male population of 200. If the English of the period wanted to cause injury, their means to do so were limited: the evidence of wills is that by 1600 nine-tenths of the population owned no weapons at all except knives, which were intended not for defence but for mealtimes. When affected by crime, commoners did not turn to noblemen for protection, as happened across much of the Continent, but reported the problem to their neighbours, who normally included a constable. Murders were no longer avenged by blood feuds, but by legal prosecutions. On the other hand, even England was a violent place by modern standards. It seems, in fact, to have been getting ever less dangerous since legal records begin: so that homicide cases between 1560 and 1640 ran at three to ten times the present level per head of population, but at half that of the thirteenth century. Violence had also become steadily more of a domestic matter: in the fourteenth century, 8 per cent of recorded homicides took place within the family, while by the seventeenth the level had risen to 20 per cent and it reached 50 per cent during the twentieth.

These overall trends, however, conceal important short-term fluctuations. In particular, there was a surge in recorded homicides and thefts between 1560 and 1620, marking the worst point of the pressure exerted by population growth and inflation. Contemporaries were conscious of living in a 'crime wave', and often deeply concerned with it. Their response was what Keith Wrightson, in the 1970s, called 'the Reformation of Manners': a systematic campaign by various county and urban magistrates to regulate and improve local social conditions. It included severe punishments for non-marital sex and the bearing of bastard children, which together threatened to increase the number of children without a family structure to feed and clothe them; attempts to relieve the poor and stop vagrancy; campaigns to abolish traditional parish feasts and festivities at which drunkenness, violence and fornication might all occur; and the regulation and closure of alehouses. There were certainly a great number of alehouses around: one was counted for every ninety-five people in Essex in 1644 and for every fifty-seven in Lancashire in 1647, and both those estimates were made after the systematic closure of many more. They multiplied as poverty grew, being both a means by which those who ran them could make a living and by which those who used them could drown their sorrows. They also, however, nurtured alcoholism and illness and consumed grain which could otherwise be turned into bread. It is hard to separate the economic from the religious elements in the 'Reformation of Manners'. Areas such as East Sussex could contain numerous religious Puritans while never instituting a programme of social reform, while towns which did undertake one were sometimes shrinking rather than suffering the strains of expansion. None the less, it does seem that the pressures of religious change and population and price rises combined in general to produce the necessary climate in which local campaigns to reform behaviour could occur.

The Scottish Lowlands were subjected in the same period to a much more intensive Reformation of Manners than England, striking at much the same targets. The difference was that the campaigns there were supported more vigorously by parliamentary legislation, and had a perfect local vehicle in the parish kirk sessions, which functioned both as commissions of enquiry and as courts in trying and sentencing offenders to penance and changed behaviour. Between 1560 and 1600 the sessions at St Andrews, on average, judged a sexual offence once every fortnight, in addition to those of drunkenness, sabbath-breaking, and so forth. The stool on which sinners sat in church to show their repentance and be shamed became as central an icon of Scottish Protestantism as the pulpit. These penances were enforced with notable equality on both women and men, and reinforced by fines which were imposed in proportion to the wealth of those punished. In addition, the same kirk sessions sought to arbitrate quarrels between neighbours and within families, especially in cases of defamation, and enforce paternal responsibilities. Whether such sustained campaigns actually made a difference to social behaviour cannot be proved – the number of offences itself calls this into some doubt. They certainly made their mark on formal attitudes, slowly establishing a stolid disapproval of the activities stigmatized by kirk sessions as hallmark of proper conduct among at least the Lowland Scottish gentry (called lairds) and wealthier townspeople, which was clearly present by the early seventeenth century. The elders who sat in the sessions became actively sought after as solvers of local social problems. All things considered, the social and religious reformation that took place in early modern Scotland was the most profound in the British Isles, and one of the most intensive in Europe.

In both nations the policing system worked because criminals were seen as disruptors of the whole community. Victims would instigate their own investigations, aided by fellow parishioners who would include constables, and the result was usually a settlement out of court: legal actions were a last resort. The people who actually got prosecuted tended to be strangers, newcomers or individuals with a particularly bad reputation. Once in court, these people were also the most vulnerable. In Wiltshire between 1600 and 1640, 68 per cent of locals accused of theft were convicted, but 93 per cent of outsiders. Likewise, it was those who offended repeatedly who got hanged. During the course of the early modern period, courts became more and more reluctant to take life: roughly half of those who were sentenced to death in England between 1547 and 1553 actually suffered the penalty, but only a quarter between 1603 and 1625 and a tenth between 1702 and 1714. The disappearance of the death penalty in modern Britain was a process with very long roots. Prison sentences were rarely handed out, because local government could not afford the cost of keeping the town and village jails clean, warm and dry enough to avoid killing any long-term residents. They were employed instead as holding pens for people awaiting trial. The usual alternative to hanging was flogging, increasingly replaced, as the seventeenth century progressed, by transportation to the new English colonies across the Atlantic.

The central government seems to have been much more scared of disorder than people at a local level, regularly sending out directions to magistrates to show the utmost rigour and severity. One aspect of this anxiety was that the death penalty was extended to thirty more crimes during the sixteenth and seventeenth centuries (as opposed to just six in the previous 200 years), while the traditional medieval escape-route for the educated – that those who proved themselves able to read were given the 'benefit of clergy' and reprieved – was abolished. A pattern was instituted which was to persist until the end of the Georgian period: of more and more offences for which people could hang, accompanied by less and less actual hanging. In some ways, the late Tudor and early Stuart governments were like those of modern banana republics – scared of invasions, conspiracies and the risk that the poor might start talking about social justice. The crucial difference was that early modern England lacked a strong military presence and possessed strong decentralized government, so that actions on the ground were usually characterized by pragmatic common sense.

The positive aspect of all this anxiety was represented by the English programme of poor relief, which was probably the best in Europe by the mid-seventeenth century. There is a paradox here, because by any test it seems that England had less actual poverty than most other European states of the age. It is true that the English seem to have thought that their problem was much worse than it actually was, but this does not alter the fact that they produced a disproportionate response. The most sensible conclusion is one that draws attention to the unusual density and standardization of administration in the English kingdom: the automatic Tudor reaction to any difficulty was to throw more government at it. By 1540, at the latest, the English had got the idea that social problems were not divinely ordained but could and should be remedied by human intervention. In addition, the country was relatively rich for the age, and so could afford to spend money on social problems, while the Reformation provided a further impetus to state action by removing medieval institutions, such as monasteries, which had dispensed charity. Calculating the actual level of poverty is very difficult. For one thing, contemporary records – tax assessments, rates to equip and pay the militia and rates to relieve the poor – had no standard way of reckoning it. For a second, it was a fluctuating phenomenon. The real problem for most people was underemployment – the ability to find work at some times of the year but not at others and the inability of many employers to pay a wage on which people could support themselves completely. A third difficulty for the historian is that Tudor and Stuart officials were not concerned to aid the poorest people in their communities but the most deserving, those who were too young, old or infirm to work or had too many children to support on their current earnings.

Overall, poverty does seem to have been worse in towns than in the countryside, where there were more odd jobs available: it is probable that a fifth of the population of the average English town could not support itself in the year 1600, and a tenth of the average village. There were, none the less, some rural black holes, such as a Norfolk village studied by A. L. Beier, where 26.7 per cent of the inhabitants could not feed themselves. The best survey of the problem in the early modern world was made at Norwich, the second city of the realm, in 1570, where it was found that 75 per cent of adult men and 80 per cent of women had jobs. The real issue, however, was that many of these could not survive on the wages that they were paid. Poor relief therefore had to be both flexible and sensitive, paying people supplements to their regular income, especially at certain hard times of the year or the decade. In the cases of people who were chronically out of work or underemployed, the basic response was to aid those who could not labour and drive out the rest. The parish of St Mary, in Warwick, had 245 inhabitants incapable of supporting themselves in 1587, and decided to help 127. The poorer market town of Thirsk, in North Yorkshire, had 161 people in trouble by 1629, and decided that it was able or willing to aid just forty-three of those. The others had to solve their own problems or clear out. Those who were granted aid were expected to pay the price of allowing themselves to be regulated, morally, socially and politically, by those who provided it; although in practice it was rare to suspend relief purely because the recipients were badly behaved. Nor was parish provision usually equivalent to a living wage, so that recipients still commonly needed additional income to survive, which was provided by informal charity and a range of survival strategies such as extended credit, petty pilfering, gleaning and alehouse-keeping.

North of the Border, we are in a different world. Scotland likewise introduced poor relief measures during the same period, but without the vital element of compulsory rates. The needy were left to local schemes, usually found in towns and based on voluntary collections. By contrast, the Scots did much better in education. From the start of the official Reformation, the Kirk had wanted a school in every parish, for all children over five, supported by the local property-owners. This was slow in coming: a national system was not established until 1616, and it was not made compulsory for forty more years, but it eventually turned the Scots into one of the best-educated nations in Europe. The difference in criminal justice was even more marked in a nation still characterized by decentralized government, strong family bonds and powerful lordship. Much of it was still meted out by a patchwork of local courts domi-nated by the nobility, while, as Keith Brown has shown, blood feuds remained a regular method of settling scores.

To carry weapons of war was a sign of pride, and neither the law nor the judges who enforced it were regarded as objective. The power of a lord to protect his kin and tenants was best displayed by his prowess in conducting a quarrel, so that a peaceable one was regarded by his dependants as a weakling who would attract predators, and thus a liability. Feuds were almost always over local matters, such as inheritances, bound-aries and revenues, but they could invade the royal court and last for generations. Both sides were usually careful to limit the damage done, so that raiding was selective and episodic. It was also informal, rarely employing the machinery of the state and of political life: nobles simply murdered their rivals instead of getting the Crown to execute them. There was an epidemic of such feuds in the late sixteenth century, the product of the price and population rise coupled with the legacy of the civil wars that followed Mary's deposition. King James and the Kirk worked between them to bring it under control, and by the early seventeenth century the custom was dying out. It was noted by the 1630s that landowners near Edinburgh, especially lawyers and courtiers who were most in touch with new fashions, were starting to build country houses without fortifications or accommodation for armed retinues.

None the less, early Jacobean Scotland was a bloodthirsty place. When only four of the eleven murderers of an Earl of Eglinton were killed in reprisal, it was thought that his avengers had shown unusual restraint. The range war between the Cunningham and Montgomery families was relatively restrained, but still devastated the Irvine valley. Unmarried women were temptingly vulnerable targets. Beyond the Highland line, things got still worse. The body count in the Gordon v. Campbell feud in 1593 ran to hundreds, and the internal squabbles of the Macleods of Assynt killed off fourteen out of the twenty-eight male members of the family. When a man won a lawsuit against some Macfarlanes in 1619, they cut out his tongue and intertwined his guts with those of a dog before slicing his throat.

So it was post-Reformation England which led the way into the British future. It was a society markedly different from that of the present day, and yet not totally alien, while measures were being taken in it that pointed directly towards later norms. In both the distinctive modern British attitude to capital punishment, and the equally distinctive adoption of a welfare state, social attitudes are embodied which were in preparation by the Tudor and Stuart English.

Famine and Plague

It has been emphasized that the period between 1560 and 1640 was one of exceptional economic pressure, to which the English found various responses. One further, entirely reasonable, reaction to such pressure was to collapse and die under it, and many took this route. When the surviving parish registers of late Tudor and early Stuart England are inspected, almost all contain years in which the normal number of burials more than doubled, and historians in the 1970s adopted the term 'crisis mortalities' for such events. The two obvious questions to ask about this phenomenon are why it occurred, and whether anything changed in it during the course of the sixteenth and seventeenth centuries.

Answers to these questions are fraught with technical problems. In the 1810s, when a national census becomes available against which local data can be checked, it is clear that a third of all deaths were not being registered. The proportion in earlier centuries was probably not very different, and so the records that we have, even where any survive, are no more than a sample of reality. Certain tactics can be adopted to identify the mass killers of the age. Where burials multiply steeply after a bad harvest, then famine is probably the cause. A steep rise in late summer probably indicates bubonic plague, which struck at this season. Several epidemic diseases, however, were not seasonal, and can only be identified from contemporary comments, which are rare and are often frustratingly vague. Where they are precise, interpretation can be difficult for modern scholars; for example, one cause of death mentioned around 1600 was the 'bloody flux' (bloody diarrhoea), which was thought to be a mysterious form of disease. It was the experience of modern famines in African nations that taught historians that it is actually the last stage of starvation, when the intestinal wall disintegrates because of lack of nutrients. Bad harvests can usually only be detected from high bread prices, and records of prices only survive for some regions. Finally, if a local mortality was exceptionally severe, then record-keeping would cease altogether, leaving no evidence for crisis mortality.

Crisis mortalities were indeed usually local in character. Most harvest failures only occurred in some regions. The greatest in the sixteenth and seventeenth centuries took place in 1596–8, and affected every part of Europe, but in England it had an impact on only 28 per cent of parishes which have left records; it almost completely spared Kent and East Anglia, because of their more diverse economies. The greatest British epidemic was that in 1557–8, almost certainly influenza, which killed between 16 per cent and 20 per cent of the English population; but it reached less than half of the parishes which have left registers. On the whole, town-dwellers were more vulnerable to disease because of their more crowded and dirty living conditions, but less vulnerable to famine because urban centres could lay up stocks of grain. Population pressure hit some places much harder than others. The number of people in England as a whole more or less doubled between 1500 and 1640, but that in Sussex hardly increased. The population of Cambridgeshire rose by about 40 per cent, but almost all of that took place in the marshlands of the north of the county, where landless people found it easiest to squat and to find a living; and these overcrowded and poor communities were the most vulnerable to serious mortalities. Even in a single parish, location and income could make a huge difference: the rich lived in better built homes set in better drained and ventilated areas, and so died less easily. It is also true that the data collated by historians does not always match the perceptions of contemporaries. When the burial data for the seventeenth century was finally collated in the 1980s by the Cambridge Group, the most lethal year of all turned out to have been 1657–8. At the time, however, nobody seems to have realized this: there were comments about the summer being 'sickly', with slow-working fevers abroad, but no sense of any real danger or disruption. As the eye travels along the other columns in the graph, however, the second tallest represents the year 1665–6, when everybody knew that they were trying to survive a terrifying outbreak of bubonic plague, which closed down two-thirds of the nation.

When all these cautions are applied, certain overall patterns do stand out. Between 1530 and 1630, every serious harvest failure was followed by at least a doubling in local deaths. This does not seem to have been the case in the previous 200 years, even given the lack of comparably good records, and seems genuinely to have been a new phenomenon, showing the impact of population pressure in forcing people towards the bread line. Between 1500 and 1650, moreover, every fifty-year period contained an average seven epidemics severe enough to disrupt the life of the nation badly. The death tolls were prodigious; probably more people died of plague in London alone in three months of 1665 than were killed in the whole of the civil war which rent England and Wales for four years in the 1640s. But this plague was not the worst to hit the city in the early modern period: that of 1563 probably destroyed a larger proportion of its inhabitants. Communities could continue to function almost normally through a famine, which by definition only slew the poor, but a severe outbreak of disease, even though the rich were still significantly less vulnerable, could bring a local economy to a halt, so that commerce could not be transacted and taxes and rates not levied.

Of all these killers, the one that created the greatest fear was bubonic plague, which has been proved in the twentieth century to have been caused by a bacillus carried by the fleas that prey on black rats; as the rats die of it, the fleas bite humans. To earlier generations it was completely mysterious; all that was known was that it had reappeared dramatically in Europe in the fourteenth century, from the east, and remained ever since, swelling into epidemics every twenty to forty years. Humans caught it with appalling ease, and it killed the majority of those who did so, in high fever and the agony caused by suppurating swellings. It was entirely responsible for about half of the crisis mortalities that have been detected and explained in early modern England, and was a contributing factor in others. Although it was a long-familiar horror by the Tudor period, the English at that time gradually developed new measures to contain it, enacted at central, regional, municipal and parish levels, in the same spirit as those they developed to combat poverty, alehouses, fornication and other perceived or actual social ills. By the early seventeenth century, these measures were firmly in place. As soon as plague broke out in a town or district, almost all those who were able to leave swiftly would do so; which by definition consisted only of the wealthier. The exceptions among this group were the clergy and office-holders, who would probably send away their families but were expected themselves to remain at their posts and work to bring the community through the approaching ordeal. Most seem to have done so, maintaining religious services and the machinery of local government throughout.

Four practical measures were adopted in the face of the outbreak, one of which was probably completely ineffectual but the rest of which were apparently very potent. The pointless one was to shut up and guard households in which the disease had appeared, locking in the healthy with the sick, until it had long ceased its ravages. Households which wanted to get rid of their infected members could have them sent to pest-houses, converted or purpose-built shacks on the edge of communities, which were effectively concentration camps for plague victims. As neither of these measures confined the deadly fleas, they almost certainly represented a needless infliction of suffering. What was far more effective was that plague-ridden communities either sealed themselves off from their neighbours or (more commonly) were sealed off from them. This process of quarantine does seem to have worked well, as long as it was strictly enforced, in limiting the spread of the epidemic. It could also work on a national scale, as the British gradually learned the rewards of suspending all contact with foreign ports in which the disease had appeared. Parishes and towns also became increasingly efficient in identifying the disease and in disposing swiftly of the dead, in mass graves served by burial parties working at night. Finally, towns came to lay up funds to cover the cost of feeding households closed up because of infection, and of meeting the increased need for poor relief as commerce was restricted or suspended during the outbreak. These funds were increasingly supplemented by collections of money taken up in churches in regions still free of infection, on royal orders, and sent to assist those that were afflicted.

The short-term impact of such mortalities on social, economic and political life could be devastating. Communities would need to repair the damage to their population, wealth and trade links, and the central government could raise no taxes in them while an epidemic was in progress. A severe outbreak of plague could seriously undermine England's ability to wage war, not merely by depleting its tax base but by striking at its soldiers and sailors; the complete failure of Elizabeth's expedition to Le Havre in 1563 was due to the depletion of her army by the disease. On the other hand, it is notable that throughout the sixteenth and seventeenth centuries the ruling elites became more and more proficient in keeping themselves out of the way of infection. Until the mid-Tudor period, leading politicians and churchmen, judges, town aldermen and justices of the peace all died in national epidemics; by the seventeenth century they seem to have become largely immune to them. Like hunger, large-scale infectious disease was becoming a tragedy of commoners, and they were easily replaced in a period of growing population. The great flu outbreak of 1557–8 just put that growth back by five years. In most towns, houses left empty by plague were filled up within a few months by immigrants from the countryside, and a few years, at most, were needed to make good the total loss of inhabitants.

Something more fundamental altered as well. After 1623, famine disappeared from England. Bad harvests were just as frequent, but were ceasing to kill people in large numbers, even though they continued to do so in Scotland until the end of the century and in continental Europe for longer. The great outbreak of bubonic plague in 1665–6 was, likewise, the last in Britain, even though the disease continued to ravage other parts of Europe until the eighteenth century. The two greatest scourges of Tudor England were therefore eliminated long before the end of the Stuart period. Discovering why is easy in the case of famine, where there are many explanations. The greatest was that the steady increase in population began to level off in the early seventeenth century, and was replaced by the 1660s with a slight drop. This was the result of greater mortality in the hard years around 1600, increasing immigration to the new American colonies, and, above all, a decline in births. The English were starting to control their own fertility, by marrying, on average, ten years later in 1640 than they had been doing in 1590 and so greatly limiting the period of time in which children could be conceived. In addition, a larger number of people than before had ceased to marry and have children at all. With a drop in population, accompanied by a continuing expansion of the economy, the value of real wages could rise again and increased food production and job opportunities make a considerable impact. Between 1600 and 1660, also, the poor relief system came into general operation, and new forms of farming and small-scale industry were adopted. By the 1660s England was becoming a regular exporter of foodstuffs for the first time, and cottagers were making lace or nails, plaiting straw, weaving and knitting to supplement or replace subsistence farming or labouring. Internal communications and marketing systems were better developed, to move food from regions of surplus to those of dearth.

The disappearance of plague is a more baffling, and contentious, phenomenon. At times in the past, 'biological' explanations have been proposed: that either rats or humans developed immunity to the disease, or that the black rats which carry the fatal species of flea were replaced by brown rats, which do not. Both arguments fail, for plague vanished in Britain before the arrival of brown rats and it is not logical that British rats or people should have developed the immunity before those in the rest of Europe while those in Africa and Asia failed to do so. The most plausible alternative is that suggested by Paul Slack in the 1980s: that the local and national systems of cordoning off infected areas were enforced with so much efficiency that in the end they cordoned off the island. This would certainly explain in turn the slow and fitful retreat of the disease from the rest of Europe, as such measures were brought into effect there. Although directed by central and local government, they required the cooperation of the whole population, as even smugglers came to understand the deadly risks of non-compliance.

If correct, these conclusions provide one of the clearest ripostes possible to one of the most influential bodies of historical thought during the 1960s and early 1970s, the Annales school of French scholars. This emphasized the great degree to which medieval and early modern human beings were conditioned by their environment and subjected to its demands; this story would illustrate instead the degree to which, eventually, they could rise to the challenges of that environment and overcome them. They did so, moreover, not because of any inspired leadership from above but because of a massive effort of collective and shared will. In doing so, they made one of the most valuable transitions from the medieval to the modern European worlds, and supplied one of the finest reproofs to the assertion that human beings are individually marvellous, but in a crowd, hopeless.

Popular Religion

The traditional narrative of the English and Scottish Reformations is one of an epic struggle between the warring creeds of Catholicism and Protestantism, ending with a victory to the latter, in a society in which virtually all people believed unquestioningly in the Christian religion. More subtle and recent formulations would emphasize the differences that existed within the two opposed faiths as well as between them, and the large number of people who remained uncommitted to either. None the less, these formulations still operate within the framework of the accepted model. There is, however, another way of approaching early modern British religion, which emphasizes the similar problems faced by all kinds of devout Catholic and Protestant when dealing with the bulk of their compatriots. This is also rooted firmly in contemporary sources, which in this respect remain fairly consistent from the fourteenth to the seventeenth centuries in insisting that the real problems of British Christianity lay in the poverty, ignorance and amorality of the clergy and the ungodliness and indifference of the laity.

Recent research has done much to investigate and conceptualize these claims, made, inevitably, by the most self-consciously devout and reformist of British Christians at each stage of this period. It confirms that this was, indeed, a Christian society, and that there is absolutely no evidence of the practice of any rival religion within it. There is a great deal of evidence, on the other hand, for the incorporation into Christian forms of beliefs and actions handed on from ancient paganism, as there is all over medieval Europe: after all, early Christianity depended on such borrowings for the shape and decorations of its churches, the timing of many of its seasonal festivals, and other major features. The Reformation was designed in part to clear away as many of these as possible, and some of the local manifestations of them can be as startling to modern historians as they were to reformers. One of the most colourful was at Clynnog Fawr, on the Lleyn Peninsula at the far north-western end of Wales, where Henry VIII's agents found that cattle were being offered at the shrine of the local saint, as if to a pagan god. The clearing of most of these borrowings out of the English and Scottish Churches had the effect of making still starker the continued survival of such relics of paganism in folk customs outside of the official religion, in which reformers had less interest. Until the end of the nineteenth century, for example, farmers in parts of western Britain, from Cornwall to the Isle of Man and the Western Isles continued to burn one animal in a herd stricken by disease in the belief that this sacrifice would protect the rest.

None the less, it remains true that Christianity was the only religion self-consciously practised by the early modern British. It is more difficult to tell how well they practised it. There were apparently occasional pockets of complete ignorance or indifference: as late as 1679 the chaplain at Newgate Prison, London, tried to comfort thirteen criminals about to be hanged, and found that they had never heard of Christ. More commonly, people had done so but had little actual knowledge of him. Famous preachers loved to harp on this theme, to the entertainment and scandal of their flocks. In the fourteenth century, John Bromyard told of how he (pompously) asked a shepherd if he knew of the Father, Son and Holy Ghost. He got the answer that the man knew the father and son well enough, for he tended their sheep, but that there was no holy ghost in his village. In the 1640s, John Shaw, given care of a parish in the Furness Fells at the top of Lancashire, asked an old man how he knew Christ, and was told that he did so only from a play that he had seen in a nearby town, which he thought wonderful but could not quite understand. Such anecdotes retain their colour, but the evidence of visitation records is that by the early seventeenth century, at least, the regular practice of catechizing young people, carried on by parish clergy, had dinned the basic teachings of Christianity into the vast majority of the population.

The problem then encountered is whether that vast majority subsequently paid much attention to the teachings. There is slight evidence for some outright disbelief among the educated, though it is always alleged by enemies of those concerned because the penalty for an open expression of atheism was death. Sir Walter Raleigh was said to have denied the immortality of the soul, and the Elizabethan playwright Christopher Marlowe was reported to have called Christ a homosexual and his apostles idiots. The records of English church courts contain several examples of blasphemous jokes told by local people, often oiled by drink. More common was inattention. The same records, and those of Scottish kirk sessions, abound with accusations of misbehaviour during services: fighting, jostling, coughing, spitting, breaking wind, joking, chatting, flirting, abusing or simply falling sound asleep. Preachers regularly complained that ordinary people were just not much interested in religion. The famous Protestant bishop Hugh Latimer, eventually burned during Mary's reign, complained that most knew the stories of Robin Hood much better than those of the Bible; seventy years later, in 1607, a minister in the Midlands said precisely the same thing.

Behind all this friction lay a major shift in the concept of religion. Until the Reformation there had been no compulsion on the British laity to attend church regularly. Churches, as pagan temples had been, were regarded as special buildings set aside for the honour of a deity, reinforced in this case by saints, in which ceremonies were kept going by special officials, in the Christian context a professional clergy. These made the regular sacrifice of the mass on behalf of the laity, while the latter were freed thereby to attend services frequently if they wished, or else to get on with their daily lives. In the years 1540–42, the parish of St Giles, in the Essex town of Colchester, kept records of attendance, and found that about half of its adult inhabitants did show up on most Sundays and major holy days, while at Easter almost all of them crowded the church. This again was an ancient, and pagan, pattern – that most residents of an area came to religious rites at great seasonal festivals – though it is not clear whether the Colchester level of regular attendance was typical. With the Reformation, however, parishioners were expected to be present every Sunday unless prevented by serious misfortune, this being the easiest way in which dissent from the established religion could be detected and punished. Alongside weekly attendance came a shift in the focus of the service, from ceremony (embodied in the mass) to sermons. Hitherto, ordinary people had been most accustomed to hear these from experts, mostly the friars, as special events; now they had to submit to them weekly, from parish clergy of greatly varying abilities in this respect. Churches were unheated, and although they were now increasingly supplied with seating in response to the new physical strains on the congregation, these were often the preserve of wealthier parishioners. While all this caused friction and discomfort, it is important also not to underestimate the appeal of a good preacher, who could represent marvellous entertainment as well as edification. In Scotland in particular, where the new religion placed an even heavier emphasis on sermons than in England, the best preaching ministers produced overcrowded churches.

The records of church courts and kirk sessions reveal a further fault-line which sometimes ran between clergy and parishioners, and sometimes between different kinds of laity, with ministers taking one side or the other. Everybody agreed that the main job description of a clergyman was to be a good spiritual leader to his community, pious, sober and responsible; but not on what that meant in practice. A great many of the laity, almost certainly the majority, wanted a kindly pastor who comforted the sick, troubled and dying, reconciled quarrelling neighbours and united and pacified the community. More zealous Protestants expected a crusading evangelist who was prepared to bruise consciences, excoriate the sinful and negligent, and praise the most godly of his flock as an example to the others. Such behaviour was always divisive, and often produced serious resentment; but on the other hand the more pacific and inclusive kind of clergyman could be denounced by his more strenuously pious parishioners for laxity and cowardice.

In their need to ensure a better-trained and better-behaved parish clergy, the post-Reformation British churches turned to the remedy that their medieval predecessor had provided: higher education. It was applied energetically, so that by 1640 the majority of ministers in every southern and midland English diocese seem to have been graduates, almost half of those in the North and Wales, and virtually all those in the Scottish Lowlands. This success, however, created new difficulties. The universities taught theology, and none of the pastoral skills needed to run a happy parish, so that the new graduates often found themselves condemned to a lifetime of boredom and frustration among rural people with whom they had nothing in common and who resented them as intellectual snobs. One young minister appointed to a Leicestershire village was informed by its elders on arrival that 'all learning was foolish other than that which would make the pot boil'. He adapted to their ways, and their language, and prospered, but many others were less flexible.

To these intellectual strains were joined others of a more practical kind. Since the parish system was settled in the first half of the Middle Ages, its clergy were supported by tithes, payments levied on parishioners in accordance with their presumed wealth, supplemented by fees for extra spiritual services and sometimes by special lands. It had always contained many livings which yielded meagre profits, and the number of these was greatly increased by the process of appropriation. This consisted of the delivery of parish benefices to the care of religious houses, which would put in clergy to whom they would pay a fixed salary taken out of the full income of the living. By 1500 a majority of the parishes in Britain had been given this treatment, so that those in which the incumbent had the full profit were comparatively rare. Even the full profit of many livings was inadequate, and so clergy sometimes increased their income by taking on more than one at a time.

With the Reformation, and the dissolution of the monasteries, the parish tithes that they had owned passed to nobles and gentry along with their lands, and were treated as another source of income. Clergy on fixed salaries ran into the great inflation of the sixteenth century, and so became progressively poorer. Conflict over the payment of tithes boomed, owing to new tensions between parishioners and landowners, landowners and clergy, and clergy and parishioners. At its worst, the latter could produce cases such as that of the minister responsible for St Katherine Cree in London during the 1630s, who informed his congregation that they were 'frogs, hogs, dogs and devils', or the one at North Stoke, Somerset, in 1631, who called his people 'gypsies and cheats'. None the less, if the job of a parish clergyman was harder, it was also more prestigious and challenging. By the 1620s the level of recruitment had returned to what it had been 100 years before, with slightly more applicants than livings. More and more sons of gentry were entering the Church, as the social status of a minister was upgraded with the level of education he required. It is a heartening reminder that men do not, indeed, live by bread alone.

However it is possible to make a case that the clergy were the main losers in the Reformation process. With the removal of monks, nuns and friars, the proportion of clerics in the population was much reduced, while lay control was imposed on those who remained and lay people increasingly felt able to think about theology for themselves. The special status of churchmen was largely removed, with the abolition of their special clothing (outside of service time), their consecration with holy oil, and their inability to marry. The laity was now admitted to the whole of a church, instead of being screened off from its most sacred part, the chancel. In 1500 the Church owned about a third of the landed wealth of Britain; in 1600 it was left with about a fifteenth. In 1500, universities were essentially priestly seminaries; a century later they were also becoming playgrounds for young gentry. The laity acquired the power to appoint ministers to a huge number of parish livings, and town councils and parish vestries instituted a new kind of cleric – the lecturer – a preacher whom they hired and paid directly. By 1640 nine-tenths of London parishes had these in addition to ministers, forming almost a parallel clergy.

On the other hand, lay people were also losers in the Reformation, which swept away religious guilds and chantries, institutions which they had controlled completely. The new laws compelling church attendance meant that they were forced to listen weekly to a parish clergyman who was no longer offering up a ritual on their behalf but preaching down to them. From the mid-1550s churchmen were given the right to control schoolmasters, and their greater degree of education meant that they could lead and dominate village communities in a way never known before. So is there an overall balance sheet that can be constructed out of these conflicting bodies of information?

Indeed there is: it was the wealthier laity who gained at the expense of the clergy, and the clergy who were recompensed with more power over the poorer laity. At village level this was signalled by the replacement of parish guilds, which could include anybody, with the select vestry, a committee which ran the parish and was confined to its richer inhabitants.

A case could also be made that women did particularly badly from reform. It swept them out of power in heaven, by abolishing the cult of the saints, of whom so many were female. It swept them out of the Church, by dissolving nunneries and ending the tradition of solitary female mystics such as Lady Julian of Norwich. Women had been equal members of guilds, but were not admitted to vestries or Scottish kirk sessions, and ceased to be appointed as parish officers. Once more, this pattern of loss was not evenly distributed; gentlewomen continued to have a voice in religious matters by writing or translating devotional works, and retained private chaplains who served and celebrated them. It was poorer women who were most obviously disempowered. Viewed simply in terms of social and economic power, the true short-term victims of the process of Reformation were the common people of Britain, and especially the female majority of them. In some respects the religious history of the 1640s was to represent a rebellion against just this state of affairs.

In the long term, the victory was to go to the forces of scepticism, disbelief and secularism. From the late seventeenth century onwards, a majority of the British slowly came to believe in a kinder and more remote Christian God, who interfered less often and less directly in the lives of humans. This new concept of deity carried with it a much reduced tendency to literal belief in the interventions upon earth of his agents, angels and devils. At the end of the same century, the British state commenced a parallel retreat from the attempt to force its subjects to attend the established Church, and they were able increasingly to treat religion, to an even greater extent than before the Reformation, as a service of which they could avail themselves at need. The religious professionals, and the instinctively devout, were left to engage with it full-time. All these major trends, leading directly up to the present, spiritually pluralist and voluntary society, were evident before the Stuart period closed in 1714.

What needs to be stressed is that before 1640 we are in a different age, a unique epoch in British cultural history when the island was gripped in the experience of religious conversion and its immediate consequences. When all the reservations have been entered about the capacity of people for doubt, laxity and blasphemy, it remains true that these eighty years represented a time when the confessional temperature was unusually high. The great rent in Western Christianity and the promises of renewal and perfection held out both by Protestantism and by the Catholic Counter-Reformation produced in contemporaries a sense of living through an age in which both the deity and his satanic adversary were exceptionally active. When the strains of population pressure and inflation are added to those produced by the changes in the Church, it is easy to form an impression of a society within an emotional pressure-cooker, requiring either a reduction of heat or a huge explosion to release the tensions that were building up within it.

Witchcraft

One spectacular expression of those tensions was the trial and execution of individuals suspected of witchcraft: that is, of harming other human beings, or their possessions, by the use of uncanny powers. It is worth emphasizing that modern Western society is most unusual in refusing to believe that this sort of harm is possible. Most communities across the world have done so, throughout recorded time, and those of ancient Europe certainly did: the death penalty for it is recorded in the codes of the pagan Roman Empire and among the peoples to the north of it who were to form most of the medieval states which succeeded it. Trials for the offence are recorded throughout the Middle Ages, in Britain as elsewhere, but they were relatively rare. Christians harboured serious doubts regarding the willingness of their all-powerful and entirely good god to allow evil spirits and evil people to deploy supernatural power against humans, and discounted some ancient witch beliefs as superstition. The burden of proof that a person was bewitched was often placed on the accuser; and it is inherently difficult to demonstrate that an act of magic has been committed. What changed everything was the evolution of Western Christian theology, during the later Middle Ages, to credit its God with having permitted the devil the ability to perform actual acts of harm against humans, using other humans as his agents. From this it was a short step, taken in the 1420s and 1430s, to believing in a newly appeared and terrifying heresy, of people who secretly worshipped Satan and were rewarded with the gift of demonic servants who would injure neighbours against whom they harboured grudges. However potent, this idea was slow to mature, only claiming a few thousand victims in a corridor running from Italy up to the Netherlands during the next 150 years.

What really set it loose across Europe was the struggle between Protestant and Catholic, in which the fight against satanic witchcraft became one aspect of the general programme of reformers and counter-reformers. As the Continent's wars of religion peaked in the period between 1560 and 1650, so did the witch trials in most regions. All this is certainly true of Britain, where the transformation of witchcraft into a capital crime, rather than a concern for churchmen, was first attempted, briefly, as part of the Henrician Reformation. It was the Elizabethan one which completed the work, joined simultaneously by that in Scotland: in 1563 Parliaments in both nations enacted statutes prescribing the death penalty for deeds of witchcraft, which were to remain in force for almost 200 years.

The total number of people put to death will never be calculated with precision, because of the loss of local legal records. The most recent expert estimates run at 400–500 in England

and Wales and anything between 800 and 2,500 in Scotland, which would give Britain approximately 4 per cent of the total number of executions likely to have occurred in early modern Europe. The higher Scottish body count is especially significant in view of Scotland's much smaller population; and has a further grim aspect in that those executed in England and Wales were hanged like any other felons, while those in Scotland were burned like heretics, though usually after being strangled. The overall totals represent small entries in the annals of early modern British suffering, especially as they stretched over more than a century. The English and Welsh body count represented the number of deaths commonly claimed by plague in a provincial town in just three months, whereas even the Scottish one, taken at its maximum possible, amounts to a quarter of the number of people killed in a few hours at Flodden or Pinkie.

This statistical judgement, however, is somewhat weakened by the fact that trials were concentrated in time and place. In Sussex, a total of sixteen people were brought to court, and just one was executed: to speak of a 'witch hunt' in that county is clearly futile. In Essex, by contrast, hundreds of people were indicted, and at least eighty-four executed. The Scottish trials were located overwhelmingly in the Central Lowlands, with a smaller number in the southern uplands of the kingdom and another found in extensions of territory running out from the Lowlands along the inlets and islands of the Firth of Clyde and all the way up the eastern coast to the Northern Isles. Prosecutions for witchcraft were certainly not a feature of the cultural backwoods: on the contrary, they were concentrated most heavily in the regions around the respective capitals: in the counties surrounding London, and the regions around Edinburgh. This fits well with the fact that they were provoked by a new theological construct, of witchcraft as a satanic counter-religion, which had been imported from abroad. The regions of the British Isles which seem most free of them were the Celtic-speaking areas: Gaelic Ireland, the Scottish

Highlands and Western Isles, the Isle of Man and Wales. As all of these were subject to the same laws that produced frequent trials elsewhere, and some (such as Wales and the Isle of Man) have good records, there must be a cultural reason for the difference; but this is a matter that has never been properly investigated. Trials were also rare in large urban centres, as they fed on the suspicions and frictions generated by small communities in which neighbourly interaction was close and daily.

The British trials were also concentrated in time. In England they spanned the period from 1566 to 1682 or 1685, but a third to a half of the total number of executions occurred in East Anglia in just two of those years, 1645–7. This was the systematic hunt led by Matthew Hopkins, the self-styled 'Witch-finder General', which was big and savage even by continental standards. In Scotland, trials also began in the 1560s, and lasted until 1727, but most were concentrated in four big hunts, lasting a few years each, between 1590 and 1663. If these were 'epidemics' of witch trials, then the 'endemic' sort, of a steady trickle of cases through the decades, also had local concentrations: most in the English Home Counties took place in the reign of Elizabeth. Over time there was apparently a slow westward drift, as in the late sixteenth century trials were most common in eastern Scotland and south-east England, while in the later seventeenth century they were at least most prominent on the western side of Scotland, and in the English West Country. By extension, this movement produced a spectacular late episode on the far side of the Atlantic, in the only mass trial in England's American colonies, at Salem in 1692.

Accusations were always generated from below, by ordinary people who accused others in their community against whom they had usually long harboured suspicions. To bring somebody to trial was normally so difficult and drastic a step that it was undertaken as a last resort, after gentler methods had failed, such as using counter-magic to break the presumed witchcraft, or befriending the suspected witch in order to get the curse removed. The legal cases therefore represent only the visible tip of an iceberg of suspicions, anxieties and enmities which never surfaced in court. Accusations seem rarely, if ever, to have been made a cover for more secular motives of dislike; they reflected, instead, a genuine belief that the people concerned had done magical harm to others and were seriously dangerous. The actual incidence of trials was conditioned by the willingness of magistrates to accept denunciations. The high number in Essex was related to the unusual zeal for social and moral reform among its officials, while that in the Scottish Lowlands mirrors the activity of the region's kirk sessions, who had the same zeal. Sussex, by contrast, had a very stable economy and society, and so little social polarization: hence perhaps the low rate of accusation. Everywhere, witchcraft was essentially one item on the hit-list of the 'Reformation of Manners', usually coming after the reduction of profanity, fornication, poverty and the number of alehouses. The results differed according to national legal systems. In England the accused were tried at county assize sessions, by juries of strangers directed by professional judges, and about 70 per cent were acquitted. Those who died were normally senile, saddled with an unusually bad local reputation, or convinced that they had actually cursed people, with success. The East Anglian bloodbath of 1645–7 occurred because the assize system had collapsed in the Civil War, leaving a gap into which Hopkins stepped, a nobody from the minor gentry, with a personal hatred of witchcraft. He invited communities to name their suspects and then employed effective methods of bullying and torture to obtain confessions, followed by trials conducted by a special commission which lacked the usual judges. The much bigger body-count in Scotland likewise reflects the fact that suspects were tried there by local committees, staffed by people who were likely to know them personally and share the animosities which had brought the accusations.

There is one very striking feature of those accused: that they were overwhelmingly female, witchcraft being the only crime for which more women were prosecuted than men. The proportion of them among defendants in Essex was 92 per cent, and 85 per cent in Scotland, putting Britain on the high side of an overall average of 80 per cent for the whole of Europe. This in itself must make the witch trials an issue for historians of women, and indeed the witch is one of the very few images of independent female power which traditional Western culture has bequeathed to the present. The other features of that image, as an elderly, poor and solitary woman, need some revision. The Survey of Scottish Witchcraft, which concluded in 2003, found that most of the accused were middle-aged, married and from the middle ranks of local society; not marginal at all, but central to the functioning of local communities. Nor was middle age in itself a suspicious feature, because many of them had first become thought of as witches when they were young. If anything distinguished them from other women in that category, it was a quarrelsome and sharp-tongued nature, which made their neighbours, of both sexes, ill at ease. Historians have expended much ingenuity on the possible reasons for the association of witchcraft and women, finding explanations in the structure of early modern social and intellectual structures. What weakens them is that the huge preponderance of female defendants across Europe is an average achieved only by flattening out important local variations. Scotland's nearest neighbour to the north-west is Iceland, which had a vicious series of trials in which over 90 per cent of the accused were male. Just across the Channel from England is Normandy, where three-quarters of those tried were men. The social, economic, political and religious conditions of Icelanders were too similar to those of Scots, and those of Normans too similar to those in the rest of France, to make structural explanations for these anomalies work. What seems to lie behind them are ancient local traditions concerning the nature of magic, which focused on different gender stereotypes. It is a reminder that the early modern trials, though produced by a distinctive set of late-medieval beliefs, drew upon very deep roots in popular belief, stretching far beyond Christianity.

The great century for witch-hunting in Europe was 1560–1660, and enthusiasm for it was waning in most regions of the Continent by the latter date, although it continued in fringe areas far into the eighteenth century. In Britain, the trajectory of trials fitted the overall pattern, as social elites in England became increasingly reluctant to encourage accusations and allow convictions after 1660, and in Scotland after 1670. In 1736, Parliament repealed all the laws of both kingdoms that had made witchcraft a crime, and declared it an imposture or illusion instead. This shift of opinion was part of a package, whereby tolerance of presumed witches went together with tolerance of Roman Catholics, and of Protestants who rejected the established Church. Likewise, the decline of a belief in the power of magic was associated with the loss of a world picture in which the Christian God was constantly intervening, to reward and punish in human affairs: as angels and devils receded in the imagination of the dominant social groups, so did witches. In all these respects, the decline of witchcraft prosecution was part of the winding down of the religious fervour released by the Reformation, just as the upsurge in it had been one product of that event. It had become obvious that for some reason the deity who ruled human affairs was not allowing either Protestant or Catholic to prevail absolutely over each other, and that communities which put members to death as witches turned out to be no luckier, happier and healthier than those which did not. In one sense, the early modern European witch trials had been the last gasp of the medieval preoccupation with purity of religion; in another, they were a short-lived and unsuccessful experiment in ways to cope with misfortune, which represented one feature of the transition from the pre-modern to the modern world.

Family Values

By the end of the twentieth century, most people in the English-speaking world had a common concept of what 'traditional' family life had been like, before the social changes of the second half of the century began to disrupt it. Married couples lived together with their children, until the latter reached their mid to late adolescence and sought work or higher education. Of those couples, the men went out to work and earned the income, and women mostly stayed at home and managed its domestic affairs, at least until the children had departed. This system meant that youngsters were given adequate attention and discipline, and the bonds thus created encouraged children in turn to care for their parents when the latter became elderly and infirm. Marriage was supposed to be based on true love and companionship, and although many unions developed strains, most couples survived these and continued to live together and care for each other into old age. Individuals varied greatly, of course, in what they actually thought of this model of family life, from profound nostalgic affection to vehement loathing; but most would have accepted it as the old-fashioned norm, and still do. How does it match up to the realities of life in early modern Britain?

The short answer is, hardly at all. Most people in the period came from broken homes, simply because the high rate of mortality meant that most had lost at least one parent by the time they reached the age of fifteen (as well as some siblings). Marriage was certainly in most cases for life, because divorce was almost impossible; but then life was short and unions regularly broken by death. Somebody who survived into old age with adequate means and a taste for marriage would probably have had at least two successive spouses. The death-rate meant that in 1600 about 40 per cent of the population was aged under twenty-one. The majority of children had left home permanently by their mid-teens, and many much earlier, as part of a long process of increasing participation in the workforce, first with family and then with employers. From the parental home they went into service or apprenticeship, with frequent changes of employment if better openings appeared. Opportunities for leisure and adventure were greater than for other age groups, but the sheer physical mobility of young people, as they sought subsistence, and the social divisions between them, prevented the development of distinctive youth cultures. The target of most, generally not achieved until their twenties, was to secure long-term employment and so achieve the economic base for marriage and parenthood if desired. It was a system ideally suited to a fragile economy which required a maximum flexibility of cheap labour. It was also an economy characterized by mobility, as people had to keep moving to find new work. This is another reason why it was the community, and not the family, which cared for individuals who became too old or sick to support themselves; their relatives, if still alive, would commonly have left the area.

The age certainly had a concept of romantic love, expressed in popular stories, but the brutal realities of life meant that an ideal partner needed to combine personal attraction with a capacity to contribute to income. A popular proverb ran 'There's more to marriage than four bare legs in a bed.' Both men and women needed to earn for a family unit to survive. Sexuality itself was generally at a low level in a society characterized by chronic malnutrition, infestation with vermin, exhausting daily labour, an almost complete lack of privacy and of commercial erotica, and a general ignorance of contraception. Parish registers indicate that the boom in conceptions occurred from late May to July when the grass got high and the ditches dry. Most children did not reach puberty until their late teens, removing most of the problem of juvenile pregnancy. This situation had a practical benefit, in that repressed sexuality meant a comparatively low level of rape; it occurred, but seemingly not often. It rarely features in the criminal records, and the personal records left by women indicate little fear of it, for example when travelling alone. The gentry and aristocracy, and prosperous middle sort, suffered from few of the impediments of the majority; they even had access to a trade in erotic literature and pictures from the mid-seventeenth century. Their sexuality was accordingly much more vigorous, and puberty came on five or six years earlier. In many respects, the effect of improved living conditions during the past 200 years has been to give the bulk of the population a sex life formerly enjoyed only by the elite.

For all these differences, family values were still an issue for the early modern British. Between 1560 and 1640, writers regularly cited the family as the cornerstone of the social and political order. Many commentators agreed that respectable family men were the people best fitted to hold public office, because the qualities needed for a successful husband and father were those of a good governor. The corporation of Thetford, in Norfolk, long tolerated the notorious laziness of one member, but expelled him in 1630 when he was convicted of fornication, for bringing the whole council into disrepute. The boom in prosecutions of sexual offences between 1580 and 1620 was not due merely to fear of more surplus and impoverished population, but to a belief that loose morals undermined the family, and with it the bedrock of social order. Both anxieties were generated by tough economic times. We need not, however, necessarily take such perceptions as reality. The same writers who held that the family was the foundation of social order cited it as the model for national government as well; but at the end of the seventeenth century, when it became politically inconvenient to see kings as all-powerful fathers, many authors came to deny the parallel. Likewise, as the pressure of population and prices eased after 1660, so did the 'Reformation of Manners'. The idea that family stability and the stability of society are straightforwardly connected is unproven; what is amply demonstrated is that people in times of social and economic pressure rally to the close-knit family as an ideal symbol of harmony and order.

Women were expected to play a full part in generating food and income, but to avoid public responsibilities. Political life, except in default of a male monarch, central and county government, and, increasingly, even parish administration, were the preserves of men. In theory, women could vote for

Parliaments and parish vestries, if they were wealthy enough; in practice they rarely did so. Before 1640, females were strongly discouraged from publishing their thoughts in print, and banned from appearing on stage. Conduct manuals all recognized the supreme authority of the husband and characterized the ideal wife as submissive, while the common law denied married women property rights, even though there were some restrictions on what a husband could do with property brought to him by his wife. It is true that the same manuals expected marriage to be based on mutual support, and gave wives the right to advise their husbands, while some denied that the latter should ever beat their spouses even as a last resort. None the less, in theory early modern gender relations were based on patriarchy, in all its plenitude. The reality, as revealed by diaries, letters and wills, is that the balance of power varied from couple to couple, and decision-making was usually shared. Gentlewomen tended to be more submissive, being more indoctrinated than commoners, more subject to parental choice, and more likely to be younger than their husbands. The records of the middling sort of society, which multiply through the seventeenth century, show constant battles for supremacy, in which the husband never seems to invoke his theoretical authority. Among the lower orders there was some wife-battering, but also husband-abusing, and neither was regarded as acceptable behaviour by neighbours. Court cases suggest that the beating of a wife tended to occur as part of a stand-up fight, rather than being a routine measure of chastisement. They also make it plain that men were inclined to use violence much more frequently against each other than against women.

Furthermore, there was no straightforward subordination of female to male, even in theory. Mothers were expected to control and discipline their children, and mistresses their servants, irrespective of the latter's sex. Widows and unmarried women could own property and run their own households, and this was quite common: they led 16 per cent of the homes in the Middlesex village of Ealing in 1599. As Alexandra Shepherd has shown, masculinity was defined not by physical strength or sexual potency but by what would now be called leadership qualities: maturity, sagacity, generosity, self-discipline and good judgement. There was a fear of excessive male intimacy, and physical homosexual acts were criminalized and incurred an ascending scale of penalties, according to the nature of the act, with death at the top. This was a legacy of the reform of Western Christendom during the eleventh and twelfth centuries which had turned Europe into a region almost unique in its savage hostility to homosexuality. On the other hand, actual cases rarely came to the courts, apparently because, in an age in which men commonly slept together because of overcrowding, it was a hard crime to prove. Likewise, both manuals and court records show that many men failed to live up to the current ideal of manhood: indeed, that ideal – of the independent, patriarchal householder – was one that a large number of them could simply not afford.

The modern concept of the family is therefore a creation of the past 200 years, reaching the middle ranks of society in the nineteenth century and much of the lower parts only in the early twentieth. It was made possible by a tremendous fall in mortality and a rise in the real value of wages. If it is under pressure now, then it may perhaps be viewed as another of history's relatively brief experiments in ways of living; and one never really designed to cope with the strains that have been placed upon it by other aspects of modernity.

Sea-Dogs and Stage-Players

Members of the modern English-reading public who do not know the name of a single one of Elizabeth I's ministers are likely to have heard of two of her humbler subjects: Sir Francis Drake and William Shakespeare. There is good reason for this. While many of the other achievements of the period were short-lived, altered beyond recognition or concerned only with the internal development of the British, the beginnings of a transoceanic empire ruled from England and the elevation of English to a language with a world-class literature have a global significance.

Soon after Christopher Columbus guided Spanish power into what proved to be a New World, Henry VII commissioned another eager Italian explorer, John Cabot, to investigate the far side of the Atlantic opposite England. The result was the permanent European discovery of the North American continent – which had been briefly encountered before by the Vikings – and it was duly claimed for England; but nothing was then done about the claim for two generations. The land that Cabot found had no easy and obvious riches, and the Spanish were generally England's best friends and allies. Traders had several opportunities for new markets in Europe, and the ruling class had a traditional hunting-ground for loot, ransoms and glory on its doorstep, in France. What changed everything, of course, was the transformation of Spain into a determined and dangerous enemy after 1570, which turned the freebooting classes of England on to its territory, and especially its American colonies, using ships for their raids instead of the traditional cavalry and infantry bands. At the same time, the old claim to North America was remembered, as that continent offered bases from which to attack the rich Spanish territory in the centre and south of the New World, and a means of checking and challenging Spanish power in the Americas by planting English colonies.

The role of the Crown in this enterprise was minimal; instead, private groups pooled their capital to launch plundering, trading or exploring expeditions. The risks were huge but so too were the profits: on his voyage around the world at the end of the 1570s, Drake earned his sponsors double their outlay just by capturing one richly stocked merchant ship. Drake in fact emerges as the most high-minded of the Elizabethan adventurers, a bit of a cold fish and a fanatic, but rigidly faithful to his queen, his nation, his Protestant religion, and his personal hatred of Spain, and capable at times of gallantry to enemies. The meticulous planner of the group was the red-haired, dashingly dressed Sir John Hawkins. The psychopath was Sir Humphrey Gilbert, who boasted of the atrocities he had committed against unarmed civilians. The fantasist was Martin Frobisher, always claiming to have discovered gold mines and vital sea passages, and always wrong. The salesman was Sir Walter Raleigh, a maniacal egotist who had the charisma and talents for persuasion to get wealthy people to pour money into his ventures.

The force that drove all of them was greed, and in their scramble to satisfy it they inflicted horrific suffering on the Spanish, Irish, black Africans and Native Americans, lied to their own government, squabbled and competed viciously with each other, and bungled most of their own schemes. By the end of Elizabeth's reign, England still had no American colonies and no fast trade routes to Asia, and the Spanish colonial empire was completely intact. The Elizabethans had carried out vital reconnaissance work and dealt blows to Spain's prestige, but, judged by their own targets, their enterprises in the New World were crashing failures.

In fairness to them, the Americas were tough nuts to crack. The Spanish had taken all the really lucrative districts, and strongly fortified them. The areas that they had left, in North America, had no precious metals, no towns or settled populations used to paying taxes or tribute, and no crops of obvious value to Europeans. What they did have were terrible winters, baking summers, and plenty of warlike natives who were determined to defend their land. It was not until 1607 that the first English colony took root there, in Virginia, where the first cash crop was successfully planted– tobacco. After that, with the example set and a sympathetic king on the throne, in James I, came Newfoundland (1610), Bermuda (1612) and Nova Scotia (1620). In 1607 also, the first trading station was established in India, by the newly founded East India Company. Between 1620 and 1640 the colonies of New England appeared, largely as a refuge for radical Puritans, and gradually discovered the potential of their harbours for oceanic trade and of their interior for products which the northern forests could supply: timber and furs. Maryland followed, as a retreat for English Roman Catholics. From 1624 a few of the outlying islands of the Caribbean, which Spain had ignored as too small to be worth exploiting, were occupied and turned into sugar plantations: the most notable was Barbados. All these achievements were the work of private individuals. This steady, patient process of settlement in the early seventeenth century, so much less celebrated and glamorous than the largely ineffectual exploits of the Elizabethans, laid the foundations of the later British Empire and the United States.

The Elizabethan period also saw a celebrated flowering of English culture in every form: literature, art, music and architecture. It is important to get this in perspective. The English were starting to learn how to paint portraits, but most of the really famous artists who worked among them were still foreigners. Their music and architecture consisted of a few competent pieces produced on the cultural fringe of Europe. The real take-off was in creative literature, and especially in the theatre, as Shakespeare and Christopher Marlowe represented the highest early peaks of a swelling of achievement which commenced in the 1580s and rose still higher in the early seventeenth century. Several factors lay behind it: the existence of a long previous tradition of native poetry, stretching back to the fourteenth century; the heavy new emphasis placed by Protestantism on the spoken and written word; the Reformation's destruction of the medieval religious drama, which channelled English theatre into a new and secular form; and the new sense of cultural nationalism produced by England's redefinition into the most powerful of Protestant states, standing at bay against still stronger, Catholic, enemies. All of these, however, were shared in some measure by the Scots, who did not experience the same tremendous take-off.

The vital additional factor in the English case seems to have been the possession of London, a capital city designed to be the centre of a medieval Anglo-French empire and now left stranded, by the loss of the French territories, at the south-east corner of a newly rearranged realm too small for it. It was a gigantic and dynamic urban centre, by both British and European standards, facing the Continent and plugged into most of its cultural currents. In the course of the sixteenth century, the population of London itself increased from about 35,000 to about 120,000, while that of its suburbs more than doubled to 180,000, making it the third largest city in Europe after Constantinople and Paris. This provided the critical mass of authors and audience needed to sustain such a cultural take-off. The Globe Theatre charged only a penny for entrance, a sum within the reach of virtually all Londoners, while the more exclusive and sophisticated Blackfriars Theatre demanded sixpence, still ensuring it the patronage of the middling and upper sorts of people. London was also the centre of the printing industry, and it was during the 1580s that printed works designed for a mass audience grew from a marginal phenomenon in English life to a regular one. Popular preaching as a weekly experience, popular pamphlets and a popular theatre all took off together in the late Elizabethan era, and represented a new and frenetic English engagement with the power of words.

In addition to all these achievements, the Elizabethan period saw the first proper mapping of the realm of England, and the codification of its eccentric and untidy system of laws into texts which gave them a new coherence and dignity. The total effect was to provide a supercharged sense of national identity, and of its new religion, which was to prove the enduring one for the British. The next notable age of self-definition for the people of the island, the Victorian one, constantly referred back to it. This result is the more impressive in that it was in large part a response to the weakness and peril of a second-rate state with no potent allies, isolated in a European world where the superpowers were all Catholic, which hung on the life of an unmarried female ruler. The mapping of the nation was sponsored by a government afraid of invasion and rebellion, while the new activity of the English as explorers and settlers was provoked by the union of both Europe's existing colonial empires, Spain and Portugal, under a hostile ruler. The new enterprise of English merchants was caused by the loss of their traditional markets at Calais and in the Spanish Netherlands, and at no time under Elizabeth did England appear as formidable as it had done under her father, let alone under the greatest medieval kings. The triumphs of Elizabethan culture were born of a sense of vulnerability and inferiority, which they countered brilliantly.

The new status and achievements of English as a literary language came at a price for the other British tongues. Cornish had held its own in the far west of Cornwall all through the Middle Ages, but now went into terminal decline. Scots had a distinguished literature, especially in poetry, which flourished into the reign of James VI. It was the Reformation that dealt it a fatal blow, because of the common Protestant bond with England, which ensured the victory of the reformed faith. This bond, and the flourishing publishing industry in London, meant that at first most Protestant books intended for Scotland were printed in the English capital, and the English language. The Bible adopted by the Scottish national Kirk was that of the Calvinists of Geneva, but in its English version. After 1600, most Scots had begun to publish in English, and Scots was crippled as a literary language. The Welsh, likewise, possessed a very distinguished medieval literature in their native tongue, produced by the professional poets retained by the landowners. The accession of the Tudors to the throne, and the new freedom given to the Welsh to reclaim their own country, initially produced a golden age of poetry. This came to an end in the second half of the sixteenth century, as the native gentry came increasingly to appreciate the advantages of cooperation with English systems of government and the rich pickings to be made in England. They began to abandon their traditional culture en masse, as outmoded, and to adopt an Anglicized lifestyle which was in turn connected to the fashions and ideas of continental Europe. During the seventeenth century, support for the traditional poets completely collapsed, leaving what could be salvaged of their work to be collected by scholars who realized that they no longer completely understood it. As in Scotland, the result was not simply an elimination of competitors to English literature, but a direct transference of talent to it: before 1640 the Welsh had produced their first truly brilliant poet to work in the English language, George Herbert. In 1500 only 65 per cent of the people of the British Isles could speak any form of English, and often did so in dialects barely intelligible to each other. By 1700, 85 per cent were able to speak a standardized English. It was a development which undoubtedly helped to bring the peoples of these islands together, and was one foundation of the later United Kingdom; but it annihilated national and regional traditions which had produced rich, diverse and valuable literatures. The world knows Shakespeare and Marlowe, but not Alexander Montgomerie, Lewis Morgannwg or the Play of St Meriasek, and more's the pity.

The British Problem
According to most current historians, what has become known as 'the New British History' began in the mid-1970s, when a distinguished scholar of political thought, John Pocock, called for a project to bring the different histories of the various British peoples together. This is not entirely true. What Pocock actually called for was a much more extensive and inclusive vision of Britishness, uniting those peoples from Britain who had settled across the oceans with those in the parent nations. The movement that appeared instead, from the late 1980s, was more concerned with the manner in which the four main component peoples of the British Isles – Irish, Welsh, Scots and English – had reacted with each other at particular points of history. It had three different causes. The first was a realization, by some prominent historians, that certain episodes could only really be understood in terms of the relationships between

those component peoples. Pre-eminent among these were Conrad Russell, dealing with the civil wars of the 1640s, and Rees Davies, considering the formation of national identities in the archipelago during the eleventh and twelfth centuries. This realization was itself propelled by recognition that great national events were more obviously driven by religious and political, rather than economic, pressures; and those were factors that the different peoples of the islands had most in common. The second cause lay in the proliferation of new history written in Irish, Scottish and Welsh universities after the expansion of higher education in the 1960s; this gave English scholars much more comparative material with which to engage. The third consisted of growing contemporary anxieties over British identities, produced by the continuing problems in Northern Ireland, the movements for Welsh and Scottish de-volution, and the moves for closer European union. All begged the question of what 'nationhood' really meant. By 1990, a 'British perspective' had become fashionable among academic historians all over the archipelago, but especially in England.

In fact, where early modern history was concerned, the result was a set of different perspectives. One was taken by John Morrill, who emphasized the common problems and crises of the kingdoms of England, Scotland and Ireland by the mid-seventeenth century. Monarchs were judged in one by what they were doing in another, and politicians in each were all reacting to events in the others. None of them actively sought complete independence from the others, even under the greatest strains, and the nobility of all three was represented at the royal court and intermarried. Morrill acknowledged that the three kingdoms could be studied separately at times, but for a total of about one-third of the early modern period were so entangled that they could only be profitably considered as a whole. The second perspective was taken by Steven Ellis, who was pre-eminently a specialist in Tudor Ireland. He suggested that the early modern period was best characterized by an exercise in English state-building. He emphasized that until the 1530s English kings had mostly been concerned with their French lands, though in gaps between campaigns there their power had also expanded to leave large borderlands in Ireland, Wales and northern England, owing the monarch allegiance but run by their own magnates. This situation was altered by the final and complete loss of the French territories, plus a serious new problem of security created by the Reformation. The latter meant that the borderlands had to be taken in, a process which took almost 200 years and was completed in the early eighteenth century. By then Protestant, English-speaking elites were in control of the whole archipelago, and could harness its resources to create a superpower in the next hundred years.

A third perspective consisted of a reaction against these ideas by Irish and Scottish historians, especially Brendan Bradshaw and Nicholas Canny among the former and Keith Brown among the latter. Bradshaw insisted that the Irish experience was unique, not just in the British Isles but in the whole of Europe. It opposed the whole thrust of early modern state formation, whereby ever stronger monarchies either absorbed outlying realms or drove them into independence. Ireland ended up neither absorbed nor subdued, the only place in Europe where religious conflict was left chronic at the end of the early modern age. To Bradshaw, Ireland *was* the 'British Problem'. Canny complained that the 'New British History' was too narrowly political in its preoccupations. To him, the societies, economies and cultures of the different peoples of the islands were so distinctive that common political and religious problems could have radically different effects. The one thing, indeed, that they clearly all shared was the impact of English cultural and military expansion upon everybody else. Brown commented that the new kind of history was useful in inducing the English to take a greater interest in the other peoples, but that it should not divert the Scots and Irish from concentrating on the unique characteristics of their own nations. Behind some of these concerns lay the danger that if English historians got really good at writing Irish and Scottish history, then specialists in the latter could be out of a job.

During the years around 2000, these fears more or less dissolved, to leave a general amity among the scholars involved and the recognition that a three-kingdom or archipelago-wide view was essential to an understanding of at least particular periods and episodes. By then, it was also apparent – at least to somebody detached from the debates concerned – that lumped together under the heading of 'the British problem' in the early modern period were actually four different, but simultaneously occurring, problems. The first was the problem of the union of Crowns, which was started in 1541 when Henry VIII declared himself King of Ireland and ended in 1603 when James VI united all three realms under his rule. Multiple kingdoms were common in early modern Europe, as Conrad Russell reminded us, but this was a very unusual bundle. England was the most centralized and heavily administered monarchy in Europe, and also had a society much more open – individualist, capitalist and socially mobile – than the norm. Scotland was far closer to that norm, and Ireland a bizarre case of English institutions imposed on a much more fragmented society. The second problem was the English one, highlighted by Steven Ellis: of an English culture and state reaching out into what had hitherto been its neighbours and borderlands in the archipelago. In the course of the period 1530 to 1630, the Welsh native elite were brought into the English system with full rewards, the native Irish ruling class dispossessed or annexed, and the Scots sucked into a common Anglicized culture and a royal spoils system centred on England.

The third problem was the Irish one, created by Ireland's stunningly anomalous position as an independent state which was not visited by its royal rulers at all between 1399 and 1689. They never went there to be crowned, took no oaths to respect its laws, and were regularly deposed without any consultation of the Irish. The Irish government was a carbon copy of the English, in each detail, but with a completely invisible ruler.

This did not mean independence in practice, but (from the 1550s) treatment as an English colony, with land and office being open to exploitation by a stream of Englishmen who worked the independent institutions for their own benefit. The English themselves were never sure of what they were doing there. They did not have a scheme for taking over Ireland directly, but spoke instead of giving it their own superior culture, which would in theory be open to all its inhabitants to enjoy. They treated the natives as full subjects of their Crown, with feudal titles and rights to formal justice; yet at the same time equated them implicitly or explicitly with Native Americans, as savages essentially different in kind from the British. They also increasingly regarded the Old English as traitors and backsliders in the work of cultural re-education and religious conversion. Unlike the Native Americans, the native Irish were allowed to remain on the land taken by the New English, because they were already assimilated into the economic processes needed to exploit their labour and skills. At the same time, almost as little effort was made to convert and re-educate them by their new masters. The result was that wars and rebellions in Ireland were much nastier and more protracted than those in Britain. The great change of the period between 1530 and 1630 was to produce two new identities in the land, a New British one, firmly linked to Protestantism and close ties with England, and a New Irish one, as firmly linked to Catholicism and greater independence.

The fourth problem, which is another that has been high-lighted by Steven Ellis, was the Celtic one, and it ran through all three kingdoms. They were, indeed, probably the only three kingdoms in the whole of Western Europe by 1485 to retain in each what was commonly regarded as a savage frontier, represented by those among their subjects who spoke either Welsh or Irish or Scottish Gaelic. Indeed, at that time it seemed as if the Lordship of the Isles, held by the Macdonald family, might grow into a fourth kingdom, thoroughly Celtic and spanning Northern Ireland and north-western Scotland.

As suggested above, the subsequent policy of Anglicization was deeply destructive to Celtic identities. Between 1485 and 1603, successively, the Lordship of the Isles was conquered by the kings of Scots, Wales was peacefully assimilated to English government, and the military power of the native Irish chiefs was broken. The old link between the Gaelic-speaking populations of Ireland and Scotland was also broken, as religion separated the former into (mostly) Catholic, and the latter into (mostly) Protestant.

By 1630, only Scotland's Celtic hinterland, the Highlands and Western Isles, remained largely intact; and that is why by then it was at last starting to emerge as a problem for monarchs. This was very much a new development, for this had been the region which had produced the first rulers of a united Scottish kingdom, and until the end of the Middle Ages Gaelic culture had generally been admired. James V, indeed, seems to have been the first king who was not bilingual in Gaelic and Scots. The big shift occurred when James VI inherited the English throne and redefined his kingdoms as based on a common Anglicized culture, linked to the Continent, with barbarism and backwardness most clearly represented in them by the common Gaelic traditions of Ireland and Scotland. Between 1603 and 1621 his Scottish government passed a series of measures which stigmatized Gaelic culture and declared the need to modernize and civilize it according to Lowland Scots and English norms. National law was ordered to be enforced throughout the land, short-lived colonies of Lowlanders were planted in Gaelic areas, and certain clans, above all the Campbells, were favoured to act as the king's peacekeepers. Highland culture was, however, no living fossil, left over from the dark ages, but tough, dynamic and adaptable: and that was really the issue.

It lacked most of the trappings that became associated with Highlanders in modern times: the kilt, clan tartans, and the use of the bagpipes as the distinctive musical instrument. None the less, it had features which were just as distinctive, in Lowland eyes. It had its own costume for men: a long shirt with a long cloak wound over and around it. It had a strong and impressive poetic tradition, of verse composed in Gaelic by the native bards. Above all, it had the clan system, whereby land was divided into territories held by native lords whose tenants shared their surname and were in theory, though only at times in fact, their junior kin. These tenants owed them military service, 'man rent', in payment for their holdings, which meant that, in a still highly militarized society, the chiefs could gather war bands at great speed. It was itself not prehistoric but a late medieval system, built up in the late Middle Ages because of the relative loss of interest by the kings in their Gaelic hinterland and a resulting problem of keeping order there. When compared with the lordships of the medieval Lowlands, it differed only in a greater emphasis on kinship. By the seventeenth century, however, the waning of medieval systems of military lordship across the Lowlands, as in England, began to make the Highland clans look very different indeed. When the sixteenth century produced the triumph of firearms in warfare across Europe, the Gaels of Ireland and Scotland adapted in different ways. The former, led by Hugh O'Neill, took on the new gunpowder-based military technology from the Continent, so that he could engage English soldiers with the same weapons: guns and pikes (long spears), supported by horsemen. The Highlanders, not able to afford these, adopted an opposite response which slowly came into force in the first half of the seventeenth century. This was to throw away their heavy medieval armour and swords, and equip their men as light and mobile infantry, armed with leather shields and two-edged, one-handed broadswords. With the advantage of slope in their favour, they could charge fast enough to get among musketeers before they had time to fire off more than one volley, at long range, and so cut them down. Given the right terrain, in which the Highlands abounded, and a good commander, this 'Highland charge' could be devastatingly effective. By the middle of the century, therefore, the attempts by James VI's regime to suppress traditional Gaelic Scottish culture had backfired; it had evolved into something that was in military terms much more dangerous than before, and even more distinct from the Lowland Scots, let alone the rest of the British. To the 'Irish Problem' created under the Tudors, a 'Highland Problem' had now been added.

What all four aspects of the 'British Problem' had in common was a relationship of cores with peripheries, existing in every kingdom but with the basic dynamism provided by the greatest core of all, the Kingdom of England as defined by its original Anglo-Saxon heartlands east of Gloucester and south of York. In the long term it was the most serious knock-on effect of the end of the Hundred Years War, as English monarchs reluctantly turned away from France for the first sustained period in half a millennium, and sought realms to the west. This would probably not have occurred had England not produced a king as completely inept, and long-lived, as Henry VI. Its precise form was defined by the Elizabethan Reformation, which ensured that it would be characterized by cooperation, rather than enmity, between the English and Lowland Scots. This in turn would not have occurred had Mary Tudor produced a healthy son, or had Henry II of France not collided with a lance and so been able to make military interventions in both Scotland and England during the 1560s. All this is a reminder that, in an age of personalized monarchy, even powerful and sustained political, cultural and religious developments may turn on such human accidents.

8

THE EARLY STUARTS (1603–42)

James VI and I

The family that took the thrones of England and Ireland in 1603 had long been known in Scotland as 'Stewart'. It was Mary, Queen of Scots, who adopted the French form of the name, 'Stuart', when she became Queen of France, and south of the border it is this version that has stuck. When James VI inherited the English and Irish thrones from Elizabeth, he acquired not just a different number (as James I) and a different dynastic name, but a different historical personality. I myself first encountered that as a child in two nursery rhymes by Eleanor Farjeon: 'James I had goggle eyes, and drank more often than was wise', and 'James I, I must make plain, was ugly, greedy, gross and vain'. He featured in the gallery of English kings as its buffoon. James VI, on the other hand, retained his reputation as one of the best monarchs that Scotland ever produced. During the past thirty years, various historians, above all Jenny Wormald and Pauline Croft, have laboured to bring these two different kings back together. To a great extent, they have now arrived at a consensual result.

According to this, James was of all British monarchs the one best suited to be an academic: a genuine intellectual and a very good author, with an adventurous and enquiring mind and a witty and realistic style. He really understood history, theology and classical literature, and had a natural interest in, and respect for, other points of view to his own. He was no coward, being a keen huntsman and reckless horseman, with a terrible temper and sharp, witty tongue. He could be cunning and devious, and it was difficult either to manipulate or to bully him. These virtues were balanced, for contemporaries, by his physical awkwardness and lack of dash: he was ungainly, untidy, informal and shy of crowds. As a result he lacked that apparent accessibility which the Tudors had cultivated so effectively, and with it their ability to project an image: today he is the only Tudor or Stuart monarch who reigned longer than ten years to whom the modern British public seems to have difficulty in putting a face. His subjects themselves worried about the scarcity of portraits of their king: in representation, as in the flesh, James managed to lack both a majestic presence and a common touch. As a politician he had real ability, loving debate and man-management, but was bored by administration. It remains now to see how he fared in different aspects of government.

The first is Anglo-Scottish relations. On taking the English throne, James had to reckon with a widespread dislike and contempt for Scotsmen among his new subjects, accumulated over centuries of suspicion and open conflict. He had both to woo his new nation and to keep his old one content, and the double burden was a severe one. Every time he gave his attention to Scottish affairs, the English would accuse him of neglecting theirs. His initial solution to the problem was a complete political union between the kingdoms. After five years it had become clear that no English Parliament would accept this on any terms that approached equality for the Scots. In revenge, and to compensate Scotland for his now almost constant residence in England, he gave individual Scotsmen large sums from English revenues and privileged places at his court. In particular, he created a new and enlarged entourage of personal servants, the Bedchamber staff, which was almost completely Scottish. This angered many of the English in turn. From 1615 onwards, James delegated supervision of much of the practical work of government in each kingdom to a favourite courtier. This relieved him of much of the administrative burden, but created a new one, especially in England, of public resentment of the favourites concerned. James's greatest achievement in this area was to preserve the union of the two British Crowns, successfully enough for it to become permanent. He did so largely by spending most of his time in England, by compensating the Scots with cash rewards and court offices, and by more or less ignoring Ireland.

The second area of activity was finance, and here both James's subjects and historians have faced a problem: that although James ended Elizabeth's wars against Spain and the Irish rebels, the English Crown continued for years afterwards to run deeper into debt. The obvious question is whether this was due to the king's mismanagement or to problems in the fiscal system – and there is no easy answer. It is clear that James did not understand the concept of limits to what he could spend; a story was subsequently told of him that one Lord Treasurer, faced with yet another royal warrant for expenditure, took the king to a room in which he had piled up the cash represented by the sum concerned. James was allegedly amazed by the quantity of money that the amount that he had signed away on paper actually meant. Unlike Elizabeth, he had a family to support – his Danish wife Anne, two sons, Henry and Charles, and a daughter Elizabeth – and royal households did not come cheap. This royal fertility was a huge asset: it had been over two centuries since an English monarch had been crowned with one male heir already in being, let alone two. On the other hand, a king who did not pay much attention to his clothes somehow managed to quadruple the royal wardrobe account in the first five years of his reign. His inner ring of household staff, the Gentlemen of the Bedchamber, numbered eighteen in 1603 and forty-eight by 1624, all drawing salaries. In his first eleven years as king he managed to quadruple expenditure on fees, annuities and pensions. The pension list actually came to eat up a third of all royal expenditure, making James's court one of the most overstaffed and extravagant in Europe. Elizabeth's last Parliament had granted enough money to pay off three-quarters of the current royal debts, while expenditure on the armed forces shrank by six-sevenths between 1602 and 1607, with the ending of the wars. All this suggested incompetence or corruption.

Many of James's English subjects were convinced that both were involved. It was obvious that royal ministers were making record sums out of the profits of office: the countryside was studded with the palaces that they were building on the proceeds. All of the Tudors had kept decorous courts, but James's was a drunken shambles by comparison. It became scandal-ridden to what may have been an unprecedented degree: by 1618 a former Lord Chamberlain, Lord Treasurer, Secretary of State, and Captain of the Gentleman Pensioners (a troop of royal guards) were all in prison because of misconduct in office. Reports flew around the political nation of events such as a party thrown by the current Secretary of State for the king in 1606, when a series of allegorical entertainments collapsed because the court ladies performing them were too intoxicated to cope. The worst (or best) moment was when the noblewoman representing Peace lost her temper with her attendants and beat them with her olive branch; the one taking the part of Victory had already passed out on the entrance steps, while those personifying Hope and Faith were throwing up in the vestibule. It was hard for people to believe that any administration run by people who permitted such scenes could be properly managed.

On the other hand, Elizabeth's extreme parsimony in making grants of land and money had created an enormous, pent-up demand for them, and James, the newcomer and outsider, had to weigh up whether he would incur greater unpopularity by refusing it or by giving lavishly and coping with the financial consequences later. He went for the short-term option. In his first year he trebled the number of knights in England, and by the end of the 1620s the size of the House of Lords had doubled: but all this merely restored the size of the peerage as a percentage of the population to what it had been in 1485. Furthermore, this was an age of conspicuous consumption and display among the English ruling elite, and the king was expected to lead in this respect as in all else. One Lord Treasurer once informed him that at the end of every evening the candles that lit his residence were burned down halfway. If, therefore, he lit them anew for each second night, then he would halve his expenditure on candles. James accepted the financial logic, but could not bear the possible damage to his reputation, of being known as a ruler too poor or mean to afford new candles every night; so the waste continued. It also mattered enormously that he was having to cope with the consequences of Elizabeth's long run-down of the Tudor financial system, which by the time of his succession had become the most backward in Europe (at least apart from Scotland's). The royal income had fallen by 40 per cent in real terms since the reign of Henry VIII; and even James could have managed comfortably within that extra margin of revenue. Two-thirds of the annual deficit was represented by the new subsidies to the Irish government, incapable by itself of supporting the soldiers needed to keep the island obedient after Elizabeth's conquest. No provision at all for this was made either by the regular revenue or by English Parliaments.

James made some real attempts to confront the problem. Three out of the four men whom he made Lord Treasurer – the Earls of Dorset, Salisbury and Middlesex – had financial ability. Salisbury was none other than Robert Cecil, Burghley's younger son and Elizabeth's last leading minister. In 1610 he attempted to give the whole system the overhaul that had been needed for forty years, by proposing a Great Contract whereby the king would surrender many of the traditional sources of Crown income in exchange for a more efficient and streamlined set provided by Parliament. This scheme eventually foundered because both James and the current House of Commons were too suspicious of each other's good faith to reach agreement over it. Royal bankruptcy was only prevented because the government had decided to raise and extend the customs dues on its own authority, without taking a Parliament into partnership. This carried the price of embittering relations severely between James and his Parliaments, which never accepted his right to do this. Along with a range of similar emergency measures, it succeeded in bringing expenditure under control in James's last eight years; but the basic problem of a failing fiscal system remained, along with a large royal debt and a political nation, represented in Parliament, which blamed the king and his servants for the whole situation. Perhaps the best verdict upon the matter is that the situation concerned, itself the responsibility of Elizabeth, would have severely tested the abilities of a king who was a born financier; but that James's spendthrift nature made it considerably worse.

By contrast, recent scholars have been generally admiring of James's handling of the Church of England. He arrived as a reformer. When the English bishops informed him that their church had been stable for forty years, and so he should leave it alone, he replied, characteristically, that a man who had been sick with the pox for forty years could still be cured. He then humiliated the bishops by calling a conference at Hampton Court Palace at which they were forced to debate the condition of English religion with their Puritan critics. He did not, however, pick the finest speakers among those critics to attend, and at the actual event he supported the bishops. The result was that the most important reforms requested by Puritans were not implemented, but many minor changes were ordered to make the Church more administratively efficient and more obviously based on preaching and Scripture than before. These did something to assuage the disappointment of moderate

Puritans; the most enduring feature of them was the production of England's Authorized Version of the Bible. James now turned on the more obstinate Puritans, allowing the current Archbishop of Canterbury, Richard Bancroft, to demand that all beneficed clergy attest their acceptance of the whole Prayer Book and all the Elizabethan articles of belief. Both he and Bancroft, however, urged the bishops not to enforce this requirement on clergy who failed to use all the official ceremonies but did not make a fuss about them. The result was the ejection of up to eighty-three ministers, about 1 per cent of the whole, leaving many quiet or occasional nonconformists still in charge of their parishes.

Having thus tamed the Puritans, James proceeded to choose excellent scholars and preachers as bishops, usually men who had served in the dioceses concerned and knew them well. As a result, his leading churchmen were of a higher quality than those of Elizabeth, and when he came to appoint a new Archbishop of Canterbury he chose George Abbot, who emphasized the primacy of Scripture, hated Catholics and wanted an aggressively Protestant foreign policy. As a result, James's primate was respected by most Puritans and popular in the nation, and especially in Parliaments. The king responded to the growing presence of the 'Arminian' faction in the Church, which stressed ceremony and physical beauty in religion and the possible salvation of all believers, by promoting some of its members to high clerical office; above all, Lancelot Andrewes and Richard Neile. He ensured, however, that they never took up more than a third of the bench of bishops, while most sees were filled by churchmen of Abbot's kind. What the presence of the Arminian group represented for him was a policy that ensured that a range of viewpoints was represented among his leading clerics and that the bishops would never be able to unite against him over a contentious issue. In particular, he used the Arminian presence as a means of leverage against Abbot and his allies when the latter attempted to put pressure on him to adopt a more aggressively Protestant foreign policy towards the end of his reign.

English Catholics initially had high hopes that he would end the Elizabethan persecution of them. He had encouraged these, to win further support for his accession, but soon reverted to the established policy, both because the weight of English public opinion had become so hostile to Catholics and the fines levied on them were so lucrative. As a result, a group of the wildest of them tried to blow him up, together with the whole of his current Parliament, in the Gunpowder Plot of 1605. Had the plot not been betrayed, it would have killed the majority of the political nation of the time, and destroyed the whole centre of Westminster; the appropriate modern comparison is not with the attacks on New York on 11 September 2001, but with the impact of the atomic bomb on Hiroshima. The knock-on result would probably have been a mass slaughter of English Catholics. Instead, tough new laws were immediately rushed through against Catholicism, but the government did not intensify persecution in practice. Indeed, it executed only nineteen priests in the course of the reign, a sixth of the toll claimed by the Elizabethan regime in a comparable period. As in the case of the Puritans, having cowed the Catholics, James was content to let them survive. His government also burned two Protestants, for heretical views concerning the sacraments, but after 1612 it deliberately called a halt to this process, apparently because of the king's own unease. In doing so, it ended the execution of heretics in England for all time. The Church of England that James left at his death was stable and flourishing, but still riddled with tensions, which had become more potentially dangerous because of the new prominence allowed to the Arminian minority. To modern eyes, it does the king credit that he was able to see virtue in both the mainstream ideas of his clergy and those of the Arminian avantgarde. What was ominous was that almost none of his churchmen were able to do so.

In high politics, James also inherited a set of problems. They revolved around the fact that most contemporaries believed, and the Tudors had almost always ensured, that the monarch's advisers needed to reflect a range of different political and ideological groups. At the end of Elizabeth's reign, however, the rebellion of her favourite, the Earl of Essex, had left church and state in the hands of a single faction, that of Robert Cecil and Archbishop Bancroft. James kept this faction in power, but, just as he showed the bishops that he was their master, so he doubled the size of the Privy Council by bringing in advisers to balance Cecil. This was done by introducing Scots and rehabilitating noble families and factions – those of the Dukes of Norfolk, and the Earls of Northumberland and Essex – which had been broken under Elizabeth. When Cecil died, James elevated another group of politicians, led by Archbishop Abbot and the Earl of Pembroke, to provide a further balance. So far, this looked like a return to business as usual, but James had to rule Scotland as well, so that the details of government would have been too much for him even if he had possessed any aptitude for them. He solved the problem by appointing leading courtiers as patronage-brokers, to hand out jobs and grants on his behalf. The reward to the brokers was to make money in bribes, or in outright payments for posts or titles, from those whom they favoured. To those on the outside of this system it could easily look corrupt, but the brokers could only retain their positions by getting good results: by filling offices with people who could carry them out effectively, and by giving titles of nobility to those who were socially qualified for them.

There was, however, another factor operating at this time. Like Elizabeth, James had a weakness for handsome and charismatic young men, but in his case it became much more pronounced as he grew older and had ever more serious conse-quences. In part, this pattern seems to have been a response to emotional deprivation. As we know, the king had a wife, and three children who survived childhood. By the 1610s, however, he had become emotionally estranged from his queen, and does not seem to have found either of his sons, Henry or Charles, to be kindred spirits. In that decade, moreover, Henry died and James's only surviving daughter, Elizabeth, married and left the country. It must have counted for something, too, that James aged badly. During the last ten years of his life he was obviously tiring, growing ever more frequently ill and thinking less clearly; the deterioration in his written works is marked. He was burning out, and increasingly felt the need of somebody to give him emotional and practical support. The new pattern first became obvious in 1607, when James formed an attachment to a young Scotsman called Robert Kerr, whom he made Earl of Somerset. Then, in 1615, he transferred his affections to an Englishman, George Villiers, whom he raised by degrees to the rank of Duke of Buckingham and to whom he remained devoted for the rest of his life.

Were these men the king's lovers? With such a separation in time it is impossible to say, but it is worth noting that James had earlier condemned physical homosexual acts in his published work as a detestable crime and a sin. How far he subsequently compromised these views can never be known, but two things are beyond doubt. The first is the sheer power of his emotional infatuation with these men, and especially with Buckingham. The second is that this provoked, in many of his subjects, that disgust with homosexuality which was a hallmark of the age. It did not help matters that neither of James's 'toy boys' had any real gifts for politics or government. Somerset fell in 1615 because he was accused and convicted of being implicated in the murder of a fellow courtier by poison. Whether he was guilty will, once more, never be known; the king was by now tired enough of him to let his enemies handle the prosecution. After Somerset's conviction, however, James got the worst of both worlds. What was needed to restore the confidence of his subjects in him after such a scandal was to put his former favourite to death, as a demonstration that nobody was above the reach of justice. Instead, whether swayed by lingering affection or by doubts over the truth of the charge, he commuted the punishment to a term of comfortable imprisonment and so did his own reputation further damage. Buckingham was more intelligent than Somerset, and had better political survival skills, but was even greedier, enriching both himself and his relations from the royal bounty. Nobody since Cardinal Wolsey had combined the roles of chief royal executive agent and personal favourite so completely.

Neither favourite dominated the king politically. Roger Lockyer has proved that Buckingham, the more important of the two, kept himself aloof from factions of politicians and acted as the patronage agent of the king instead. He could only get men jobs if James did not already have his own candidates, and only delay their dismissal if they were revealed as unworthy of office. He had, moreover, to work within the whole formal system of rights and reversions that had accumulated under Elizabeth. It is also now plain that James made policy and Buckingham then followed it. All told, the role of the favourite was to take much of the strain of administration from the ailing monarch. To those on the outside of government, however, it looked very much as if Buckingham was doing the governing, and with no other qualification than the king's sexual passion. He and Somerset did a great deal to worsen the reputation of the regime for sleaze and corruption.

An interim verdict on James can be proposed at this stage: that in hindsight he appears remarkable and in some ways admirable, with many personal and political virtues. His essential problem was that, like Henry VII, he was an able ruler who did not correspond to the model of what the contemporary English expected a king to be. This becomes still plainer when examining the two remaining areas of royal activity: parliamentary affairs and foreign policy.

Crown and Parliament under the Early Stuarts
The topic of English parliamentary history between 1603 and 1629 may be described as a minefield, in both an economic and

a military sense, a situation resulting from the perceived importance of the issues that have become bound up in it and the number and high quality of the historians who have clashed over them. The 'classic' view of it was established in the late Victorian period by Samuel Rawson Gardiner, who portrayed it as a contest between the Stuart kings, who aimed at a stronger monarchy and a more narrowly defined and closely controlled national Church, and the House of Commons, which strove for greater influence over Crown policy by the people's elected representatives, and a more accommodating and decentralized national religion. Between 1975 and 1978 Gardiner's picture was attacked by a group of scholars, most prominently Conrad Russell, Kevin Sharpe and Mark Kishlansky, who were given the nickname of 'revisionists'. They argued that neither monarchs nor Members of Parliament were striving for greater power over each other, and that no consistent and coherent opposition to royal policies existed in Parliaments. They emphasized the continuing crucial importance of the House of Lords and suggested that apparent struggles between the Crown and a parliamentary opposition were usually contests between different factions among royal courtiers and councillors. Those quarrels that occurred, they suggested, were the product of misunderstandings and practical problems, rather than deep-rooted ideological differences. In the 1980s a group of historians emerged who disputed several aspects of the revisionist case: its most prominent members were Derek Hirst, Thomas Cogswell and Richard Cust. They held that ideology was still very important in the struggles inside Parliaments, and that the tensions that it generated were serious. They insisted that more than mere bickering within the government was at stake, and that profound issues of trust and responsibility were being raised.

This summary of a famous debate generates three obvious questions: to what extent have the contending historians in it been proved right or wrong?; what were the problems that vexed early Stuart Parliaments?; and were the Stuarts genuinely different from the Tudors in their relations with the representatives of their people? The third may be answered most easily, and with a resounding affirmative: the year 1603 marks a genuine watershed in British parliamentary politics, because of two huge new issues that began to emerge in that year. The first was the need to reform the royal financial system, while reckoning with a political nation completely unaware that reform was needed. The second was the crowning of a king of Scots as monarch of England and Ireland; and one, moreover, who wanted a true union of his Scottish and English realms. This immediately made MPs much more wary than before of the extent of royal power and the manner in which it intermeshed with, or overruled, parliamentary consultation and consent. As in the case of the financial problem, the Elizabethan conquest of Ireland added a further strain to the situation. James blatantly manipulated the Irish electoral system to change the composition of Ireland's House of Commons, creating many new boroughs in Protestant areas to reduce Catholic representation to a minority. This probably made English MPs even more sensitive to possible royal attempts to exert control over the composition of their own house.

The English faced this new situation with an unfortunately vague set of constitutional principles and precedents. All agreed that sovereigns could not, under any normal circumstances, levy taxes or make or alter laws without the consent of Parliaments. Everybody also agreed that this rule might be infringed in an emergency, but not upon precisely what constituted an emergency. There was likewise universal agreement that any legitimate government had to rest upon 'divine right', in other words to enjoy the approval of the one true God, and that realms were effectively families, of which kings were the head. What was not clear, or accepted, was whether that familial model meant that subjects had the relationship to their monarch of a wife, who was expected to counsel or admonish her husband, or of children, who had a right to expect good treatment in response to good behaviour, but were not expected to offer useful advice. Nor was the notion of divine right ultimately any better defined, because it begged the question of how much obedience was owed to an ungodly ruler. It was a problem repeatedly faced in different parts of post-Reformation Europe, as populations found themselves under a sovereign with a different kind of religion, and no generally accepted answer to it existed.

Under Elizabeth, the threat of the succession of the Catholic Mary, Queen of Scots, had caused some leading English politicians to draw up contingency plans in the case of Elizabeth's sudden death, whereby the next monarch would essentially be chosen by Parliament. Once Mary was dead and a Protestant succession ensured, however, leading ministers, churchmen and judges began instead to cry up the power of the Crown against opponents such as Catholics and Puritans. The reign of Elizabeth itself, therefore, provided examples both for those who wished to emphasize the descending power of the monarchy, and its ultimate power over all subjects, and its ascending power, as an institution ultimately responsible and accountable to the people it governed (or at least the elite among them). Both views of government had, however, been built into English politics since time immemorial, one or the other predominating at particular moments or among particular groups. In practice there had been no serious clash between them under the Tudors because rulers and ruled had usually managed to make a working relationship in practice.

Things were different under the Stuarts, because James I's status as King of Scots, and the need to reform the royal finances, immediately raised serious constitutional issues. James's very succession to the throne was itself in contravention of parliamentary law, because (thanks to Henry VIII) a statute had been passed excluding the Scottish royal family from it, and never repealed. In confronting such problems, the king had the wrong personality. He needed to play down issues of principle, concentrate on common interests and practical needs, respect customary rules and patterns, and keep himself aloof from political wrangling as far as possible. Instead, being an intellectual and a keen debater, he drew the attention of his Parliaments to the constitutional implications of practical issues and broke through customary procedures that he found restrictive. He cried up his own powers in a way which he probably intended as a debating position but which many of his subjects mistook for dogmatic assertions, and he tried to contribute directly and personally to discussion.

As a result, matters that were difficult in themselves, such as English resentment of the number of Scots who held posts at court and the failure of Parliaments to find a workable solution to the Crown's financial problems, became caught up in questions of high constitutional principle. As early as 1604, the House of Commons attempted to force James to define what powers he thought that he had over the national religion, and was prevented only because the Lords refused to cooperate. In 1612 the king dissolved a Parliament in fury, believing that he could no longer work with it, something that no Tudor had ever done. Two years later he called another, and this immediately ran into trouble over the favouring of Scots at court and the royal increase in customs dues. Both James and the Commons rapidly deployed their two ultimate weapons against each other. The MPs refused to vote taxes unless the king responded to their grievances, and the king dissolved the whole Parliament before it had passed a single law, earning it the shameful nickname of the 'Addled Parliament'. This really was a new, and frightening, political world. The next Parliament, in 1621, revived the medieval tactic of impeachment, whereby royal ministers were formally accused of misgovernment by the Members and put on trial. After 1610, James had a chronic dislike of English Parliaments.

None the less, recourse to them never completely broke down during his reign. He respected the most important conventional limits to royal power, never imprisoning a subject without trial and never imposing entirely new taxation without parliamentary consent. When in 1607 a clergyman called John Cowell wrote that the king's authority was superior to any law, James explicitly disowned him. In 1610 the Commons challenged his right to create new kinds of crime by royal proclamation, whereupon he consulted his judges about the issue and accepted their verdict that the MPs were correct. He may have experienced problems with his Parliaments on a scale not known to any English monarch since the Middle Ages, but they always remained within bounds that allowed for the making of better relations given only time and a normal amount of good luck. As it happened, James was to be given neither: instead, in the last seven years of his reign, he was to be caught up in a crisis which intensified every tension already present in English political and religious life: and its point of origin lay on the far side of Europe.

As part of James's unconventionality as a king, he had a personal dislike of war, and indeed he set a record in both his realms for reigning at such length without ever waging one. Instead he wanted to win glory by becoming the peace-maker of Europe, and this was reflected in the marriages that he sought for his children. His daughter Elizabeth was wedded to the most dynamic and ambitious Protestant prince in Germany, Frederick, the Elector Palatine. This tied his family and his kingdoms to the cause of international Protestantism, and was popular among his subjects. Much more controversially, he tried to marry off his sons, successively, to a Spanish princess, so balancing his daughter's union with a link to the greatest Catholic power on earth. In that manner, he hoped to draw together the two great contending branches of Western Christianity, and reduce tension, and the potential for bloodshed, between them. In this, as in so many other respects, James looks more admirable through modern eyes than those of his subjects, many of whom reacted in horror at the prospect of a Spanish queen. Reluctance on the part of Spain doomed the project, but developments abroad brought all his well-intentioned diplomacy an even worse result. In 1618 his son-in-law Frederick accepted the throne of Bohemia, offered to him by its Protestants who had risen in rebellion against their hereditary king, an aggressive Catholic who was also heir to the various lands of Austria and to the title of Holy Roman Emperor. Frederick was thereby presenting himself as the hero of Protestant Europe. The Emperor responded by calling in help from his relative, the King of Spain, and the combined Catholic forces drove Frederick out of Bohemia.

None of this should have been a problem for the English, as Bohemia was far too remote to make any intervention there credible, and Frederick's title to it was very doubtful. What changed everything was that the Spanish swung west, to attack Frederick's hereditary lands in Germany and to renew their former war against the Dutch. The Emperor launched his own soldiers against other Protestant German states. What had been a squabble on the eastern side of Europe had turned by 1621 into a major European war, in which the lines were drawn between Protestant and Catholic. James was inevitably pulled in, both as the leading Protestant monarch and as Frederick's father-in-law. Had he been a natural war-monger, he would have faced an almost impossible situation, because the heartland of Frederick's realm, the Palatinate, lay in the central Rhine Valley, hundreds of miles from the sea; and England had never been capable of launching military expeditions deep into Europe. James dealt with this by pursuing a consistent and logical policy: to persuade the Spanish to stop their attack on Frederick's lands, by offering them friendship in return, while threatening war if they refused. This involved preparing to fight, by sending soldiers to the Palatinate and warships to the Mediterranean, and calling a Parliament and asking it for funds, while negotiating with Spain. As a strategy, it was too complex and ingenious, and it backfired. The Spanish encouraged James to believe that they would make a deal with him, while Parliament grew suspicious, with reason, that they would vote huge sums for a war that would then not happen, leaving the king to pocket the proceeds. As a result James and the House of Commons fell out again, and he dissolved the

Parliament, leaving the Spanish free to call off any agreement with him and complete the conquest of the Palatinate in 1622.

Being thus unable to make war, the Stuarts next attempted to use diplomacy once more. In 1623 James's son and heir, Charles, and his favourite, Buckingham, went to Spain in person to negotiate a marriage between Charles and a Spanish princess which would bring about the return of the Palatinate to Frederick. Once again the Spanish turned English ineptitude to their advantage, forcing their own terms upon their unexpected guests. Charles returned to England without a bride or the Palatinate, but with a promise to emancipate English Catholics, which was completely politically unacceptable to most of his father's subjects. He promptly repudiated the agreement and he and Buckingham henceforth became ardent proponents of a war with Spain to regain the Palatinate. The result was the Parliament of 1624, the most successful for almost twenty years because the majority of its members united with Charles and Buckingham to force this war upon the king, voting almost £300,000 to launch a naval expedition. Once more, however, James did not declare war, trying to escape it instead by getting others to fight it for him. He used the money from Parliament to send soldiers to assist the Dutch and German opponents of Spain, while trying to enlist the aid of the only power in Western Europe which possessed an army large enough to tip the balance of power against the Spanish – France. James's hope was that the traditional French rivalry with Spain would count for more than the common Catholicism of both monarchies. Once more he employed a marriage alliance as his means, asking for the hand of the French king's sister, Henrietta Maria, for his son Charles. Once again his diplomacy failed in its object. The marriage was actually agreed, but on terms that did not commit the French government to an alliance against Spain but did commit the English to suspending the persecution of Roman Catholics. At this critical moment, in March 1625, James suddenly expired. He had been in poor health for years, but would probably have survived this latest illness had his physicians not employed such a drastic set of remedies; they effectively tortured the king to death.

This ought to have made the situation much easier, because the new monarch, Charles I, was eager to launch a proper war against Spain, using seaborne strikes in the Elizabethan manner. His first Parliament was, however, made confused and suspicious by the evaporation of all the money voted by the last one, and by the imminent arrival of a Catholic queen, accompanied by a relaxation of the penal laws against English Catholics. Nor did Charles want to launch his attack on the Spanish before the French were committed to help him. At the same time, he made his father's former favourite, the Duke of Buckingham, supreme both in the court and in the royal counsels, to an extent that James himself had never done. The result was that the Parliament was dissolved without supplying money. Seeking to gain popularity and foreign allies by a military coup, the government raised funds by levying a compulsory loan from its people, and sent an expedition to sack the most important Spanish port, Cadiz. This had actually been done under Elizabeth, but since then Cadiz had been strengthened and England's commanders had become less experienced and gifted. The result was a humiliating repulse.

In the next year, 1626, Charles called a second Parliament, to get money for a further effort. The Commons responded with a straight offer; that funds would be voted if Buckingham, who was now generally blamed for the regime's failures, left public life. To Charles, both parts of the deal were unacceptable: he would not abandon Buckingham, and the sum offered by the Commons covered only a third of the cost of another expedition. Without French help, there was no prospect of making headway against the Spanish, and the French had delivered their princess to England without any accompanying military alliance. Charles's strategy now switched to putting pressure on France to make one, by using the single means that he possessed to do so. The French Wars of Religion had left the nation divided between a Catholic majority and a tolerated and armed Protestant minority. In the late 1620s, much of the latter rebelled again to protect their privileges, especially at the important seaport of La Rochelle. By sending aid to the rebels, and renewing the persecution of English Catholics, Charles and Buckingham hoped to win new popularity as champions of Protestantism at home and abroad, and also force the French to fight Spain, by showing how much trouble England could make if they did not. To raise the cash for such an expedition, the government resorted to a new kind of forced loan, levied nationwide and systematically in the manner of a war tax. It provoked much unpopularity and some outright opposition, but was effective, raising over £250,000. This was enough to raise an army to save La Rochelle, which Buckingham himself led in 1627. The expeditionary force was, however, poorly organized and inadequately equipped, and the money proved insufficient for its needs; it returned, having failed in its objective and suffered terrible losses.

The government had now added £1 million to its existing debts, despite dangerously large sales of Crown land which had, effectively, completed the dispersal of the real estate of the medieval English monarchy. It was also at war with both Spain and France, the two strongest powers in Western Europe, and without any means to fight either. The royal army was left unpaid and billeted upon civilians across southern England, while seventy-seven prominent men who had refused to pay the forced loan were jailed without a formal process of law. The king had to call a third Parliament in 1628, and this time the Commons proposed a different deal: war taxes in return for a ban on forced loans, billeting of soldiers, and imprisonments without trial. Once again, however, the accounting of the MPs was out, as the £280,000 they offered was too little for an effective war effort. Moreover, the 'Petition of Right' in which the Commons embodied their requests made the novel constitutional claim that certain rights, enjoyed by the subject, were as integral to the English state as the powers of the Crown. It was the culmination of those anxious attempts to protect the people and define and so limit the king which had commenced almost as soon as the Stuarts took over England. When the House of Lords sided with the Commons, Charles had either to agree or give up his war, and so gave in with notable bad grace, provoking fervent displays of popular rejoicing and of support for the actions of the two Houses.

Buckingham now prepared to lead a new expedition to rescue La Rochelle, but was stabbed to death by one of his officers, who blamed him both for personal grievances and for the misbehaviour of the royal government. The expeditionary force was thrown into complete disarray, and La Rochelle surrendered to the French royal army, depriving Charles of his lever on the French government and wasting the taxes just voted by Parliament. Both his foreign policy and his war effort were in ruins, and he gave up, seeking henceforth to buy peace with both France and Spain by giving up disputed colonial claims in the Americas. These treaties were completed by 1630, leaving England safe from attack and from bankruptcy, but with none of the king's war aims accomplished after a total expenditure of almost £2 million.

The peace-making process should have extended to the king's relations with Parliament, especially as he could recall the successful one of 1628 in the next year without the need to ask it for new taxes. Relations between the royal government and its critics had, however, been seriously embittered. Charles felt betrayed by the Commons because they had consistently failed to vote enough money for his wars while trying to interfere with the way in which he ruled; less directly but still potently, he blamed them for the murder of his beloved friend Buckingham. Many MPs had found the new king's regime to combine incompetence with high-handedness, a mixture designed to alienate most people. Two flashpoints remained as the wars wound down, and they were to prove fatal. One was the issue that had been left over from James's reign: that the Crown was only surviving financially in normal conditions by levying increased dues on foreign trade which no Parliament had recognized as legal. The other was new: that Charles had shown an undoubted, and unprecedented, partiality for the so-called Arminian faction in the Church of England, promoting them from the moment of his accession to a dominant position by 1629. Some of the churchmen in that faction had repaid the king for his support by preaching in favour of his more controversial measures, such as the forced loan. People who already disliked the Arminians because their ceremonious style of religion seemed too Catholic could now resent them as apparent supporters of arbitrary government as well. When his leading critics in the Commons tried to force through resolutions condemning the government for both its religious and its financial policies, and suggesting that the royal ministers had committed treason against the nation, Charles threw the Parliament out. He did so with a declaration that no further Parliaments would be called for a relatively long period.

The chronic difficulties in Charles's first three Parliaments had introduced a language of crisis into English political life. Revisionist historians have proved that there were not in practice two opposed parties, representing the followers and critics of the government. The problem is, as post-revisionists have demonstrated, that political rhetoric tended increasingly to assume that there were. Since 1600 a whole set of new vehicles for political information had become important, reflecting a growing public appetite for news and debate: the printed newspaper had appeared, and newsletters, verse satires, libels and pamphlets had become common. The mass lobbying of MPs, with the publication of petitions to them, had begun. In the face of this growing need to give an account of itself and argue down criticism, the government of Charles had responded by trying to raise the Crown above debate, and ceased trying to explain itself at all. Both the regime and its critics wanted Parliament to work harmoniously, and were increasingly angered and frustrated by the fact that it seemed to be failing repeatedly to do so. Neither the king nor the opponents of his policies had the ability to understand and manage each other. Both wanted to agree upon a set of workable guidelines for national politics, but found that no guidelines seemed to work any longer.

The Tudor model of politics collapsed in the 1620s, leaving the ruler of England unable to work with Parliaments, and therefore to wage war or have new laws made. The revisionist historians of the 1970s and 1980s were correct that this development was not the product of a greater will to power on the part of either the monarchy or the House of Commons. It was, rather, the result of the strains produced by the accession of a new, foreign, royal family and the creation of a triple kingdom, combined with those of a financial system in prolonged and severe decay; by 1600, indeed, it was the most backward and inefficient system in Europe, other than that of Scotland. Charles I had opened his reign with a war effort which was seriously underfunded: the decline of the value of the Tudor subsidy had accelerated in the new century by a further third to a half between 1610 and 1628. What seemed to be votes of huge sums by Parliaments were producing thoroughly inadequate results.

The essential problem was not, therefore, one of growing strength and ambition on the part of different components of the body politic, but of growing confusion, weakness and anxiety. This was not a peculiarly English problem: as contemporaries realized, all too vividly, representative institutions across Europe were starting to collapse during the period because they were ceasing either to restrain or to satisfy the needs of rulers. This compound of difficulties was worsened by the tensions generated by religious differences and by the accidents of fortune and the misjudgements of leaders. There should be no doubt that the problem represented by the Spanish seizure of the Palatinate was particularly difficult and that the policies adopted by both James and Charles in response were diplomatically, militarily and politically flawed. Here the opponents of revisionism come into their own in emphasizing that genuinely important ideological issues were generated by these practical difficulties. There is no doubt that by 1629 the familiar mould of English politics had been broken. Everybody now understood that it had either to be mended or to be replaced; and even a repair job would take considerable ingenuity and effort.

The Personal Rule of Charles I

The years in which Charles I governed England without a Parliament, between 1629 and 1640, represent one of the periods of British history over which the least agreement has been achieved by specialists. To be precise, the disagreement has until recently consisted of most of the other experts ranging themselves against the views of one, Kevin Sharpe. Professor Sharpe has, however, produced the fullest overall study of the subject to date. In the traditional view of the period, formulated by Samuel Rawson Gardiner in the late nineteenth century, the Personal Rule was a time of unpopular, inefficient and at least potentially despotic government, brought to an end by public opposition. The big question is whether that view is unjust and inaccurate: Kevin Sharpe has argued that it is, while his critics pronounce it to be substantially correct. What is perfectly clear is that the Personal Rule was a unique period in English history. Politically, it was the quietest decade of the seventeenth century, and indeed the last period of internal peace for 100 years. It was also the first of a series of experiments to replace the system of government which had broken down in the 1620s, and accordingly the one which attempted to make the fewest changes to that system.

As the name 'Personal Rule' suggests, the king himself was central to it. Charles I was probably the smallest man ever to rule England or Scotland, standing five feet tall or a little less. His speech was afflicted by a stammer, certainly due to nerves, because it cleared on those few occasions when he lost his fear of speaking. To make all this worse, he grew up in the shadow of the kind of elder brother whom we can all do without: Prince Henry, of normal height, equipped with perfect diction, limitless self-confidence and enormous popularity. Henry died in 1612, to general horror and disappointment, leaving his runt of a sibling to take over. No wonder Charles suffered from crippling shyness and had only limited interpersonal skills. He tried to remedy these shortcomings by cultivating rigid self-control, presenting an exterior of freezing calm and dignity to the world. Whereas most former monarchs had sought to gain respect by flamboyance and communication, Charles preferred to deploy silence and reserve as political tools; he had three locks put on his private apartments. He wanted a daily routine as regular and predictable as possible, which incorporated a lot of prayer, as he tried to gain further reassurance and advice from the God who had intervened to put him on the throne. As part of this persona, he was a conviction politician of terrifying rigour, viewing the art of the possible as the pathway to Hell. If, as king, he was directly responsible to his God, then to act against his own conscience, which he took to be God's bidding, was to risk damnation. Accordingly he felt bound in honour to listen to any advice, and then to ignore it and follow his own inclinations. His greatest curse, as person and ruler, was that he couldn't understand the feelings of others. This mattered in general politics, as he could only view those who opposed his policies as deluded or wicked. It also counted in individual situations, such as that of Lord Cottington, one of his ministers, who asked the king for time off from his duties to attend his own wife's funeral, and was refused.

The second member of the cast list for the Personal Rule was Charles's French wife, whom the English called Henrietta Maria. In many respects she was an excellent consort. It was an unusually happy royal marriage, the queen being small, affectionate, fertile (she produced three sons and two daughters who survived childhood) and loyal. She was vivacious and fun-loving, rescuing the court from being as dull as Charles would have made it left to himself. She became a magnet for dashing young nobles, including some who were at times opposed to royal policies and ministers, so broadening the viewpoints

represented among courtiers. Her single enormous trouble
was her Roman Catholic religion, which meant that to many
British Protestants their king was literally sleeping with the
enemy. Had the queen been tactful about her beliefs, the
problem would have been reduced, but she was proud of them
and did her best to convert any courtier willing to listen, with
occasional success. Again, personal tensions between the royal
couple would have served to diminish fears of her influence
over her husband, but their obvious love for each other only
enhanced them. Despite her personal virtues, Henrietta Maria
was a public relations disaster.

Ranged around the king and queen were the bulk of the
royal ministers: the Earl of Portland, Lord Cottington, Lord
Finch, Sir Francis Windebank, Bishop William Juxon and Sir
John Coke. All were efficient, hard-working administrators
with different views on most aspects of policy; all that distinguished them from earlier ministries was a lack of the more
evangelical sort of Protestant with whom Puritans might
identify. Charles gave them the security that Mary and the
young Elizabeth had accorded to their servants, ending the
feuding between factions that had gone on since the 1590s. In
addition, two other figures were associated with the regime:
William Laud, whom Charles made his Archbishop of
Canterbury in 1633, and Thomas Wentworth, who was sent
first to run the north of England and then to govern Ireland.
Their letters did much to provide previous generations of
historians with their basic picture of the period, as they talked
of the need for the king to rule with ruthless efficiency and
without truckling to popular opinion, of the disease of
constant opposition and disaffection in the realm, and of the
corruption and laziness of the royal ministers. Wentworth
summed up their view of politics in 1632 by describing himself
as 'a sailor in a storm'. It is time now to see whether this view
was correct.

Charles I was a ruler who believed in learning from mistakes.
His father had been criticized for timidity, untidiness, loquacity

and a respect for too many points of view; on becoming king Charles was therefore warlike, dignified and withdrawn, and inclined to adopt and follow a single viewpoint. After the disasters of the late 1620s he drew some new lessons: to avoid making war and calling English Parliaments until the whole structure of government was overhauled and repaired; to ensure that his actions remained within the bounds of customary law; and never again to have a single all-powerful favourite. Being Charles, he rigidly implemented each objective. As almost nobody in his government was an ideologue, it is hard to know what, if any, theories underpinned his new way of ruling. The exception was Wentworth, who believed that the prerogative powers of the Crown needed to be reasserted, having been whittled away by subjects' rights since 1600. How much his view was shared by the king's other advisers, we cannot now tell. The 1630s was certainly a great decade for parliamentary government, producing the only completely successful Parliaments of the reign, in Scotland and Ireland. Only in England was the king now allergic to them, but there his allergy was very plain. His behaviour suggests that he would not call one there unless an emergency rendered him absolutely desperate for money. This ran counter to the beliefs of all his ministers, including Wentworth, who urged him to summon Parliament when the Crown was at its strongest and could afford the time and trouble to wear down opposition. The king's attitude does raise doubts as to when, under any normal circumstances, he would have been willing to face an English Parliament again.

An immediate initiative was launched to make central and local government both more standardized and more efficient, which generated a snowstorm of paper but only limited practical results. The militia became no more effective, and attempts to spur JPs into greater efforts soon faltered; the Privy Council could not cope with the amount of feedback it was now demanding even had local government been willing to provide it. The great success story was finance, the Tudor system being worked with enough ruthlessness to raise the regular income by a third, to £900,000, providing a regular surplus. Every branch of the revenue was made to yield more, and a series of one-off expedients was adopted, based on the king's medieval rights as monarch, feudal lord and landowner, which helped to halve the royal debt. The problem of defence was solved by Ship Money, a rate which Tudor monarchs had levied on coastal counties, during emergencies, to pay for the navy. In 1635, Charles's regime extended it to the whole nation and made it an annual levy. The result was an administrative triumph, as in five years the rate provided almost twice the amount yielded by all the parliamentary taxation of the 1620s. All of it was dutifully spent on ships, greatly increasing the quality of the royal navy and the Crown's prestige abroad. Dutch fishermen agreed to pay Charles for licences to ply their trade in the North Sea, while the French removed their own fleet from Atlantic waters.

The problem with the levy was, of course, its legality, as it was by no means obvious that it could either be imposed upon the whole nation or demanded without any military emergency to be countered. The official justification was the threat presented to English merchants by North African pirates, but that was less serious than in previous years when the money had not been demanded. When a Buckinghamshire squire called John Hampden mounted a legal challenge to it, Charles scrupulously asked all of his twelve judges for an opinion. The result was embarrassingly close, seven of them finding firmly in favour of the king. In some counties it seems to have reduced payment, but in others it did not, and Ship Money was now firmly established in case law.

Charles's prime foreign policy objective remained what it had been in the 1620s: to get back the Palatinate for his sister and her family. Once again, two successive strategies were attempted: to persuade the Spanish to hand it back and the French to help reconquer it. By 1637 enough Ship Money had come in for England to look like an effective naval power again,

and a treaty was drafted with France for joint offensive operations. It might have worked, for France itself was now locked
into an open and prolonged struggle with Spain, and Charles
had a fleet capable of harrying coasts and seaways. He was
apparently on the verge of showing Europe that he could wage
war effectively without needing to reckon with Parliaments.

In religious affairs, his plan was to produce a Church of
England that was better supervised, managed, funded and
repaired than at any time since the Reformation. His problem
was that he was Supreme Governor of the most badly defined,
slackly administered, deeply divided and volatile Church in
Europe. Any attempt to exert greater central control over it
was going to worry a lot of people, and any attempt to define
or enforce its beliefs and practices would trouble a lot more. In
one sense, the king's solution was simple: as noted earlier, he
completely identified himself with the Arminian faction in the
Church, whose tastes for beauty, ceremony, order and sacra-
mental worship all accorded with his own. They were shared
fervently by his favourite churchman, William Laud,
Archbishop of Canterbury from 1633, a man who, like a
plump white mouse, scurried around the corridors of power,
gnawing at one political, religious or social issue after another.
He and the king both wanted to bring as many clergy as
possible under the direct control of the national Church. Since
the Reformation, the number which were outside its formal
structure had multiplied steadily: now 'lecturers' appointed to
preach by urban corporations and wealthy parishes were to
hold formal parish livings, only nobles were allowed to hire
personal chaplains, and the children of foreign Protestant
refugee congregations had to attend the Church of England.

Charles and Laud also aimed to re-endow that Church by
better management of its lands, an increase in the tithes levied
on laity to pay parish ministers, and an augmentation of the
salaries of the poorest clergy. They intended to enforce use of
the ceremonies prescribed in the official Prayer Book of 1559,
and decrease the multitude of individual interpretations of its

liturgy which had hitherto abounded in the parishes. Communion tables, which had stood in various different places within parish churches, were to be moved to the east end, like a Catholic altar, and railed in. King and archbishop wished to get churches better repaired in general, as fit houses for ritual, and to shift the emphasis of worship from preaching to catechizing and ceremony: to ensure a more communal, standardized and inclusive national religion. A strict observance of Sunday as a day of prayer and charity alone, associated especially with Puritanism, was officially condemned, and all clergy expected to announce that games, dances and feasts could be held after evening service. Finally, the royal intention was to make the clergy better behaved, educated and pious, and more independent of the laity: a spiritual elite which would help the king rule for the good of all his subjects.

In enacting this programme, king and primate had to reckon with the ramshackle structure of the Church of England, which was to a great extent a patchwork of semi-independent dioceses. Durham, Peterborough, Salisbury and Exeter were in the hands of bishops who were largely unsympathetic to the reforms, and in several of the others the physical and ritual changes were only selectively enacted. On the other hand, Norwich, and Bath and Wells, turned out to have prelates who actually went much further than Laud had asked in enforcing them. The one at Norwich, Matthew Wren, was so zealous that the king actually moved him to a less populous and sensitive see. To some extent, Laud could iron things out by sending in his own, metropolitan, visitation to inspect what was happening, but this often lacked the local knowledge and the follow-up muscle of the diocesan machinery.

Nor was leadership from the top as determined as it might have been. The number of ministers deprived for refusing to conform was small compared with that under James: less than twenty in all. Charles himself stopped any increase in the tithes of the City of London, rather than offend the people on whom he most relied for loans, while Laud did not enforce the official ceremonies comprehensively on Oxford University, of which he had been made chancellor. Nor was anyone hanged or burned for opposition. The government did try to cow any potential opposition in 1637 by holding a spectacular show trial of the three most vociferous critics of the reforms, a minister, a lawyer and a doctor called Henry Burton, William Prynne and John Bastwick. All were fined and imprisoned after having their ears cut off on a public scaffold. This was the most brutal punishment inflicted by the Personal Rule, and indeed Charles's reign was notable for a lack of political executions: there were none in its first sixteen years, which was a record not reached for almost two centuries before. This abstinence certainly reflected the king's own mildness of temper, but the mutilation inflicted on the three men was still counter-productive, its squalid and humiliating nature arousing public outrage.

The impact of the changes is difficult to ascertain. Clergy, unsurprisingly, often found aspects of them attractive. Puritans, with equal lack of surprise, deplored them as running directly counter to all that they had wanted from the Church; as an Arminian, Laud regarded Puritanism as the force within English Protestantism to which he was himself most vehemently opposed. Local public opinion became hostile when popular ministers were punished for nonconformity, when good lecturers were sacked because no parish living could be found for them, or when the changes to ritual and church decoration were expensive or destroyed long-established custom. Otherwise there is little evidence of reactions, and where it does survive the most common pattern is one of division and uncertainty.

It may be suggested, however, that there was one important group which, collectively, might have found much to concern them: the English ruling class. One of the features of the Reformation had been, after all, an enormous shift of wealth and power from churchmen to the richer laity. The nadir of the Church's fortunes had been reached under Elizabeth, when its members were weakest – politically, socially and economically – in relation to the nobility and gentry. James started to reverse the process, favouring churchmen at court and putting some into local government, for example as justices. Charles greatly accentuated the change. He became the first ruler since 1558 to give a high political office to a prelate, making William Juxon, Bishop of London, his Lord Treasurer. As part of the religious reforms, gentry were forced to renegotiate leases of church lands, and some saw their family seats in the chancels of parish churches demolished in order to move the communion table there. Former archbishops had entertained local landowners as a part of their function as leaders of county society; Laud scorned to do so. When the gentry of particular counties petitioned against aspects of the reforms, their requests were flatly rejected, on the grounds that laity had no business to intervene in ecclesiastical affairs. Squires who had formerly thought the local parson pompous and intractable, tended to find him unbearable after the Laudian initiatives had reinforced the clergy's sense of independence and importance. Laud himself set a spirited example of the way in which churchmen might campaign for a better society. Gentry hauled into the royal council's Court of Star Chamber accused of enclosure found him there, rebuking them. Those brought before the parallel Court of High Commission for moral offences confronted him again; and all this was in addition to his religious role. At a basic level, a richer and more powerful Church could only be reconstituted at the expense of lay landowners, irrespective of their religious views. None the less, it is possible to find examples of individual nobles and gentry who liked the reform programme in its own right; and had it been given time to settle down, and been associated with a prosperous and successful royal regime in all other respects, then most might have been reconciled to it.

In the last analysis, the question of how popular the Personal Rule was, until its last year, is impossible to solve. The channels that could have expressed public opinion – Parliaments and newspapers – were both missing. It proves nothing to follow the example of some scholars and cite the private grumbles of Puritans, such as the over-quoted Robert Woodford of Northampton, as examples of a general response, as Puritans were the very people whom one would expect to be most offended by the reforms. It is certainly true that opposition could be very well concealed: Sir Symonds D'Ewes was a conscientious collector of Ship Money who never seems to have expressed any doubts about it to his friends, but in private notes he called it illegal and a 'fatal blow' to liberty. He was, however, still an unusual individual, more politically aware and more Puritan than most, and it is again uncertain to what degree he can be treated as representative.

What is clear is that the Personal Rule was not a single period. Between 1629 and 1636 English government still ran on fairly normal early Stuart lines, with some new initiatives and changes of emphasis. From 1637 it turned into something novel, as Ship Money and the religious reform began to bite and the gap between Parliaments slowly became more and more unusual. From that year onwards, however, the regime was also becoming locked into a crisis in Scotland, which was to drive it into ever less popular courses and greater humiliations, and eventually to bring it down; and it is impossible to tell the story of these years without that external factor, or to judge how English government might have fared without it. It can be concluded that the Personal Rule was always intended as a stop-gap period of recuperation, rather than as a permanent way of governing. There is every sign that Charles now feared English Parliaments, but none that he wanted to dispense with them on principle. What he seems to have hoped is that firm and successful government would eventually restore the loyalty of his people and silence his critics. By doing what he took to be his God's will, he expected that he would enable that God to make sure that things turned out well. In the last analysis, it may be suggested that historians cannot know where the Personal Rule was leading, because the ruler did not know himself.

The Collapse of the Stuart Monarchies

At the end of the 1720s, the satirical author Jonathan Swift had
one of his characters sum up the political history of England
during the previous hundred years as 'only a heap of conspir
acies, rebellions, murders, massacres, revolutions, banish-
ments, the very worst effects that avarice, faction, hypocrisy,
perfidiousness, cruelty, rage, madness, hatred, envy, lust,
malice and ambition could produce'. In many respects that is a
reasonable judgement. In the first four decades of the seventeenth century, England had probably been the most peaceful
monarchy in Europe. Between 1640 and 1720, it suffered two
civil wars, five invasions, three revolutions, six rebellions and
thirteen changes of regime which involved some measure of
physical force. The source of all this instability, as Conrad
Russell first emphasized in the 1980s, lay in the union of three
Crowns created in 1603, and the propelling force for it came
from the kingdom which had been the least troublesome for
most of the early Stuart period: Scotland.

Just as the arrival of James I in England created serious
strains for that polity, so the removal of James VI from his
ancestral kingdom produced problems for the Scots. On the
whole, he handled these with the same flair that he had
brought to ruling Scotland before. He only actually returned
for one visit, but he stopped his countrymen feeling abandoned by giving English money and offices to many of them,
and a high profile for them at his new court. He also employed
money saved by the removal of his household on to an English
budget as a slush fund to placate the nobles he had left at home.
This mattered, because the Scottish aristocracy was under
economic pressure. During the sixteenth century, much of it
had rented out lands on long leases to gentry, in an attempt to
provide long-term financial security; a policy which backfired
when the rents agreed were hit by the great inflation which
affected Europe in the later part of the century. At the same
time, both James and Charles greatly enlarged the size of the
noble estate by creating many new titles. James also attempted

to bring the two British kingdoms closer together, especially in the vital matter of religion. After his removal to England he persuaded the Scottish Parliament and the General Assembly of the Kirk to accept bishops again, although with less power over other churchmen than in England. Subsequently, he also got them to allow certain ecclesiastical ceremonies, and the observance of traditional festivals such as Easter and Christmas, which had been abolished in the more radical Scottish Reformation but retained in the English one. Those latter reforms, however, aroused so much opposition that James's government in Scotland did not enforce them on ministers who found them unacceptable.

That should have set up a boundary mark for Charles, of the point beyond which the Scots could not safely be pushed or cajoled, but it was one which he chose to ignore. The new king was not only absentee, but unknown, having left Scotland at the age of three and never been back; and he immediately took steps which highlighted the dangers of rule by a non-resident stranger. He tried to strengthen the royal finances by raising taxes and restricting the gifts to nobles. He tried to strengthen the Kirk by revoking all royal grants of land made since 1540. It was not his serious intention to take back all the estates concerned, but to force the laity to rene-gotiate the terms on which it held former Church land, so that the Kirk could get better endowments from them. It was far from clear that the king had the legal right to do this at all, and although the whole scheme eventually proved un-workable, and collapsed in a mire of disputes, it had given a bad shock to the nation's political elite. Then Charles plunged Scotland into his wars with Spain and France, ruining its trade in conflicts which did not serve its own national interests at all. Through all this, the Scots remained loyal, biding their time until their new monarch turned up to be crowned and they could meet him at first-hand. He did so in 1633, and showed himself arrogant and insensitive, making clear in particular his preference for the English mode of worship and churchmanship, and especially the Arminian, which to Scots looked particularly popish.

After this, a growing number of Scots who were unhappy with Charles's way of ruling waited for an opportunity to confront him over it; and he now supplied them with the perfect one. The Reformation had left Scotland, unlike England, with no single liturgy, and Charles's tidy mind could not allow this situation to continue. Between 1634 and 1637 he therefore had a national Prayer Book compiled, by a few Scottish bishops who consulted him and a few Scottish advisers at his court. It placed a heavier emphasis on ceremony than had hitherto been the custom in many parts of the reformed Kirk, and would make Scottish practice in some respects more similar to the English; though at one point it actually adopted a formula for the sacraments that was closer to Catholicism than contemporary English worship. As such, it was bound to cause major controversy, though had Charles been prepared to wear down opposition by long and detailed discussion in a Parliament and General Assembly, as his father had done, he might well have got at least most of it accepted. The crucial point was that he didn't try, but imposed the book by direct royal decree, with every expectation that it would be enforced on all ministers. Once again, the legality of this action was dubious and his own Scottish Privy Council was unhappy about it, but Charles was not interested in its opinion. His behaviour in this regard was accompanied by another initiative, to give bishops a leading role in Scotland's government to an extent not known even before the Reformation. It seemed to many Scots that churchmen were now being used as royal agents to control both kirk and state on behalf of a monarch ruling without proper concern for consent.

As a result, when the Prayer Book was introduced in 1637, riots and protests erupted across the Central Lowlands, the area of greatest population and wealth and the seat of government. The Privy Council hoped that these would induce Charles to change his policy, but he at first refused. The result was one of the key documents of Scottish history: the National Covenant signed by the protestors in February 1638. It was a defiant restatement of collective pride, emphasizing the unique virtues of the Kirk and arguing that it could only be reformed with the participation of Parliament and General Assembly. It called on the king to return it to its earlier condition, leaving open whether this should be as it was in 1625 or before. The Privy Council was generally favourable to the document, and even some bishops thought it had merit. Slightly less than half of the political nation had apparently gone over to the malcontents, for the Covenant was supported by thirty-nine out of eighty-one Scottish peers.

Charles responded by cancelling his projected alliance with France in order to deal with the Scots, sending them a negotiator, his closest surviving domestic relative, the Marquis of Hamilton. Hamilton worked hard to persuade the Covenanters that the king was reasonable, and to persuade the king to be so. He told Charles, as tactfully as possible, that if he did not agree to what the Covenant asked then he would have to fight its supporters, and – prophetically – that this would risk his rule over all three kingdoms. The king, however, was not prepared to agree, as such a surrender would effectively broadcast his loss of control over the Kirk. The result was the worst of both worlds: the king allowed Hamilton to call a General Assembly to discuss reform, while the Covenanters became convinced that Charles could not be trusted. Nor could he; he was already planning a military strike against Scotland, and only agreed to the Assembly when he found that an army could not be ready that summer.

As a result, the elections became a party contest between Covenanters and Royalists, and the Covenanters won, as the result of a factor which had never occurred to the king. He had expected the nation, at worst, to split in half like the nobility. Instead, two other groups overwhelmingly backed the Covenanters: the lesser landowners, or lairds, and the townspeople. These were the most nationalist and most fervently

Protestant social blocs, and the lairds had become rich on the profits of the lands leased from the nobility. They represented most of the voters, were concentrated in the richest parts of Scotland and surrounded the seats of government; as the Scottish Crown had never kept a standing army, its representatives were helpless if these people turned nasty. The General Assembly that they voted in was overwhelmingly Covenanter, and persuaded by its leaders that the king was opposed to their wishes. Accordingly, they broke royal control of the Kirk by deposing the bishops altogether, which was an effective declaration of war. War was, of course, what Charles had planned if the Covenanters did not back down, and he now simply activated the plan for an invasion that he had suspended in 1638.

The obvious question is, what Charles I thought he was doing. As he never spelled it out or drew up a blueprint, it can only be surmised from his actions. From the start, he had behaved as if his Scottish kingdom was a half-civilized backwater, to be tidied up as swiftly as possible and turned into an appendage to England. He appears to have expected the Scots to obey him in all things, and believed that his possession of two larger and richer kingdoms would enable him to steamroller them if they refused. In view of what he took to be his overwhelming superiority in resources, he could hardly have seen the need to give up what he took to be his most important duty, to run a national Church as he believed right. He was about to become the latest in a long line of rulers, from the Romans to the Tudors, to underestimate the people of Scotland.

One of Charles's worst weaknesses as a ruler was his fear of having royal policies debated and questioned in public, even if to do so would strengthen them and win them support. This was almost certainly why he would not submit his Scottish Prayer Book to a Parliament or General Assembly and he now became the first English monarch, since Parliaments were first instituted in the realm, to launch a full-scale war without calling one to gain political and financial support. Instead he relied on his regular income, and borrowing, to fund it, and the new strength of the royal fiscal system allowed him to do so for one year. The army that he led to the Scottish border in 1639 was deficient in training, discipline and equipment, but the expeditionary forces launched by Elizabeth usually had been no better; and Charles's was much larger than those. His problem was that he had not expected to face much resistance at all, having relied on attacks from Ireland and the navy, and risings by loyal Scots, to break up the Covenanter war effort before he invaded. Instead, these diversionary measures had all failed, and he found himself faced by an army almost as large as his own, raised by imposing on Scotland the efficient Swedish system of local committees to raise money and recruits.

This was the turning point of his reign. Had he decided to attack, he might very well have won. Had he sat still, in the strong position that he occupied at Berwick, his opponents would probably have run out of supplies within a few weeks, and disintegrated. In either case, his three kingdoms would have been at his mercy, to consolidate his policies in each as he chose. Instead he lost his nerve. His generals and counsellors were shocked by the strength of Scottish resistance – which they now overestimated instead of underestimating it as before – and he was not the leader to inspire them to fight despite their reservations. Both sides were glad to make a deal whereby they called off the war and agreed to talk the whole dispute out again from the beginning. The problem was that as soon as winter came they both got their courage back. A new General Assembly of the Kirk confirmed the acts of the last, and added a condemnation of bishops as contrary to Scripture itself. Then a Scottish Parliament, likewise dominated by Covenanters, endorsed these reforms and filled the gaps opened in the government by the eviction of the bishops with their own supporters. In retaliation, Charles decided to fight again.

The regular financial system could not sustain a second year of war, and so the king reluctantly agreed to call a Parliament to obtain funds. When it met in April 1640, however, the Commons asked for concessions in return, such as the abolition of Ship Money, and after a few weeks of bargaining Charles lost patience and dissolved it, earning it the enduring nickname of 'The Short Parliament'. Realistically, as Conrad Russell has pointed out, the king now had no alternative to giving the Covenanters all that they wanted, abandoning his policies in Scotland to keep them intact in England. Charles, however, still wanted to renew the war, and one councillor in particular agreed with him. He was Thomas Wentworth, who had been sent to rule Ireland on the king's behalf for most of the 1630s. His actions there had made a sharp contrast with those of previous Stuart royal deputies, who had traditionally snubbed the Old English settlers and allied with New English incomers in order to steal more land from the native Irish. Wentworth, recognizing that Ireland had no settled land law, used this weakness to grab estates from all three groups in order to enrich the Crown, the Church and himself. In the process he made the kingdom pay for itself at last and raised from it a powerful army for royal service. He cowed opposition with trumped-up charges, and earned himself the nickname of 'Black Tom Tyrant'. As Charles decided to renew the war with Scotland in 1640, he called over Wentworth, encouraging him with the title of Earl of Strafford, as just the kind of hard man the hour demanded. Strafford (as he now was) lived up to his reputation, persuading his master that the Irish army could be used to make up for the expected deficiencies of the English one, landing in Scotland to take the Covenanters in the rear.

Once again the Scots pulled off a masterstroke, this time by carrying out a pre-emptive strike. They invaded England in August, with an army well recruited and supplied by the same revolutionary system of local committees. Strafford's Irish forces were not yet ready, and nor was Charles. His regular fiscal system was indeed collapsing without parliamentary aid, and a third of his soldiers had no weapons. His army broke in half, as he sent the portion of it which was fully equipped up to meet the Scots, who outnumbered and outgunned them, and broke them in the first engagement. The Covenanter army then sat down on top of London's coal supply, at Newcastle and Durham. Of all Charles's councillors, only Strafford now wanted to go on fighting. The king was forced to agree to a truce on terms by which he became responsible for paying the upkeep of the occupying Scottish army as well as his own, and agreed to call an English Parliament in order to make a lasting peace settlement. When what was to be known as the Long Parliament met in November, Charles still expected its Members to supply money to enable him to beat the Scots. Instead, they refused to proceed with the war, furiously condemned his whole system of government since 1629, and forced him to abandon his existing ministers.

Why was this? In part it was due to the remarkable skill of Covenanter propaganda. The invading Scots denied that they were rebels, insisting instead that they were petitioners, loyal to their king but asking him for better government. They likewise told the English that they came as friends and liberators, simply to ensure that public opinion in England could be freely expressed through a Parliament once more. At the same time they released a clandestine stream of propaganda into England, warning its people of a conspiracy to subvert both Protestantism and liberty, throughout the British Isles, of which the king was a tool or dupe. By contrast, Charles's actions were of a kind suited to produce the worst impressions. Once again, his dislike of debate had prevented his government from being able to inform his subjects, systematically, of why it was in their interests to fight the Scots.

On dismissing the Short Parliament, he had commenced desperate talks with the Spanish, to borrow some of their soldiers – from the most feared Catholic army in Europe, and the one still occupying his sister's realm – to crush the Scots. These came to nothing, but news of them leaked. At the same time, the queen was mobilizing Catholic support for her husband at home. In character, his Personal Rule had reduced the executions of priests to a tiny number, but had fined

Catholics in general with a new efficiency to swell royal coffers. It was doubtful, therefore, how much gratitude they owed him, but many rallied to the call of Henrietta Maria in the hope of earning Charles's favour. All this did much to lend credence to the Covenanter charge of a popish conspiracy, as did the fact that for some years the king had entertained a papal envoy at court, the first since the Reformation. These developments all lent new weight to those who had always argued that Arminianism was itself a means of reintroducing Catholicism by stealth. The sense that royal religious policy menaced traditional norms and freedoms was reinforced by Charles's decision to allow Convocation, the assembly of the Church of England, to carry on sitting once the Short Parliament had dispersed, when customarily the two institutions sat side by side. The Convocation concerned enacted a series of measures to reinforce Arminian control of the Church.

Most important of all, perhaps, was the extent of the king's military failure. Because of the superiority of English resources, the Scots had only managed to inflict shattering defeats on the English thrice before, in 685, 1297 and 1314; and in all those cases they were fighting on home ground. Never before had they forced the English to sue for peace on their own soil. To an age in which many people believed profoundly that worldly events reflected the direct will of an interventionist God, this unique humiliation strongly suggested that Charles was peculiarly lacking in divine favour. This was particularly evident because the king had stirred up the struggle with the Covenanters for religious reasons, and the taint of it was extended to the churchmen who had abetted him in both kingdoms: the twin campaigns of 1639 and 1640 acquired the enduring nickname of 'the Bishops' Wars'.

To those with more secular instincts, it indicated that the government was in dangerously incompetent hands. This is probably the single greatest reason for the Long Parliament's comprehensive rejection of the policies and personnel of the former regime. A settlement might have been reached in 1641 in which Charles accepted a new financial system, new guarantees for his subjects' rights, a non-Arminian Church, and new ministers chosen from the critics of the old. This chance was, however, prevented by the Scots, without whose support Parliament would be at the king's mercy again, and who wanted it to take two key initiatives in return. One was to reform the Church of England to make it more Scottish, getting rid of bishops and the Elizabethan liturgy. This would, of course, safeguard the Covenanters' Kirk, but it split the Long Parliament between those, mostly traditional Puritans, who wanted to take this step, and many others, especially in the Lords, who wanted to retain the Elizabethan Church. The other initiative was to ensure that the man whom the Covenanters regarded as their most dangerous enemy, the Earl of Strafford, was pushed out of public life, preferably by being executed.

Had Charles been prepared to sack Strafford immediately, and have him locked up, there would have been no crisis, and the earl would probably have survived. Instead he insisted that, in law, Strafford had done no wrong, and chose to make the matter a test of his own authority and view of government. Technically, Charles was correct, and so the Commons adopted against Strafford the very dubious mechanism of an Act of Attainder, that declared people traitors who had rebelled or conspired and then fled so that they could not be put on trial. This had never been used before against somebody who was actually available to be tried. It is possible that the Parliament would not have passed it had not mobs of Londoners intimidated the Lords, and the king not alienated waverers by trying to frighten the Parliament with the covert threat of using his army to cow it. Charles had the right to veto the Bill but, faced with the will of the two Houses and angry crowds, his nerve gave way again. Strafford was beheaded in May 1641, breaking Charles's record as a king who did not kill politicians and scarring the king's conscience for the rest of his life. In a very real sense the blood that gushed from the earl's neck was the first of the English Civil War; more than that, it started a cycle of violence that was to last for over 100 years. Not until the 1750s would the sequence of vengeance and counter-vengeance that commenced with Strafford's death be fully played out.

In the first stage of this feud, the king's resentment was directed against the 'junto' or group of politicians who had proved most influential in obtaining the death of the earl, led by figures such as the Earl of Warwick and Lord Saye and Sele in the Lords, and John Pym and John Hampden in the Commons. Even before the calling of the Long Parliament, these men had developed a commitment to limit and constrain royal power in England. Whether this was an inevitable ambition on their part may be doubted. All were associated with an evangelical Protestantism bordering on or shading into Puritanism, and had Charles turned out to be a Protestant zealot, with a love of preaching and a hatred of Catholicism, they would probably have cheerfully supported a stronger monarchy. As it was, the king's Arminian beliefs had alerted them to the dangers of its existing strength; conversely, the Arminians, aware of their minority position in the Church and dependence on royal favour for advancement, had worked for a more powerful Crown. After Strafford died, moreover, the 'junto' had an additional reason for working to constrain royal freedom of action: that Charles would never forgive them for the judicial murder of his loyal servant.

Once again, Charles tried to learn from mistakes. He had been too rigid before; now he made a series of sensational surrenders to buy off most of his critics. In England he consented to the greatest constitutional changes for almost four centuries: agreeing that no more than three years could henceforth pass without a Parliament in session; that the Long Parliament could only be dissolved with its own consent; and that the Tudor Courts of Star Chamber and High Commission, whereby the royal council had sat as judicial tribunals, be abolished, along with the regional councils. He took a new set of ministers and advisers drawn from opponents of the Personal Rule who were not in the 'junto', and appointed non-Arminian bishops, leaving Laud shut up in the Tower of London. On the strength of these, the Scots went home and both armies were paid off by the English Parliament. In the late summer the king went to Scotland himself, gave a bonanza of honours to the leading Covenanters and signed away virtually all royal powers over the Scottish Kirk and state. He hoped that in return the Scots would give him a free hand to deal with the English; which seemed more likely because of the disappointment of the Covenanters with their English allies for failing to carry out the expected reform of the Church of England. As he returned south in the autumn, Charles could have real hopes that the Long Parliament would grant him a new financial settlement and then go home, leaving him to consolidate his power anew. So it might have done, had he been ruler of only two kingdoms; but, like everybody else in Britain, he had forgotten the Irish.

Strafford's final achievement had been to unite the different religious and ethnic groups in Ireland against himself so effectively that they all helped to feed ammunition against him to his enemies in Britain. Once he was dead, their brief alliance dissolved. The Catholics, especially those of English descent, applied to the king again for security for their lands and religion and opportunities to gain office. To grant these would have secured the peace of the land, but Charles dared not do so for fear of infuriating most of the English, Scots and Protestant Irish. What he did instead was to assure some Catholic leaders privately of his personal goodwill, while putting Ireland under the rule of a panel of aggressive Protestants allied to the Long Parliament. Those who held to the old religion now began to fear a renewed attack on it, and this was accentuated in the summer, when the Long Parliament casually pronounced final judgment in a legal case, brought by a settler called Sir Henry Stewart, which concerned events on Irish soil. The matter was a small one, and its implications probably not discerned at

Westminster; but they were immense, for the English Parliament had just extended its authority to the other kingdom, and the Parliament concerned was vehemently hostile to Catholicism. Some Catholics now began to plot a rebellion to win real security for Irish self-government and for their own religion and property. It was intended to repeat the success of the Scots in winning back control of their own affairs, and was launched upon an almost wholly unsuspecting Irish government, and Protestant population, in October.

It proved to be a terrible mistake, for in two vital respects it fell short of the Covenanters' achievement. It failed to capture the whole land, and in particular left the capital, Dublin, in the government's hands. Furthermore, whereas the Covenanter rebellion had been almost bloodless, the Irish Rebellion of 1641 precipitated the greatest civilian massacre in the history of the British Isles. On joining it, local Catholics often took the opportunity to seize back lands occupied by Protestant settlers, and to rob them to exact compensation for the profits lost from it. The settlers increasingly resisted, and were killed, while others who were driven off, stripped of their possessions, died of exposure. Soon slaughters of local Catholics were commencing in retaliation. The total number of those who died in October to December 1641 will never be known: it could come to anything from 3,000 to 12,000. Fearing that they would be caught up in the Protestant counter-attacks, for the first time in history the Old English, the Catholic descendants of medieval settlers, joined the native Irish en masse against the government. As a wave of panic-stricken refugees burst upon English shores, the rumoured figure of Protestant deaths alone reached 100,000. The British in general clamoured for bloody retribution, and both Scots and English prepared to send over armies. In England this development precipitated an acute new political crisis. By all traditional rights, the power to raise and control the force sent from England lay with the monarch; but Charles's opponents in Parliament dared not entrust him with it for fear that, having put down the Irish rebels, he would turn it upon those whom he detested at home. For the last two months of the year, the 'junto' and its allies fought to convince the Long Parliament that the king was not fit to exercise one of the sovereign's oldest rights, convincing a slight majority of the Commons and a minority of the Lords. Eventually, they decided to put further pressure on Charles to submit by preparing for a legal attack upon his queen.

His response, in January 1642, consisted of two successive panic reactions. The first was to attempt to break his enemies, once and for all, by arresting their five leading figures in the Commons, including Pym and Hampden, and charging them with treason. The attempt failed, and the corporation of London and a clear majority of the Commons now concluded firmly that the king could not be trusted. His second was to flee London for the provinces, determined not to return except with an army to protect himself. This in itself forced his opponents left behind in the capital to raise soldiers to defend themselves against him. Both were literally afraid for their lives, Charles now convinced that the 'junto' intended to destroy both him and the monarchy and his enemies believing that their monarch was either involved in, or being manipulated by, an international Catholic conspiracy to annihilate Protestantism and English liberties. Both were wrong, but these rival strains of paranoia brought about the complete collapse of the English political system.

By handing his opponents London, the king almost lost the conflict at the start, for by late summer his enemies had used its resources, and those of the rich surrounding counties, to mobilize a much larger and more compact strike force. Charles's adherents were still scattered across the realm. He was saved by the Welsh, whose loyalty gave him a compact area of solid support. He was able to cross England to Shrewsbury, and settle there, with the Welsh covering his back and sending reinforcements, to gather the soldiers pouring in from many parts of England. By October he had an army as large as that of Parliament (as his enemies now termed themselves): the Irish had precipitated, the Welsh had ensured, and the Scots had failed to prevent, a conflict which was to go down in history as the English Civil War.

9

CIVIL WAR AND REVOLUTION
(1642–49)

The Course of the Civil War

The Great Civil War of the English state ended in the victory of
the Long Parliament, but four years were needed to achieve that,
from the summer of 1642 to that of 1646, with isolated castles in
Wales and in the Bristol Channel holding out for the king until
1647. This pattern of events begs two major questions: why did
the king lose, and why did he take so long to do so? In recent
years a brisk debate has broken out over the first of those,
between Malcolm Wanklyn and Clive Holmes. The former held
that the outcome of the war had depended on the achievements
and errors of commanders; while Holmes argued that it was
inevitable as Parliament had better resources and exploited them
more effectively. Who seems to be the more correct?

It may be proposed that Parliament had three enormous
advantages, the lack of any of which would have doomed it to
defeat. The greatest was that the Scottish Covenanters came to
its rescue when the war seemed to be turning against it, for fear

that a victorious Charles would then seek revenge upon them for their humiliation of him in 1640. This gave Parliament the resources of a complete extra kingdom, the only one with a land frontier with England across which troops could easily be moved. Most of the north of England was controlled at that time by the Royalists, so that the king's war effort was effectively being stabbed in the back. The Scottish army which invaded at the opening of 1644 was enormous, containing 22,000 infantry alone when the total size of any single English force raised on either side in this war was less than 18,000 men. Its arrival was the decisive factor in the loss of most of the north to the king within eight months. Ever after that, the total manpower available to Charles was smaller than that at the disposal of his enemies. In most battles, and all the largest, his supporters were henceforth facing superior numbers.

The second major reason for Parliament's victory was its firm control of London and the south-eastern quarter of England. The capital now contained 400,000 people in a land in which no other city had more than 20,000, and was the centre of the nation's commerce and financial credit. It also had the established institutions of government and the central law courts, and the printing industry. To hold it gave not only huge material advantages but great prestige at home and abroad. The London and Middlesex militia provided a constant pool of manpower to reinforce armies in emergencies, while the presses meant that all through the war Parliamentarian newspapers and pamphlets outnumbered those published by Royalists by at least three to one. The wealth of the whole region meant that London, the south-eastern counties and East Anglia could each raise a separate field army. It was also the biggest industrial area of the nation, especially in armaments, while within a month of the outbreak of fighting, Parliament had secured the land's three main magazines of arms and ammunition, at London, Hull and Portsmouth. For the first year of the war, the king's operations were repeatedly halted for lack of military supplies. London was also the core of the national trading system, and indeed

Parliament always controlled the main ports of the south and east coasts, from Hull around to Poole, plus Plymouth, Gloucester and Pembroke, each of which could jam a local commercial network.

The third great advantage that Parliament held was the royal navy, whose support was won because its popular admiral, the Earl of Warwick, was a firm Parliamentarian, and then confirmed by a large pay rise for the sailors. This put the seas around Britain at Parliament's disposal. Its warships could disrupt trade from Royalist ports and cut Charles's communications with the Continent, especially important as he desperately needed to import weapons and munitions to make up for his initial shortage of them. It also meant that when his adherents conquered territory, they found it impossible to take all the seaports. Places such as Pembroke, Plymouth, Lyme and Hull could stand up to siege indefinitely because they could be constantly supplied and reinforced by the navy. By contrast, Royalist ports were always in danger of being attacked from both land and sea at once, a factor which led to the loss of several, including Tenby, Warrington and Liverpool. More generally, Parliament's sea power meant that whereas East Anglia and Kent were far enough from the king's quarters to be safe from attack, there was no part of Royalist territory which was secure because Parliamentarian warships could always get around behind it. Parliament could garrison its hinterland lightly and turn it into a source of supplies, money and recruits. The king's most remote areas, on the other hand, had to be kept filled with soldiers to guard them against an amphibious operation. These garrisons ate up a lot of resources on the spot, denying them to the field armies.

It must be obvious, then, that Parliament had considerable advantages. None the less, not only did Charles take a long time to lose the war, but for a couple of years he seemed to be winning it. To understand why this was so, it is necessary to consider the advantages that his war effort possessed, and the first of these was that if Parliament could call on Scotland, to some extent he could call on Ireland. This was, it is true, a less considerable asset. For one thing it had no land frontier with England, so that aid from it had to be ferried across a sea guarded by Parliament. For another, it was divided and damaged by its own civil war, resulting from the rebellion of 1641. During the second half of the conflict in England, Charles tried repeatedly to turn the Catholic rebels into his allies, but as most of the British regarded them with loathing after the massacres of 1641, he could never make concessions that would win their help without losing most of his existing supporters. Instead, he made a truce with them and recalled the royal army in Ireland, to balance that sent by the Scots. It was no real match for the Scots, because it was much smaller, supplying about 7,000 infantry to the Covenanters' 22,000. Moreover, instead of arriving in one hammer blow it had to be shipped over in parties and at intervals to reinforce existing Royalist armies. Half of it was destroyed almost at once in a local battle in Cheshire. Still, the standard of its soldiers was very high and they did bolster the Royalists at several points and provide the core of a new field army.

Furthermore, Charles used Irish resources with much more spectacular effect to overturn the balance of power in Scotland. The Royalists there were too weak and divided to accomplish anything alone, but eight months after the Scots invaded England, an Irish Catholic, the chief of the Macdonnels, shipped over his clan to attack Scotland. They were superb fighters, who soon found a brilliant general in a disenchanted Covenanter, the Marquis of Montrose, and after a year they had won control of the country. They inflicted terrible damage on the Covenanter regime, killing about 1 per cent of the adult male population of Scotland, ravaging large areas and sacking two cities. They not only prevented the Scottish army in England from receiving reinforcements, but forced much of it to return home. Unfortunately for Charles, their success was too late and too temporary. The Irish arrived in Scotland after the Covenanters had struck their decisive blow in England, and by the time that they fought their way to victory, the Royalists cause in England was already lost. They were then themselves defeated by a Scottish force returning from England, and driven out of the land. Their decisive contribution was to prevent the Scots from achieving the influence in English affairs which their intervention was intended to bring them. The distraction provided by the war in Scotland meant that after the Covenanters rescued Parliament from defeat or compromise, they had to leave it to win the war itself, and to take most of the credit.

The second advantage of the Royalists was that they attracted the support of much more of the nobility and greater gentry than Parliament: the party which emphasized ceremony and hierarchy, in church and state, simply appealed more to the traditional leaders of society. The Stuart kings had doubled the size of the House of Lords, and while about half of the noble families that survived from Tudor times were Parliamentarian, the newcomers overwhelmingly became Royalist, and gave the king about two-thirds of the peerage. In an age in which land was by far the greatest source of wealth, these people owned more of it than anybody else. The richest sent Charles their spare cash, while the less wealthy donated their family's gold and silver plate, to be melted down. Land and lineage were also the main sources of prestige, so that great landowners were still respected local leaders, and could use their influence as well as their wealth to recruit soldiers. This asset was sufficient in the short term to offset Parliament's control of the main mercantile and financial centres.

In some ways the comparative poverty of much Royalist territory could actually be an advantage, as long as the king had money from somewhere. Poor areas have been good recruiting grounds throughout history, as their people need to join up to make money. No wonder Wales became known as the 'nursery' of the king's infantry, and at the Shropshire village of Myddle twenty boys joined the royal army because they were promised four times the earnings they could make at home.

The landowning classes were also the traditional source of army officers, so could provide a better supply of experienced commanders to the king, and the realm's best horsemen. For the first year of the war, Charles had both more and better cavalry than Parliament, severely limiting its striking power. All these were wasting assets. Parliament's officers soon learned on the job, and it slowly built up its cavalry arm, while in the long term the financial system of London and the agricultural riches of the south-east were a more durable means of raising money than the family wealth of Royalist grandees. Once again, however, the Royalists compensated, this time by ruthlessness, as they taxed and conscripted from their areas with a savagery that Parliament did not need. This tactic had further long-term weaknesses, as it naturally rendered them unpopular, but as long as it provided the materials of war it was effective enough.

Furthermore, the Royalists responded to their own handicaps by showing more willingness to innovate. Being deprived of the main iron-producing area of the nation, which lay in the Weald of Kent and Sussex, they developed those of the West Midlands and Forest of Dean. Combined with imports, this cracked the problem of supply, so that after 1643 they were never short of weapons or ammunition again. Deprived of command of the sea, they relied on fast privateer ships which could outrun Parliament's navy, keep open communications with Ireland and the Continent, and prey on merchant vessels. If Parliamentarian ports could jam local trading centres, then Royalist fortresses could cut off trade to those ports in turn. The king's officers were initially more willing to innovate. Some Royalist towns were rapidly given defences of the latest European type, proof against cannon shot and with bastions for flanking fire. The king's most charismatic commander was Prince Rupert of the Palatinate, a son of his sister Elizabeth, who arrived from the Thirty Years War with the latest European ideas. He introduced the Swedish tactic of the full-scale cavalry charge, and the technique of mining beneath the defences of a fortress to bring them down; both with devastating effect. One again, all these were wasting assets, as Parliament came to imitate and develop them; but initially they achieved remarkable results.

Logistical disadvantages, however, simply mean that the side suffering from them cannot afford to make mistakes; if the other side makes all the errors, then that party's superior advantages are thrown away. In this sense it remains true that the Royalists lost the Civil War because they failed to win its biggest battles. There were three of those, at Edgehill, Marston Moor and Naseby, and had Parliament been roundly defeated in any of them then it would probably have had to surrender or make a compromise peace. Edgehill, in October 1642, was the first major engagement. The king's cavalry wings easily routed their enemies, and had their reserves immediately fallen on the exposed Parliamentarian infantry, then the latter would probably have disintegrated. Instead, the king's horsemen all made the crucial error of chasing after their fleeing enemies, leaving Parliament's foot soldiers to inflict serious damage on their Royalist counterparts and produce an indecisive result.

Marston Moor, in July 1644, was the biggest action of the war, between the Scottish expeditionary force, joined to two Parliamentarian armies, and Prince Rupert's field army partnered with the northern Royalists. Rupert, finding himself outnumbered, drew up his soldiers in a defensive formation, across difficult ground, to shatter an enemy attack; but all afternoon his opponents made no move. When evening came, he gave the order to stand down, and it was then that the allied army struck. On his left wing Rupert's preparations were still in place, and the attackers were routed, but the right one was taken by surprise and overwhelmed, leaving the rest of his forces to be outflanked and broken up. Had he not gone off guard, he would probably have won the day. At Naseby in June 1645 Charles's main field army attacked that of Parliament, charging uphill into a force almost twice its size. On the right wing his horsemen broke through, but on the rest of the field, the superior numbers of the enemy proved irresistible and most of his army was eventually annihilated. His left wing was so weak because two months earlier he had detached 3,000 of his best cavalry, needlessly, to cover the West Country. Had those still been with him at Naseby, they would have given him the crucial extra numbers to break the Parliamentarians on both flanks and hit their infantry from both sides. Again, a single misjudgement had caused a Royalist defeat.

It seems, therefore, that both Malcolm Wanklyn and Clive Holmes were correct, although the argument here has not exactly been made in their terms. The logistics of war, and the British and Irish context, were crucially important, but so were strategic and tactical decisions. This war, like so many, was both a matter of counting men and money, and one of snap decisions taken by men under stress, on which the fate of a nation turned.

The Nature of the Civil War

In the mid-twentieth century the English Civil War was viewed by most experts as the result of long-term changes in society, producing tensions which eventually surfaced to blow up the existing political system. Since then, most specialists have come to place more emphasis on the strains of a triple kingdom, and on the mistakes made by politicians at Westminster in the winter of 1641–2. In this model, a relatively stable society was shattered by explosive drilled into it and then detonated by a few people at the top. None the less, the pre-existing strains within society still matter, because, to follow that geological metaphor, the explosion would break the rock into which it was inserted along natural lines of weakness. Of these fissures, there is no doubt that religion was the most important, and did most to determine the nature of the conflict. It remains a basic truth that Puritans formed the bedrock of Parliament's local support, while those who wanted to preserve the Church of Elizabeth and James tended to take up arms for the king. Most Catholics remained neutral, but their community still made a contribution to the Royalist war effort out of all proportion to its numbers; partly from ingrained conservatism, and partly because Puritans were its most bitter traditional enemies. Social factors also mattered: as we have seen, many more of the traditional ruling elite were Royalist than Parliamentarian. It is important to emphasize, however, that the issues over which the war was fought were not those of class, but of religion and of the distribution of power between the component parts of Parliament.

In addition, there were many other local factors. In some counties, such as Cheshire, Lancashire and Leicestershire, power had long been disputed between rival factions of landowners. When the war came, and one of these picked a side, its rivals were likely to choose the other. Big urban corporations such as Chester and Newcastle were dominated by wealthy merchants who had been given trading privileges by the Crown, and therefore tended to support it; conversely, lesser merchants and retailers who wanted to break into these monopolies tended to be Parliamentarian. At York, where the ruling elite was Parliamentarian, it was the interlopers who were Royalist. Where a great local magnate commanded wide respect, such the Earl of Newcastle in the north-east, the Earl of Derby in the north-west, and the Earl of Warwick in Essex, many people would follow his choice. In Wales, western Cornwall and perhaps Cumbria, a language barrier operated which meant that English, or at least standard English, was not the usual means of communication. There the inhabitants were clearly less inclined to view Parliament as the embodiment of the realm, and accordingly supported the king wholesale: by contrast, all other English counties were divided.

It is important to appreciate that these factors are in practice very difficult to separate out. Rather, they combined to create different local political cultures, which were themselves sometimes riven by debate and division. It is often impossible to tell why an individual supported a particular party, let alone a community. The model of the rock is also inherently flawed, because the explosion at Westminster had the effect of closing traditional fault-lines as well as enlarging them. Herefordshire and Somerset are examples of counties where the traditional rival power blocs were fractured and replaced by the conflict. In Yorkshire, gentry who had avidly persecuted Catholics now took them as comrades because Puritans had suddenly come to seem more dangerous to the monarchy. In the Lonsdale Hundred of Lancashire, landlords and tenants who had long quarrelled over rights and dues became equally devoted Royalists. Local disputes over whether or not traditional festivals and folk customs should be abolished, or over hunting rights and forest law, which had bitterly divided communities, rarely correspond to the wartime polarity.

Notoriously, the war split families apart: a third of the gentry houses of Somerset suffered this fate, while the Verneys of Buckinghamshire were unlucky enough to be divided father against son and brother against brother. The geological model also fails to take account of the large number of people who changed sides in the course of the war, including many individuals and a few entire garrisons. Nor does it reckon with neutralism. A third to two thirds of the leading gentry of each county seem to have played no discernible part in the conflict, and many of those who did were clearly bullied or cajoled into doing so by others. The zealous partisans on each side reduce to about six to eight individuals in most counties. In the first year of the war, the leaders of twenty-one counties signed local pacts to suspend or prevent hostilities within their borders, so that those who wanted to fight needed to go elsewhere. In every case, however, these agreements eventually collapsed as the warring parties had more need of local resources.

In many ways the comment of a Frenchman upon his nation's Wars of Religion applies equally well to the English Civil War: 'At first we fought like angels, then like men, and finally like devils.' Parliamentarian generals like Sir William Waller, who could refer to 'this war without an enemy' and urge a Royalist counterpart to fight 'in a way of honour, and without personal hatred', were replaced by those like the rising cavalry commander, Oliver Cromwell. He could describe the king's soldiers as 'God's enemies', and rejoice that they were 'stubble to our swords'. When this war got nasty, it could be very unpleasant indeed. When a small Parliamentarian garrison at Hopton Castle, Shropshire, surrendered to a local Royalist force in early 1644, its common soldiers were slaughtered and buried in a mass grave. In Devon, the king's local commander had both prisoners of war and people who resisted taxation systematically starved to death in captivity. After destroying the royal army at Naseby, the Parliamentarian troopers turned on its female camp followers, killing over a hundred of them and disfiguring many others. Altogether, perhaps one in five adult males bore arms in the course of the conflict, and perhaps one in twenty died as a result of it. None the less, compared with most European wars of the age, it was still a gentle one. No group of soldiers numbering over twenty was killed in cold blood, there were no wholesale massacres of civilians when towns were stormed, and rape remained, as it was in peacetime, both strictly forbidden and rare in practice.

The universal civilian experience of the war was to pay for it. Both sides, in their increasing desperation, carried out the long-overdue reform of English war taxation, and imposed demands of a weight and efficiency never known before, the equivalent of raising a Tudor subsidy every few weeks. The assessments used were those drawn up for Ship Money, but at a rate which removed each month a quarter of a propertied person's pre-war income. In addition, everybody was hit by the excise, a sales tax levied on commodities vended in shops and markets, and many communities had to pay extra amounts to fortify their towns or move convoys through their neighbourhood. Farms could be ruined if their horses were conscripted for military service, on promise of payment that never came, and their other equipment confiscated in lieu of taxes that they could no longer provide. Soldiers whose pay was falling short, and some who were merely criminal, often looted the communities whom they were supposed to protect. All this damage was done before the enemy actually showed up: then towns captured by storm could be plundered bare, and cereal crops burned and livestock slaughtered in raids intended to remove the economic infrastructure of an area held by the enemy. At least a tenth of all provincial townspeople had their homes destroyed, and up to 200 gentry lost theirs; overall, perhaps 2 per cent of the population were left homeless. Many contractors did well out of supplying Parliamentarian armies, but even in Parliament's quarters many more people suffered than gained by the war. London was best situated to survive it unscathed, and there bakers, brewers, arms dealers and printers all prospered. On the other hand, the city in general plunged into a major recession, and smaller and more exposed urban centres, even those that saw no fighting, must have suffered proportionately worse.

The war was not the most economically damaging that the English, Welsh and Cornish have ever undergone: both World Wars of the twentieth century far surpass it in that regard. The damage that it inflicted on property is minute compared with that imposed by Hitler's air force. It was, however, in proportion to population the bloodiest war that the peoples of the realm of England have ever suffered, and the most disruptive, physically and ideologically. There were always, indeed, two civil wars in progress during its duration: that between the contending parties, and that between those who wished to fight it and the bulk of the population, who had never desired it, barely understood it, and only wanted to get through it with the minimum of damage to all that they held dear.

The English Revolution

By the end of 1646, the three Stuart kingdoms were each dominated by a completely different regime, installed by violence: England by the Long Parliament, Scotland by the Covenanters, and Ireland by the Confederate Catholics who had risen in 1641. All owed nominal allegiance to Charles I, who controlled none of them, and both the English and Scottish governments were committed to the destruction of the Irish Confederacy, while the Scottish one still felt itself obliged to seek a reformation of the Church of England. The two British regimes were deeply resented by many of their subjects, while the Irish one was still locked into a savage civil war. Everybody in the archipelago must have recognized that this situation could not endure for long.

Of the three regimes, that of the Long Parliament had the most secure grip on its territory, and the greatest resources; but it was still vexed by serious problems. The defeated Royalists included most of the traditional leaders of social and political life, who were now excluded from any role in central and local government for the foreseeable future. The Scots were demanding the price of their wartime aid, in ecclesiastical reforms and in hard cash. Because a large army was needed to hold down the Royalists, the heavy war taxes had to be continued, but these were very unpopular: in 1646 and 1647 twenty-five county petitions were presented to Parliament asking for their removal. Despite them the government was still disposing of twice as many soldiers as the taxes alone could support, so it was £2.8 million in debt. The Church had been wrecked by the ejection of about a third of its clergy, for Royalism or mere local unpopularity. The worst harvest failure of the century was commencing, and would continue for three years. Most threatening of all, the king had concluded the Civil War by surrendering to the Scottish army in England. Despite his tendency to panic at critical moments, Charles had an underlying dogged courage. Most other monarchs would have fled abroad after total defeat by rebels, but he chose to remain in his own land, and carry on fighting by negotiation. His first hope was to turn the Covenanters against the Long Parliament, and he spent the second half of 1646 as their prisoner, attempting to reach an agreement with them.

Between the summer of 1646 and the spring of 1647, the leaders of the Parliament produced a programme that seemed to deal with all these challenges. They abolished the bishops and Elizabethan Prayer Book and substituted a presbyterian system of church government and a liturgy which did away with most formal ceremony and prayer. This pleased the Covenanters, who were also paid their war expenses from the proceeds of the sale of bishops' lands. As Charles had proved unable to agree to reforms of the English Church that were as extensive, the Scottish government handed him over to the Long Parliament and took its soldiers home. At the same time, Parliament set about disbanding most of its own army, intending to substitute a militia which would be supported by local rates and to ship off the best of its remaining soldiers to reconquer Ireland. All this was intended to isolate the king, who would then be forced to accept the settlement thus achieved, abandoning the Royalists to accommodate them-selves to it and making a considerable reduction of taxes possible. This effort became the work of a set of politicians led by Denzil Holles, who secured a steady majority of supporters in Parliament, the City of London and the provinces. The result would have been a constitutionally limited monarchy of the sort that Charles had already conceded in Scotland in 1641.

A minority existed in the nation which was very much opposed to the settlement being imposed. It included anybody who wanted the right to worship outside the established church, in congregations gathered around ministers of their own choice, or anybody who was prepared to accord others this right. The settlement prescribed after the war was intended to create a national religion which, like the pre-war one, was enforced upon everybody in the nation; but wartime condi-tions had produced an effective period of toleration, in which independent congregations had been able to appear among Puritans who had scruples about the brand of worship and belief being prescribed nationally. These congregations wanted to continue, and to them were joined those people who sought some overall reform and rationalization of the political and legal systems. Such demands were orchestrated and publicized during the post-war period by a group based in London which became known to its enemies as the 'Levellers'. At times, it seemed to consist of three intellectuals, John Lilburne, William Walwyn and Richard Overton, armed with a printing press. At others, it appeared to be an imposing popular movement, which could field thousands of supporters for demonstrations. The truth was that it was both – and all points between – according to the moment and the issue.

It would not have mattered much, save to historians of ideas, had one other minority group not taken up similar interests, that is, Parliament's most important body of soldiers, the New Model Army. This had been formed in 1645, and was the force that won the battle of Naseby and struck all the other decisive blows in the defeat of the king. It was the most successful product of a general process produced by the war, by which both sides divested themselves of most of the nobles and greater gentry who had provided their leading officers at the opening of hostilities. In their place they promoted men of lesser social rank and proven military talent. The king engaged in this practice to a slighter extent, and could conceal it better by giving his new men titles; but even among Royalists it was significant. Peter Newman examined their field officers and found that of the total 55 per cent did not rank as gentry and 77 per cent were not esquires, the class that provided traditional local governors. The New Model represented this tendency at its most dramatic: none of its members had noble titles when it was formed and by 1648 only 9 per cent of its officers were gentry of any kind.

This social mobility was associated with a notorious tendency to radical ideas. Probably only a minority of the army wanted to worship outside the national church by 1647, but this still represented a large number of armed men. None the less, the New Model would probably have peacefully disbanded or gone to Ireland, as Holles and his allies wished, had the latter been prepared to address its material needs. The soldiers wanted their large arrears of pay, and also a legal indemnity for any actions committed during the war. The problem here was that the available money was almost certainly not enough to provide the arrears, and now the Holles group blundered by trying to bully the army into submission and disbandment without satisfying its requests. During the course of the summer of 1647 the New Model went into mutiny. Many of its more moderate officers departed or were ejected, and the remainder led their men in seizing the person of the king and then surrounding London. Holles and his friends fled, and power at Westminster passed to a coalition allied to the soldiers, and known as Independents.

The Independents and army officers now presented the king with their own plan for a settlement, known as the Heads of Proposals. It was gentler to Charles, the Royalists and traditional religion than any terms which the Long Parliament had been prepared to offer at any previous point since the war. The king lost his powers over government for a shorter time, the Royalists suffered fewer penalties and bishops and the Prayer Book were allowed back into the national Church. The price of these concessions was to have shorter and more frequent Parliaments, elected according to a regular franchise and more equal distribution of seats, and a Church in which the bishops lacked coercive powers, the Prayer Book was not enforced, and Protestants who wished to worship in their own congregations could do so. Recent historians have been almost unanimous in agreeing that this was the best chance that Charles was given after his defeat to settle the nation, and that to refuse it, as he did, was a grave error. This is understandable, but is a judgement delivered not only with the benefit of hindsight but according to modern beliefs. The notion of a national Church from which people were able to contract out at will, in any parish, was one repugnant to most of the English, Welsh and Cornish at that time and virtually all Scots; as part of this pattern it was also literally damnable to Charles himself.

Faced with the king's obduracy, the unity of the soldiers began to fragment, some of them taking up the Levellers' call for wider political and religious freedoms. It was restored in November, when Charles escaped from army custody to the apparent security of the Isle of Wight, which had an apparently sympathetic governor, and then signed a deal with the Scottish Covenanters. The prospect of having as a neighbour an England where heretics could flourish in legal freedom had shocked a majority of the Covenanters at last into deciding to declare war on the English Parliament and its soldiers. All that they asked of the king was the establishment of a presbyterian Church of England for a trial period of three years, after which the settlement could be reviewed; and this he was prepared to grant.

The preparations for a new Scottish invasion encouraged every group that was dissatisfied with the regime that had ruled ever since the army's coup to join an armed rebellion, and the result, in the summer of 1648, was the Second Civil War. In the course of it, many Royalists, some former Parliamentarians, most of the English navy and large numbers of provincial people all took up arms to aid the Scots against the Independents and the New Model Army; and the New Model beat them all. Because none of their efforts were properly concerted, they could be contained and defeated one by one, by a compact, experienced and dedicated body of soldiers operating on internal lines of communication. An English expeditionary force then installed in Scotland a new government composed of those Covenanters who had opposed the treaty with the king. Charles could only watch the process helplessly, as the governor whom he had trusted held him a close prisoner on the Isle of Wight, on behalf of the Independent-dominated Long Parliament.

None the less, the New Model's victory was a difficult and hard-fought achievement, and its soldiers came out of the war with a determination to ensure that Charles, who had started it, never again wielded authority. This demand flooded up from the junior officers and their men, carrying away with it first the colonels and then the generals. It split the Independents, many of whom still wanted to reach an agreement with the king which would restore as much of the pre-war system of religion and government as possible. A majority of the Commons and almost all of the remaining Lords decided to carry on talking with him. As a result, in December the army seized the capital and purged Parliament down to the minority of MPs willing to call the king to account. The Commons had now been filled up with new men, faithful to the wartime Parliamentarian cause, and numbered 461; but of these only 71 were prepared to accept the soldiers' action.

Charles's trial took place in January 1649, and could have ended in his abdication or deposition had he been prepared to recognize the authority of the court; but he would not and so was executed on 30 January. Because an alternative king could not be found – the legal heir, the king's eldest son, was safe in the Netherlands and promptly proclaimed himself Charles II, vowing vengeance – the monarchy was abolished. Because too few Lords would cooperate to make up a quorum, the House of Lords was abolished too. In their eagerness to get at the person who had tried so hard to destroy them, and whom they had come to call the 'Man of Blood', the soldiers had wrecked the constitution. It was a genuine revolution, carried out simply to commit an act of tyrannicide. The Bible, which was the main source of ideological inspiration for most of the army, had little to say about republics but much about doing away with wicked kings.

Charles I ended his life a crashing failure, and such failures have few friends among historians. Indeed, to defend him means persuading an audience to award him three out of ten instead of zero, but some defence can be mounted. It is possible to point out that had he not mishandled the Scots he would never have lost control of England and Ireland; that during the Civil War he acquired a new sense of the need to appeal and explain himself to his subjects, and that after it he was almost certainly more popular than the Long Parliament; that his ideals were not bad in themselves; and that his gentleness was impressive. He was not so different in his personality and tastes from many more successful contemporary rulers, and it could be that he was simply in charge of the wrong set of kingdoms. The true tragedy of his position was that he could not accept that a Church of England over which the monarch had no control, through bishops, was one worth having. This was because by abdicating his responsibility for it he was essentially betraying his duty to his God. In the last ditch, in December 1648, he was willing to give up his power over the armed forces and political appointments but not permanently to alter the form of the Church; and it was this that signalled to the army that he had not changed his ways. In that narrow sense, he died a martyr, giving up his life for a concept of religion which, as in most people of his time, was bound up with his whole view of politics, society and humanity.

The Politics of Religion in the 1640s

One of the great intellectual developments of the 1980s was a recognition that ideas have an independent life of their own, and that human beliefs, decisions and reactions are often, in objective terms, irrational. The writing of history is in itself traditionally often an attempt to make sense of apparently irrational events, and the new 'cultural history' that commenced in that decade tried to get to the heart of the problem by reckoning with the most intangible and powerful of ideological forces: faiths, fashions and moods. In part it was a self-contained development resulting from the actual progress of historical research, especially into local records, which suggested by the 1980s that economic forces did not, in fact, lie behind most political and religious changes. It was also, however, the result of broader developments. The primacy of economic forces in human affairs had been the main tenet of Marxism, an ideology which seemed to be expanding all over the world in the middle of the century but which collapsed as a political force towards the end of it. Instead, Islamic and Christian fundamentalism both reappeared as potent ideological forces, and local ethnic and religious hatreds convulsed regions from Ireland to India and Central Africa.

One impact of these changes was a new appreciation of the importance of religion in the politics of the 1640s. As said, it was both the most important single factor in the formation of the Civil War parties, and one which interwove with other attitudes to life. It is least easy to discern in the case of the Royalists, many of whom seem to have lacked more than a conventional religiosity, and to have supported the traditional Church as part of a general affection for established ways. In some, however, and above all in Charles I himself, religious faith was paramount, and its influence was the more important the further towards the radical end of the political spectrum people were situated. This has recently been emphasized in the case of groups who had been seen by historians before in more secular terms. It is true that the issues over which the New Model Army went into mutiny in 1647 concerned material conditions of service; but most recent commentators have pointed out that the soldiers who resisted most fiercely were those most opposed to Parliament's impending religious settlement. The Levellers were seen for most of the twentieth century as the forerunners of the Victorian Chartists, or the modern Labour Party or Green Party. It is now obvious that they made increasingly extreme calls for reform of the political system because their original aim, to gain the right to worship outside the national Church, was refused successively by every component of the existing system.

This pattern carried over into the republic established on the execution of King Charles. Consistently, those individuals in the localities who gave it the most active support were members of independent congregations, who saw the republican government as their best bulwark against an intolerant and monopolistic old-style Church of England. In 1649, a small but active movement appeared under the name of Diggers, which sought among other things the right for poor people to cultivate common land. They were viewed for much of the twentieth century as primitive communists, but their ideologue, Gerrard Winstanley, was primarily a mystical

Christian, seeking a personal union with his God. This is equally true of the loose collection of individuals branded by their enemies with the label of Ranters, who came to public attention in 1650, allegedly preaching such doctrines as the non-existence of Hell. In the early 1970s they were portrayed as counter-cultural activists, loosely equivalent to modern hippies, but now seem more like yet another manifestation of mystical Christianity. That so many new ideas could be voiced was largely due to another development made possible by the excitement generated by the Great Civil War and the collapse of effective regulation of belief as authorities had to give their whole energy to the conflict. It was the wholesale exploitation of printing presses for the communication of ideas. In the 1630s, these pumped out an average 624 books per year in England. In 1641 the figure rose to 2,042 and in 1642 to 4,038, and almost never sank below 1,000 for the rest of the century. Common people, and women, gained a voice in published works during the 1640s that they never subsequently lost.

As Blair Worden has pointed out, the tragedy of the whole age was that virtually nobody in it believed in genuine religious toleration in the modern sense. To almost all Scots and Irish, all English Royalists and most Parliamentarians, toleration was a dirty word. It was something to be granted only if all other options had been closed. In the 1620s Puritans fought hard to deny it to Arminians, and then protested vigorously in the 1630s when the Arminians harassed them in turn and rejoiced when the chance did come to crush Arminianism in the 1640s. The only true liberty, to the average Puritan, lay in salvation by divine grace. Today, people talk about the virtues of religious freedom in social terms, but the early seventeenth century was more concerned with the fate of souls than of societies. To tolerate a bad religion was clearly to flout the will of the one true God, a step which was literally soul-destroying. Likewise, nobody in early Stuart England had believed in freedom of the press: all wished, instead, for it to be made to express their point of view. *De facto* toleration was achieved, from 1647 onwards, because all those Protestant groups who now wished to worship outside the national Church were driven together by a common fear of being wiped out by an intolerant presbyterian system. They were kept in alliance with each other by the fact that they remained unpopular minorities, dependent on the army's support to survive. The hope of most of those army officers and politicians who supported this liberty of conscience was that sooner or later a better national Church would rebuild itself from the ground upwards. An external diversity of belief and practice could be allowed among godly Protestants as a temporary expedient. People were not permitted to hold such dogmas as they pleased but those which might lead eventually towards a properly reformed Church.

Although limited by modern standards, for its age this idea was still revolutionary, and it did indeed create a nation of exceptional religious diversity which was to persist until the present. This diversity was, however, precisely the result the various British religious groups in the 1640s did not want. If there is a God in heaven, and the course of history is broadly a reflection of His wishes, as all the religious factions of Civil War Britain certainly believed, then it must be acknowledged that every single one of them had got Him wrong.

10

THE COMMONWEALTH AND PROTECTORATE (1649–60)

In the course of the 1990s, it became fashionable for some historians of ideas, such as David Norbrook and Markku Peltonen, to emphasize a republican tradition in early modern English thought. This may have reflected disenchantment during that period with traditional non-democratic elements in British political life, such as the monarchy; it certainly added excitement to discussions of early modern ideological history. Some confusion was created, however, by the tendency of these writers to term 'republican' anybody who believed that power was ultimately accorded to rulers by the ruled, and that some of the latter, at least, should have a measure of control over their representatives. This belief is completely compatible with monarchy: indeed it underlies the whole concept of 'mixed monarchy', in which a sovereign shares some power with representative bodies, and is simply the 'ascending theory' of royal authority which was one of the themes of medieval and early modern political thought. Ever since the late fourteenth century at least, English thinkers had mixed an ideology of inherent royal power with one of responsible citizenship, drawing for the latter upon a language derived ultimately from republican Rome and filtered through the experience of medieval Italian city-states. It is a measure of how little genuine republicanism had lodged in the English political psyche that when a revolutionary regime actually abolished the monarchy and the Lords in 1649, it did so without any pre-prepared and shared ideology that justified the act or any blueprint for a government to replace it. Over the following few years, a number of authors, none of them disposing of any great influence, came up with different justifications for a republican regime, and models for one. The chronic political and constitutional instability of the 1650s reflected the inability of those who led this *de facto* republic to settle upon either an ideology or a model for it with which they themselves – let alone those whom they ruled – were content.

This is the more remarkable in view of the tremendous practical achievements of the English Commonwealth, as the new regime was officially termed. It began life completely surrounded by enemies, at home and abroad, who regarded its very existence as illegal and immoral. The minority of MPs remaining in the House of Commons purged by the army, and the executive council that they appointed, proceeded to defeat the lot. Between 1649 and 1653 their regime submitted Ireland to a more thorough conquest than that which had been made by Elizabeth. Almost simultaneously, between 1650 and 1652, it completely conquered Scotland, being the first and last English government ever to do so. It then set about uniting the whole of the British Isles into a single political unit represented by an imperial Parliament at Westminster. Between 1651 and 1653 it turned to the European theatre of operations, picking a fight with England's main commercial competitors, the Dutch. During these three years the Commonwealth drove them out of their powerful position in the carrying trade between England and its colonies, and hammered their war fleet in a succession of battles. As a result, the great powers of Europe began one by one to recognize the legitimacy of the upstart English state.

Before turning on its foreign enemies, the Commonwealth dealt with those at home, on both political wings. The king was followed on to the headsman's block by a number of prominent Royalists, while the Leveller leaders, who had turned against the new regime as insufficiently democratic, were locked up. Soldiers in the republic's own army, who demonstrated or mutinied against their terms of service, and seemed to be infected by Leveller ideas, were suppressed and their spokesmen shot. The government took a firm stand against the most radical ideas, by allowing the local Digger communities to be dispersed and passing a law which declared the beliefs attributed to the Ranters to be blasphemy. In dealing with the Irish, Scots and Dutch, the Commonwealth could draw on all the advantages which the Long Parliament had enjoyed in the Civil War, now much enhanced. It deployed the entire machinery – fiscal, administrative, military and naval – which it had built up to win that war, and retained the heavy and efficient monthly taxation that sustained it, now applied to the wealth of the entire English state. This was much inflated by massive windfalls, in the shape of the lands confiscated from the Crown, cathedrals and leading Royalists. Such assets, in turn, enabled it to borrow heavily on the London money market, while huge areas of land taken from the conquered Irish provided another means of paying off soldiers and creditors. As a result, it was able to build up its armies and fleets to a strength that none of its enemies could match.

In the case of Ireland, the Commonwealth was simply reasserting the traditional claim of the English monarchy to rule it, acting as usurper of all that monarchy's former powers. Even in alliance, the Confederate Catholics and Irish Royalists could not field an army big enough to face that which the Commonwealth shipped over. All that they could do was retreat into their walled towns, which the heavy guns of the invaders could break open, and then into the countryside where they were hunted down as brigands. The Scots were a different matter. The radical wing of the Covenanters, whom the Parliamentarian army had installed in power in 1648, could not abandon the dream of their movement, of converting the religion of the English and Irish into a form similar to their own, and so securing their Kirk for ever. They therefore proclaimed the exiled king Charles II as ruler of all three kingdoms, and brought him to Scotland on their own terms in 1650, whereupon the Commonwealth decided on a pre-emptive strike. Once again, the Scots dared not face the English army in the field except at what seemed to be an exceptionally favourable moment. When that came, at Dunbar, they were outmanoeuvred and crushed, giving the Commonwealth half of Scotland. The rest was nibbled away until in 1651 the king broke out and led the fourth Scottish invasion of England in eleven years, hoping to raise the English Royalists. Instead, his army was annihilated at Worcester: he escaped abroad, but the conquest of Scotland was rapidly completed. Just as in the decisive stage of the Civil War, the Parliament's generals had enjoyed crucial material advantages but deployed them with brilliance, not making a single error. The greatest of them all was the East Anglian squire who had emerged from the Great Civil War as Parliament's main cavalry commander, and was now raised to the supreme position in the republic's armies: Oliver Cromwell.

Having seized the other two kingdoms, the Commonwealth, as John Morrill has emphasized, carried out changes in both which went far beyond any attempted in England. The Scots and Irish lost their Parliaments and governments, while the Irish Church was stripped of bishops and cathedrals and it and the Scottish Kirk were forced to allow godly Protestants to form independent congregations if they wished. The Scottish nobility was deprived of its judicial rights and most of its control over tenants, and some of it was completely ruined: the Earl of Traquair, who had been the Lord Treasurer in the 1630s, had to beg on the streets. As John Morrill has suggested, Ireland suffered perhaps the greatest exercise in ethnic cleansing in early modern Europe – only the fate of Bohemia after the revolt of 1618–20 comes close – and underwent the most complete political integration with Britain that it has ever known. Forty per cent of its territory was transferred from people born there to Protestants from England. The share owned by Catholics was reduced from a clear majority to 15 per cent. In both nations, moreover, the English conquest inflicted terrible damage to populations which had already been reduced by the preceding years of civil war. From one tenth to one fifth of the adult males of Scotland died as a result of the conflicts between 1637 and 1652, and at least one fifth of all the inhabitants of Ireland were killed, fled, or perished of disease or hunger in the same period. Most of these losses were sustained during the Commonwealth's invasions.

All this served to confirm to most people at home and abroad, in an age in which great events were generally thought to reflect the will of God, that however abhorrent the regime might be there was some divine purpose behind its existence. By 1653 the only threat to it could come from within its own ranks; but that threat was very serious indeed.

Constitutional Experiments

Newcomers to the political history of England in the 1650s generally find it one of the most confusing episodes in the national story: a succession of short-lived regimes and constitutions with no apparent connecting thread of logic. Such an impression is largely a result of traditional historiography, which has concentrated upon the actions of governments and Parliaments in the period, and above all on the enigmatic figure of Oliver Cromwell, who presided over most. The key to an understanding of these years lies in a body of people that has been relatively neglected by scholars, partly because of a comparative lack of material and partly because of an academic preference for studying formal organs and offices of power. This is the army that commenced its life as the New Model in

1645 and became the force that had made the English Revolution. If it had little sense of an ideal form of government, it had a very good one of the kind of social and political outcome which it wanted any government to produce. Between 1647 and 1660 it had a consistent list of reforms it expected from any regime which it was prepared to support: a transformation of the legal system to make it faster, cheaper and easier for ordinary people to understand; regular Parliaments elected on a reformed franchise; and a broadly based national Church without the compulsory tithes which traditionally supported parish ministers and with freedom for radical Protestants to form their own miniature churches outside it if they wished. In 1647 the army had tried to get the king to agree to it; after he refused, it continued to search for a different form of government which would.

In doing so, it suffered from two handicaps, which combined to produce a chronic impasse. The first was simply that its programme was too extreme, especially in religion, for the vast majority of the English to accept. It could command the allegiance of a minority in each level of society, and cumulatively this provided enough civilian allies to staff local government, but no more. The second handicap was that the soldiers could not bring themselves to face the reality that their reforms would not be imposed by any body that came close to representing the wishes of the English in general. Rather than enact them by the directions of a military tribunal in the manner of many modern revolutions, they continued to look to Parliaments elected from gentry, lawyers and wealthy merchants – groups which had a particular vested interest in the old order that the army wanted to reshape – to provide them. The soldiers were uneasily aware that they had seized power in the name of popular liberties but against the will of most of the people; their hope was that time, God and re-education would win the majority of the nation over. It did not help their cause that while their reform package was clear enough in outline, their proposals were either vague or contradictory when it came to practical details; for example, what could replace tithes?

The results were as follows. For four years the army applied pressure to the purged remnant of the Long Parliament to enact its reforms, with increasing confidence as its victories multiplied. In April 1653, led by Cromwell, it lost patience and threw the MPs out. Its officers then, for the first and last time, came close to the only sure means of achieving their aim, by nominating a Parliament themselves for the work instead of getting it elected. Unhappily, in their desire to give the resulting body some social weight, they named to it many individuals from the traditional governing classes, as well as many genuine radicals. The assembly concerned, popularly known as Barebone's Parliament after one of its members, suffered none of the sloth of the purged one but was afflicted by division instead, and collapsed in December. By then, some of the officers had another solution ready: to have regular Parliaments, elected from reformed constituencies and a standard franchise and without any Royalists, and to manage them as a rider does a horse. Two components were built into the new constitution, called the Instrument of Government. The first was a presidential figure, the Lord Protector, who was Cromwell himself, working closely with the second, a powerful executive council, staffed mainly with men sympathetic to the army's programme. During most of 1654, Protector and council used their own powers to impose a number of measures that prepared the way for the army's reform package, and in September they called a Parliament. To their horror, it refused not only to complete the reforms but to recognize the legitimacy of the Instrument of Government itself. In 1655 Cromwell dissolved it, and his government then imposed a direct experience of local godly reform on the nation, by dividing it into provinces governed by leading army officers, the Major-Generals. They were expected to work with local enthusiasts to ensure that the poor were relieved, the peace kept, and crime, vice and ungodliness punished, to an unprecedented degree. After more than a year of this, in September 1656, the government hoped that the English had been sufficiently impressed and cowed for a more compliant Parliament to be elected under the new system.

The second Protectorate Parliament was indeed different, but not in the way the army had hoped. A majority of it, which included some of Cromwell's own civilian advisers, offered a counter-deal: to recognize and supply the government if it abandoned the reform programme and accepted a form of counter-revolution instead. This would consist of a restored monarchy, with Cromwell as king, a restored House of Lords, with enemies of the regime excluded, and a better-defined and better-policed Church of England. When the army officers came to him to protest, he told them angrily that this was the best offer that they had ever got. Only some, however, were convinced, and from February to May 1657 the Protector hesitated over the problem. In early May the news leaked that he was on the point of accepting the Crown, whereupon his three most senior generals told them that they would not support this, and the regiments around London mobilized to petition against it. This concentrated Cromwell's mind, and he got in his refusal just before the petition arrived. Instead he brokered a compromise. He did not accept the crown or title of king but adopted increased powers, a royal robe, a sceptre, a throne and the right to create knights and hereditary peers. An Upper House was formed, but of supporters of the government rather than the old aristocracy, and a synod to tighten up the church was promised and never called. The Protector hoped that this would give enough to satisfy everybody. On the contrary, it satisfied no one, and when the Parliament was recalled in 1658, both it and the army became restless. Cromwell dissolved it after two weeks, and then listened to his councillors arguing fruitlessly over possible alternatives, as he slowly fell into a fatal illness which carried him off in September.

At this point it may be worth asking whether such a sequence of failures really mattered: after all, equipped with an unbeatable army, an effective administration and sufficient local supporters, the regime could apparently go on trying out and discarding constitutions and Parliaments indefinitely. Sooner or later, this logic suggests, the army officers would find one of each that would do their work. The problem with this suggestion is that time was not on their side: instead there were two different time bombs ticking away underneath them. One was religious. The whole system of liberty of conscience was based on the premise that given a long enough period in which they were forced to coexist, the different groups into which the old Puritanism had shattered would learn to work together, and reconstruct a better national Church between them. By 1658 this was actually happening, as in several areas former non-Puritan Protestants, Presbyterians, members of independent congregations who favoured a national Church, and even some of the new sects who had not wanted a Church of England at all, such as Baptists, were starting to cooperate. Such a development, however, was emphatically not a sign that the religious temperature of the English was starting to fall: on the contrary, these old opponents were sinking their differences in order to join forces against a terrifying new threat.

This came from the north, traditionally the most conservative of all English regions. There the disturbances of the 1640s had inflicted unusually severe damage upon the established church, leaving many parishes with no ministry. In this emergency, some country people and inhabitants of small towns began to think things through for themselves, discussing the Bible and radical and mystical ideas that had filtered through from the larger centres of population. By the beginning of the 1640s, they had reached the conclusion that no settled ministry was needed at all for salvation: all that was required was for devout Christians to meet together and wait for the spirit of God to move one or more of them. Having tried out this technique, they found that it seemed to work. The discovery spread rapidly through the fells and dales of the North Country, and in 1654 its proponents were ready to come south to preach their message. They had now embraced the whole of the army's reform programme with the major addition that the Church of England was to be wholly abolished, and with it the universities which trained clergymen. Within four years they had penetrated every county in England and some in Wales, finding adherents in town and country alike. They represented the most spectacularly successful popular heresy that the English had ever produced, and one to which their enemies gave the name of 'Quakers', after the religious ecstasies into which some of its proponents entered. If the army – already so inclined to radical beliefs – were to take up their cause, then it could very easily be carried into power. By late 1658 many who still believed in a national church, or even a settled ministry, feared that the nation would collapse into violence between the Quakers and their allies and those determined to resist them. In that sense England was growing steadily less stable.

The other ticking bomb was financial. The Commonwealth had fought its wars on a basis of heavy taxation and huge land sales; but the effort required was too much even for that, and by 1654 the state was heavily in debt and at the end of its credit. The Protectorate made matters worse, because of two miscalculations. The first was to court popularity by reducing the level of direct taxation, while not reducing the number of its soldiers to one that the new level could support. It was gambling on winning the acceptance of the political nation, which would enable it to reduce the army to a sustainable level and receive further grants from Parliaments. Neither occurred, and the soldiers' pay slid ever further into arrears as the years passed.

The second mistake was to declare war on Spain, an action itself prompted by financial difficulty. In one of the very rare debates that they held which was recorded, Cromwell and his councillors decided that they could not afford to pay off the fleet sailing home at the end of the war with the Dutch in 1654. They decided to solve the problem by sending it out again to attack the Spanish colonies in the Caribbean. The hope was that the Spanish monarchy, long committed to a war in three European theatres, would be prepared to write off some of its many overseas possessions, which would be lucrative enough to yield the English government an immediate profit. To those who thought the scheme ridiculously foolhardy, Cromwell and his supporters replied that God would surely favour a blow against an intolerant Catholic state. The critics were correct: in 1655 the English fleet was beaten off its main objective, and had to settle for seizing the smaller island of Jamaica, which required great expense to hold and develop it. The Protectorate was now locked into a full-scale struggle with a furious Spain, which was both very expensive and damaging to English trade. A subsequent alliance with France brought more victories, and the acquisition of a Channel port, Dunkirk, to replace the great medieval trophy of Calais. Dunkirk was, however, itself both costly and unprofitable, and the English economy slid into recession, even as the government, unable to make peace, faced the possibility of bankruptcy. The only sure ways to avert this were either to tax without Parliament, which even the soldiers thought ideologically unacceptable, or to find a way of working with a Parliament at last.

The second course was the one taken by the new Lord Protector, Cromwell's oldest surviving son, Richard, who had succeeded his father in default of any other candidate behind whom the dead Protector's followers could unite. He had been brought up outside political life, and so a large part of his acceptability lay in the fact that nobody knew quite what to expect of him. He soon showed his quality, having all of his father's courage and verve but very different ideas. He called a Parliament and asked it to settle the nation and supply the government, making it clear that he had no personal interest in the army's reform programme. In April 1659, he launched a coup to break the power of the soldiers, calculating that a third of its colonels would support him and a third hesitate, leaving his supporters able to attack and overpower the third who held to the soldiers' old ideals. When the moment came, his miscalculation became clear, as regiment after regiment commanded by his supporters ignored their colonels and marched off to join those gathering to oppose him: the army as a whole still clung to its old ideals. The Parliament was dissolved and Richard Cromwell fell from power, taking the Protectorate with him.

The army now recalled the MPs who, of all those that had sat during the previous ten years, had seemed most amenable to its wishes: the purged remnant of the Long Parliament, which had at least abolished the monarchy and Lords and allowed people to worship outside the national Church. Its hope was that their time in the wilderness would have made its members more receptive to the soldiers' wishes. What followed was a fast-forward version of the events of 1648–53. First came a miniature equivalent to the Second Civil War, called Booth's Rebellion, in which former Royalist and Parliamentarians joined forces to resist further radical change. The army had taken four months to suppress the risings of 1648; it stamped out that of 1659 within four weeks. A yet more rapid rerun now followed. It had formerly taken four years for the army to get disappointed with the purged Long Parliament and throw it out; now it took four months to do so, and by October the MPs were expelled again. What seemed most likely to happen next was a Second English Revolution, as junior officers called for the rapid introduction of further reforms, and some began to speak of abolishing the church and some of the central law courts altogether. Many civilians suspected that the Quaker manifesto was about to be put into action.

Instead, for the first time, a section of the army turned against the rest – the one that was holding down Scotland, commanded by George Monck, a former Royalist who had changed sides to become a personal protégé of Oliver Cromwell and had been promoted by him to the Scottish command. Monck's political attitudes remained flexible, but he turned out to have a rigid devotion to the Church of England, which he now believed to be in danger. He formed a flying column of supporters to ride around the separate army bases, arresting the many officers who sympathized with the soldiers in England. He replaced them with loyal men promoted from the ranks, and brought in Scots to fill up those, so creating a counter-revolutionary force. The army of England was still larger, and mobilized against him in November, but heavy snow made operations difficult through the winter and Monck cleverly bought time by offering to talk. Because Scotland was still overtaxed, his army was well paid, but that of England, crowded into inadequate quarters around Newcastle, felt the English fiscal and administrative system giving way behind it at last. It was underpaid, undersupplied and led by a provisional government of generals who had no clear and agreed plan for political action. At the end of the year, the regiments in England began to mutiny and disintegrate, and some of them called back the purged Parliament – now derisively known as the 'Rump' – yet again. The MPs now definitively ended the revolutionary era, by dismissing most of the army officers and men who had called for the reform programme. They then summoned Monck's army, believing it to be their only reliable armed force, to march south in order to defend them and enforce their will on the English.

When Monck and his men arrived at the capital, however, they found a thoroughly unpopular Commonwealth government adrift amid a turbulent and resentful populace, and saw no reason why they should continue to support it. Instead, they invited back the surviving MPs who had been purged at the end of 1648, with instructions simply to dissolve the Long Parliament legally and call another, which would settle the nation as it chose. When this 'Convention Parliament' was elected, in April 1660, it contained almost nobody who wanted a republic to continue. Within a few weeks it restored the monarchy, with Charles II invited back as king, and the House of Lords, composed of the traditional aristocracy; the pre-war Church of England, with bishops, cathedrals and the Prayer Book, duly followed, and Ireland and Scotland were allowed to recreate their own royal governments and national Parliaments.

These events can be read in two quite different ways. On the one hand, it is entirely legitimate to argue that the first and last republic that Britain has ever known was an entirely artificial and unnatural creation. It was imposed by a most unusual and unrepresentative group of people, the New Model Army, against the sustained will of the great majority of the population of England, Scotland and Wales. This army had been created and given ideological fuel by a unique set of experiences, and only its military power and its collective will allowed the republic to endure as long as it did. As soon as that power and that will collapsed, the traditional political and religious order returned almost immediately, as a process of nature.

On the other hand, it is equally justifiable to point out that revolutions are rarely made by the majority of a population, but by relatively small cadres of determined people who seize power and then subdue or re-educate the rest. In that sense, what happened in Britain was entirely normal, and a process of further radicalization and alteration ought to have ensued, as it almost did in 1659. This perspective would emphasize the financial errors of the Protectorate in undermining its stability, but above all the personal action of Oliver Cromwell in putting George Monck in charge of the army of Scotland instead of a soldier who had been part of the revolution of 1648–9 and shared its ideals. In that sense, only a historical accident wrenched the British Isles from their natural course of development into a yet more revolutionary republic. Readers may choose whichever of these verdicts seem the most compelling to them as individuals; and in doing so, of course, they will reproduce some of the instincts and beliefs that opposed people at the time.

Oliver Cromwell

The huge scale and unique nature of Cromwell's achievement speaks for itself: he was a soldier who never lost a battle or failed in a siege, the only commoner ever to be offered the Crown of England, and the only person ever to be offered that crown who preferred to rule without it. He also remains one of the most puzzling people in British history.

John Morrill has carried out the only genuinely original research into Cromwell's career in recent times, dedicated to the period before he came to power, and decided that three successive experiences formed him as a man. The first was loss of status, when a promising early public career, sponsored by a rich uncle, ended in 1630 with Oliver being reduced to a working tenant farmer. The second was religious conversion, to a classic Puritanism, which brought him to the attention of godly aristocrats and assisted his political and social rehabilitation. As a result, he became a zealous Parliamentarian at the outbreak of war and underwent his third experience, of rapid promotion to a general's rank and national fame. He emerged with a powerful sense of having been given a special mission by his God, and with the devoted loyalty of the army which was to make the English Revolution.

As Colin Davis has demonstrated, it is hard to define precisely the sort of religion in which Cromwell believed, within the broad spectrum of mainstream English Puritanism. He patronized all kinds of Protestant clergy who were prepared to accept the Church as reformed after the Civil War, and was also committed to liberty of conscience for godly Protestants who wanted to contract out of it. He was never interested in programmes, forms, creeds, structures or disputations, and was not a theologian any more than he was an intellectual in general. He was no stereotypical Puritan, having a personal love of dancing, music, smoking and practical jokes, and was unusual among the godly of his time in failing to give much importance to the devil. Instead he had a vivid personal relationship with an all-powerful God, and was prepared to recognize that some religious opponents had godliness in them that might leave them open to salvation. When Protestant extremists were locked up for attacking orthodox doctrine or disturbing ministers, he tried to release them as soon as possible or to ensure that they were kept in comfortable conditions. Catholics fared even better under his rule than they had under that of Charles I; only one priest was executed in the course of it, and that was against Cromwell's will. His dislike of persecution seems therefore to have been deep and genuine, as was his desire for the comprehension and reconciliation of different Protestants; the real problem was, as said, that his regime failed to persuade the nation to embrace either.

As a statesman, he had little interest in theories of government, and never drew up a blueprint for one. That had the defect of making him completely reliant on others for ways and means to rule the land, and when those around him ran out of ideas, he was politically paralysed. He embraced the broad principles of the Parliamentarian cause, and of the New Model Army, respecting the existing ranks of society but believing that godliness and goodness could be found in all, and vaguely recognizing the need for a better provision of education and of legal and social justice. He was prepared to work with or lead any form of government which seemed likely to fulfil the ideals of his soldiers and their civilian allies, and which placed restrictions on the power of the head of state; and he welcomed and emphasized those restrictions just as avidly when he himself was that head.

All this seems admirable, if woolly. The associated problem, which has made Cromwell's career endlessly controversial, is in attempting to discern where flexibility and open-mindedness shade into duplicity, deviousness and manipulation. He was a brilliant politician, whose success, like that which he enjoyed as a soldier, depended on confusing and outmanoeuvring his opponents before launching a decisive strike. His classic pattern of behaviour was to conceal his thoughts and intentions during a long period in which he took opinions and considered options, and then take sudden dramatic action. Repeatedly, he allied with individuals and groups at particular periods, only to discard them when they became inconvenient or redundant, and to blame them for failures of policy. He had the habit of giving people of widely differing views the impression that he sympathized with each of them, inevitably embittering many when his subsequent actions proved otherwise. He altered the tone of his speeches significantly according to the audience at which they were aimed, portraying himself as a godly radical at one moment and a conservative the next. He kept altering his public representation of key events in his own career, such as his expulsion of the remnant of the Long Parliament in 1653, to suit the political needs of the moment. When he favoured a policy which he found to be unpopular, such as the legal readmission of Jews to England, he first tried to get somebody else to take responsibility for it and then removed it from public debate while enacting it by indirect means. While preserving Catholics from persecution in practice, he was quite capable of whipping up feeling against them in Parliament when he seemed likely to gain political advantage by doing so.

Historians can often, quite genuinely, know more about people who are long dead than those who lived alongside them could do. Cromwell is not one of these. Very few of his contemporaries doubted the sincerity of his religious faith and of his commitment to liberty of expression for a broad spectrum of Protestant belief and to limitations on the powers of those who governed in church and state. What troubled many of them was the extent to which these ideals became tainted by the ruthlessness and cunning with which he wielded authority and steered his way through politics. In an age in which public life was full of able, self-made newcomers thrown up by civil war and revolution, Cromwell stood out to his contemporaries as somebody whom others found unusually unpredictable, inscrutable and slippery. Many of them remained uncertain of how self-centred, self-deceiving, exploitative and untrustworthy he really was; and so must we be.

Cromwell and Posterity

In the generation after his death, Oliver Cromwell had virtually no friends at all; he had managed to pull off the unfortunate trick of becoming the leader of a lost cause without seeming romantic. He had died in office rather than as a martyr or war hero, and those who had supported him could make him a scapegoat for the failure of the republic. He had in fact no influential admirers for well over a century, until the American Revolution rekindled an interest in republicanism in the English-speaking world; the Evangelical Revival made a strenuous, godly Protestantism socially respectable again; pious army officers began to feature as heroes of the expanding British Empire, and independent Protestant churches expanded enormously in number and political power. All this recreated a natural constituency of support for the Protector, and it was supplied with its key text in 1845 by Thomas Carlyle, who had grown up in an independent Church with a Calvinist belief in a predestined number of godly in each generation. To Carlyle, the Puritans had been the creators of Britain's subsequent greatness, and Cromwell literally the chosen of God. Carlyle's edition of Cromwell's letters and speeches established him for all time as a sincerely religious man with an acute desire to do right. It revealed his fears and doubts, his moments of elation and depression, and made him accessible to a modern age in a way in which most previous rulers, who have left no such personal records, are not. It became the bedrock on which future biographies of him were built, and also, with *Paradise Lost* and *The Pilgrim's Progress*, one of the three classics of Puritan literature.

As a result, Cromwell became the towering figure of seventeenth-century English history, a moral success even though a political failure, who had saved his country from tyranny and shown it a dream of a better future which eventually it achieved. He was a champion of the people who had yet not threatened the rich and titled, and a defender of freedom and tolerance who had also acted as a defence against real revolution. As such he was pretty well the perfect hero for middle-class England in the late nineteenth and early twentieth centuries, and could be appropriated by a string of authors with widely differing political views. To be sure, some conservatives, at all social levels, still remembered him as bad man, a few extreme socialists regarded him as a person who had betrayed a revolution by preventing genuine social reform, and Irish nationalists increasingly demonized him as a conqueror and a butcher. In Britain, however, his popularity only increased with time: with the coming of the third millennium he came third in the national poll to find the greatest Briton of the entire second millennium.

The online database available in 2008 had more than 2,000 titles that included his name, and there were more than 160 biographies of him held in British copyright libraries. To specialists, however, only five really mattered, and all those have been published since 1991: by Barry Coward, Peter Gaunt, Colin Davis, John Morrill and Martyn Bennett. What was really significant about them was their virtual unanimity: although they made different emphases, they showed us the same Cromwell, who is the one who has dominated the British imagination ever since the time of Carlyle. The reason for this is very simple: he is the man who features in his own letters and speeches, and what historians are doing is accepting the image that Cromwell presented of himself. Of all of them, it has been John Morrill who has perceived this problem most clearly, and posed the question why modern biographers always believe Cromwell rather than his critics, seeing him as a genuinely admirable person who movingly reveals his true thoughts, rather than as a master of spin. Professor Morrill himself could not reach an answer, and the solution may be simply that biographers make the letters and speeches the central evidence for their interpretation and work outwards from them. It is especially interesting to see what changes when scholars approach the man from a different direction. Sean Kelsey has published a deeply sympathetic portrait of the Commonwealth government of 1649–53, which shows Cromwell and his army, by contrast, as perpetrating a series of acts of injustice and misrepresentation. Christopher Durston, looking at the regime of the Major-Generals, has suggested that the Protector was an inept and unreliable leader, whom events took by surprise and propelled from one policy to another.

What is needed is somebody prepared to reverse the usual construction of a study of Cromwell: to start by recovering the context of his actions and seeing how everybody else involved in it viewed them. Only at the end would such an exercise consider his self-representation, in the light of the other perceptions and as a process of engagement with them. Such a method is clearly unworkable for a biography, being just too big a job: it needs to be applied to specific important episodes instead. In default of it, the Victorian Cromwell will continue to dominate both the scholarly imagination and the national one in the near future.

CONCLUSION

When did the Middle Ages end in Britain? The very concept of a medieval period was invented by fifteenth-century Italians to give special lustre to their own time and achievements: by claiming to have recovered much of the learning of the ancient world, lost or neglected in the intervening centuries, they sought to portray their age as what came to be called a 'Renaissance' or 'rebirth' of knowledge, qualitatively better than any before. Even in Italy itself, that concept has often proved problematic, and the work of giving it precise dates even more so.

Instead, the transition from the characteristically medieval to the characteristically early modern is commonly associated with three other processes, each one firmly rooted in medieval practices and ideas, but producing a distinctively different kind of cultural world. The first is the permanent division of Western Christianity by the Reformation; the second is the European discovery of the Americas, and of a sea route around Africa to Asia; and the third is the development of printing as a device of mass communication. All three were lengthy processes, and each has a different time scale attached. In England, the dividing line has been placed at 1485 because that year removed the Plantagenets, the realm's longest-lived medieval dynasty, from power. In a traditional way of history-writing which privileged national political events, this made sense. Nobody ever believed that Henry VII ushered in modernity as soon as he won the Crown at Bosworth, but that moment made a convenient starting point. Everybody agrees that by 1600 the Middle Ages were over, no matter that bits of them had faded out in the long years between. For Scottish historians, the choice of starting date was less clear because the same royal family carried on; some have preferred 1460 or 1488 to conform to changes of reign, and some 1500, to switch with the century.

It may be possible to do a little better than that. Henry VII was a thoroughly eccentric kind of English ruler, but there is virtually nothing about him that makes him more modern than his three Yorkist predecessors. Even more to the point, Henry VIII commenced his own reign with a self-conscious reversion to best medieval practice, both in his role models and in his policies and attitudes in every branch of government. Of the three markers of emergent early modernity, the printing revo-lution made its slow beginnings before the Tudors took power and had no considerable impact before the sixteenth century. Henry VII certainly makes a good fit with the transoceanic discoveries, by becoming the ruler who, in 1497, gained England its claim to much of North America; but this was achieved by accident, in quest of a trade route to Asia, and had no practical consequences for almost another 100 years. That leaves the Reformation as the dividing line which really counts: not only can it be dated with some precision but it fundamen-tally transformed English political, social and cultural life as well as religion, and had a direct knock-on effect upon Scotland. In two other respects, also, the late 1520s mark a break with the medieval English experience. Although the Wars of the Roses ended in a military sense with the defeat of Perkin Warbeck's rebellion in 1497, Yorkist claimants to the throne, represented by the de la Pole brothers, remained active after then. Not until Richard de la Pole was killed fighting for the French in 1525 was the last of them removed. After that, the Tudors sometimes pruned the edges of their family tree of people who were dangerously closely related, but none of these individuals were consciously reactivating the old vendetta of York against Lancaster. Moreover, 1525 was the last year in which an English ruler seriously considered an attempt to recover any of the large areas of France which his or her medieval forebears had ruled. Ever after that, the focus of England's foreign policy shifted to securing the Channel, while turning more expansive ambitions northwards and westward instead, to Ireland, Scotland and lands across the oceans. For all these reasons, it can be suggested that the Middle Ages ended in Britain between 1525 and 1530, because of developments in England and Wales which were to have a rapid impact upon Scotland as well.

Certainly the injection of a religious element into British politics from 1530 onwards constituted a major shift. Sir Geoffrey Elton may have exaggerated when he termed the reforms in the machinery of central administration between 1535 and 1541 'the Tudor revolution in government', but the simultaneous establishment of the royal supremacy over the English Church and of the Kingdom of Ireland, the removal of all religious houses and confiscation of their land, and the full incorporation of Wales into regular English government, added up to a tremendous refashioning of the English monarchy and state. Thereafter the strains of confessional rivalry, and the emerging primacy of Protestantism in England, produced a range of important results, including the Scottish Reformation and the end of Anglo-Scottish hostility, the Irish Counter-Reformation and the development of religious tensions into the major destabilizing force in that kingdom, and the emergence of literature in English as a major branch of European culture, and the decline of that in Scots, Welsh and Cornish. During the same years the growing strength of English local government enabled the realm to cope with the worst effects of a Continent-wide increase in population and prices and a major climatic downturn. Simultaneously, the failure to keep updating England's medieval system of central government, especially in its fiscal machinery, created serious weaknesses at the heart of the state. It left the nation trapped in a gap between the erosion of its medieval strength as a land power and the development of its later supremacy as a naval power, while still saddled with its medieval pretensions as one of Europe's leading monarchies. The adoption of a new identity as the world's most important Protestant state had the effect of supercharging those pretensions, while not supplying any new resources to support them.

The main potential accession of strength resulting from the change of religion was the ability of England to annex to it the strength of the Scots and Irish, the former as allies and the latter effectively as colonial subjects. A promising initial attempt to do both, between the late sixteenth and early seventeenth centuries, subsequently backfired when the Scots became more radically Protestant than the English, and so attempted to remodel England according to their own needs, while the Irish largely remained Catholic, and so a serious threat to British stability. Four different solutions to the problem were attempted in the course of the mid- seventeenth century. The first was that of Charles I: three independent kingdoms, linked by loyalty to his person and a shared presence at his court, and coming increasingly to adopt slightly different versions of a ceremonious and hierarchical Christianity which shared qualities of Protestantism and Catholicism. The second was that of the Long Parliament and Scottish Covenanters: an Anglo-Scottish partnership of evangelical Protestants which would dominate the entire archipelago through twin national Parliaments. The third was that of the Irish Confederate Catholics: an independent and Catholic-led Irish kingdom, sharing a monarch with equally independent kingdoms of Scotland and England, each of which possessed a distinctive Protestant Church but tolerated Catholicism. The fourth was what was actually achieved under the Commonwealth: a united republic of Britain and Ireland, ruled by evangelical English Protestants. The achievement was short-lived, however, because the rulers of the republic were able to secure neither the willing support of their subjects in any of the three nations nor a stable form of government.

On the whole, the English and Scottish kingdoms coped well with the new strains of religious division in the sixteenth century. They were aided by the fact that, because both possessed successful governmental structures, the growing economic pressures of the time actually worked in their favour by making parish and county leaders cooperate with government rather than turn against it. Both were also fortunate in possessing monarchs of above average ability, though those in Scotland were more accident-prone than most. What imposed dangerous new strains upon both kingdoms was the union of their Crowns, at the same moment as the sovereigns of England acquired an expensive and unstable new neighbouring realm in a conquered Ireland. This situation required rulers who were both able and had an instinctive rapport with their subjects. Fortune did not provide them, as both James and Charles turned out to be the wrong kings for the time and the job, although the former had considerable intelligence and the latter genuine personal virtues, and both fine ideals.

What turned out to be most dangerous in both realms was actually the most enduring legacy there of the Middle Ages. If the medieval machinery of government was adapted to new needs with more or less adequate success, the ideology of royal governance was left too dangerously ill-defined to cope with unfamiliar problems. It consisted of a vague mixture of inherited languages which emphasized at the same time the God-given powers of monarchy, the need of sovereigns to take counsel from subjects and respect their rights, the duty of subjects to be responsible and active citizens and to offer advice to their rulers, the natural division of society into unequal but co-dependent parts, the concept of a nation as both a unified body and a collection of estates, and the need of virtuous people to resist wicked, tyrannical and ungodly governors and counsellors. At moments of acute tension, the potential incompatibilities of these elements could act as powerful corrosives within a body politic which left ill-defined the extent of royal authority in both normal conditions and emergencies and the division of responsibilities between monarch, Lords and Commons.

By 1660 many of the problems of the post-Reformation British kingdoms were on their way to solution. The pressure of a rising population and prices was vanishing, and fear of famine, poverty and crime was declining in most regions as a result, aided by the changing administrative responses which both nations had made. The economies of each were more prosperous and diverse, and England had acquired a safety-valve for population and an increasingly important stimulus to trade, in its trans-Atlantic colonies. The great swelling of religious excitement and expectation in the period between 1560 and 1640 had been lanced by the bloodshed and instability of the following two decades. Godly enthusiasm was now suspect to, rather than admired by, most of the leaders and most of the populations of both kingdoms. The dangerously varied nature of belief, practice and ideal within the post-Reformation Church of England was being eased by the removal from it of the most radical Protestants, the gathered Churches and the Quakers. What had been a tension-ridden established religion had begun to turn, during the years of civil war and republic, into a pluralist religious society. The Scots and Catholic Irish had learned, to their heavy cost, that the English without a king were even more dangerous than with one. Most of both the Scots and the Irish were henceforth devoted supporters of the Stuarts. The Scots no longer wished to intervene in English or Irish affairs, and desired either to be left alone or to achieve closer political and commercial (but not religious) ties with England, to remove any grounds for disagreement between the two realms.

On the whole, however, the two decades before 1660 had been more remarkable for showing which solutions to Britain's various problems would *not* work than those which would. In other important respects, the tensions of the post-Reformation order were peaking at this point. Trials for witchcraft were actually rising in both nations in that year, and those in Scotland were developing into the biggest single witch-hunt in its history. This upsurge would, in the event, be final, and during the following generation convictions for the offence would go into rapid decline all over Britain before ending for ever. In 1660, however, this still seemed very unlikely. Similarly, if religious enthusiasm was becoming unfashionable in many parts of society, sectarian tensions were still at fever pitch, and would lead in a few years to the creation of dissent from both the established churches on an unprecedented scale. Most important, the three great strains in the Early Stuart British polity were still completely unresolved: the question of whether the ultimate power in each land was vested in the sovereign alone or the sovereign in Parliament; the relationship between the Church of England and Kirk of Scotland and compatriots who were discontented with the nature of established religion; and the relationships between the three kingdoms in the Stuart polity. No consensus of ideas or sense of shared guidelines existed for any of these amongst the British, and the new generation of Stuart kings were to prove themselves as incapable as the last two of achieving any. Nor were they any more capable of representing the established national religions, unequivocally and fervently, in the manner of most rulers of the century. All of these problems were to be resolved, permanently, in the 1690s, but thirty turbulent years were needed to reach that point, and sixty more before the settlements achieved then were completely secure.

Both the opening and the terminal dates of this book are therefore skewed. The first, 1485, falls well before the end of the true Middle Ages in Britain, and the four succeeding decades represent arguably a preparation for the great changes to come, and certainly a culmination of the traditional polity and society which were now to be transformed. The second date of 1660 marks the beginning of the process by which the reformed kingdoms and nations of Scotland and England, created by that transformation, were successfully repaired after their complete breakdown. That process was not to achieve even the first stages of success for another three decades. We may agree that Britain passed out of the Middle Ages in the sixteenth century, but by 1660 it was still seeking a lasting new form.

FURTHER READING

Chapter 1 – Henry VII

For many years the standard heavyweight biography was S. B. Chrimes, *Henry VII* (Eyre Methuen, 1972), which was better on the administrative history of the reign than its other aspects and did nothing to rescue it from a reputation for greyness. Now we have Sean Cunningham, *Henry VII* (Routledge, 2007), a warmer and more thorough account. Another historian well qualified to produce a new treatment of the reign is Steven Gunn, who published an overview of it in the *Oxford Dictionary of National Biography* (Oxford University Press, 2004). Other aspects of his work are 'The Court of Henry VII', in Steven Gunn and Antheun Janse (eds), *The Court as a Stage; England and the Low Countries in the Later Middle Ages* (Boydell, 2006), and 'Henry VII in Context', *History* (2007).

Two historians whose views are quoted in the text, and have had some impact on the ideas provided there, are Alexander Grant, from his lively pamphlet *Henry VII*, 2nd edn (Routledge, 1989), and Christine Carpenter, from her important and polemical textbook, *The Wars of the Roses* (Cambridge University Press, 1998). A short and useful treatment to supplement that by Sandy Grant is Roger Lockyer and Andrew Thrush, *Henry VII*, 3rd edn (Longman, 1997). Also valuable for an understanding of Henry and his regime have been Ian Arthurson, *The Perkin Warbeck Conspiracy* (Sutton, 1994); Benjamin Thompson (ed.), *The Reign of Henry VII* (Harlaxton Medieval Studies, 1995); Mark R. Horowitz, '"Agree with the King": Henry VII, Edmund Dudley and the Strange Case of Thomas Sunnyff', *Historical Research*, 79 (2006), pp. 325–66; and P. R. Cavill, 'Debate and Dissent in Henry VII's Parliaments', *Parliamentary History*, (2006).

Chapter 2 – Henry VIII

The last fully researched, heavyweight biography was J. J. Scarisbrick, *Henry VIII* (Eyre and Spottiswoode, 1968). More recently, we have good profiles of the king and reign in Michael A. R. Graves, *Henry VIII* (Pearson, 2003) and Eric Ives's entry on Henry in the *Oxford Dictionary of National Biography* (2004); a collection of essays in Diarmaid MacCulloch (ed.), *The Reign of Henry VIII* (Macmillan, 1995); and helpful textbook surveys in John Guy, *Tudor England* (Oxford University Press, 1988); Susan Brigden, *New Worlds, Lost Worlds* (Penguin, 2000); and Richard Rex, *The Tudors* (Tempus, 2002). David Starkey, *Henry: Virtuous Prince* (HarperPress, 2008) is the first instalment of what should be the full biography to replace Scarisbrick. Glenn Richardson, *Renaissance Monarchy* (Arnold, 2002) puts Henry into a European perspective.

Specialist studies of Wolsey's ministry are represented by Peter Gwyn, *The King's Cardinal* (Barne and Jenkins, 1990) and S. J. Gunn and P. G. Lindley (eds), *Cardinal Wolsey* (Cambridge University Press, 1991). There is a useful insight into his treatment of heresy in Craig W. D'Alton, 'The Suppression of Lutheran Heretics in England 1526–1529', *Journal of Ecclesiastical History* (2003). The famous textbook by Sir Geoffrey Elton was G. R. Elton, *England under the*

Tudors (Methuen, 1955), which went into its third edition in 1991. Sir Geoffrey's ideas about the reforms of the 1530s were embodied in *The Tudor Revolution in Government* (Cambridge University Press, 1953), and challenged in Christopher Coleman and David Starkey (eds), *Revolution Reassessed* (Oxford University Press, 1986). The result was a debate between Elton and Starkey in the *Historical Journal* in 1987–8. Elton's legacy to Tudor historians was discussed by a collection of contributors in the *Transactions of the Royal Historical Society* (1997). Further reflections on the nature of Henrician government can be found in the textbook by John Guy, above, and in David Starkey, 'Court, Council and Nobility in Tudor England', in Ronald G. Asch and Adolf M. Birke (eds), *Princes, Patronage and the Nobility* (Oxford University Press, 1991); Greg Walker, 'Henry VIII and the Invention of the Royal Court', *History Today* (1997); S. J. Gunn, *Early Tudor Government* (Macmillan, 1995) and 'The Structures of Politics in Early Tudor England', *Transactions of the Royal Historical Society* (1995); David Loades, *Power in Tudor England* (Macmillan, 1997); J. P. D. Cooper, *Propaganda and the Tudor State* (Oxford University Press, 2003); and Roger Schofield, *Taxation under the Early Tudors 1485–1547* (Blackwell, 2004). The fleet is well covered in David Loades, *The Tudor Navy* (Scolar, 1992).

Anybody still under the illusion that a scholarly consensus can be achieved over the course, cause and meaning of Henrician court politics should read the following: John Guy, *The Public Career of Sir Thomas More* (Yale University Press, 1980) and *Thomas More* (Arnold, 2000); David Starkey, *The Reign of Henry VIII* (G. Philip, 1985), and *Six Wives: The Queens of Henry VIII* (Vintage, 2004); Barbara J. Harris, *Edward Stafford, Third Duke of Buckingham* (Stanford University Press, 1986); E. W. Ives, *Anne Boleyn* (Blackwell, 1986); R. M. Warnicke, *The Rise and Fall of Anne Boleyn* (Cambridge University Press, 1989), 'Anne Boleyn Revisited', *Historical Journal* (1991), and *The Marrying of Anne of Cleves*

(Cambridge University Press, 2000); Glyn Redworth, *In Defence of the Church Catholic: The Life of Stephen Gardiner* (Blackwell, 1990); the debate between Eric Ives and George Bernard over the fall of Anne Boleyn in the *English Historical Review* (1992); the discussion between Eric Ives and Ralph Houlbrooke over Henry VIII's will in the *Historical Journal* (1992 and 1994); the debate between George Bernard, Eric Ives and Thomas Freeman over Anne Boleyn's religion in the *Historical Journal* (1993–5); Joseph S. Block, *Factional Politics and the English Reformation* (Boydell, 1993); Diarmaid MacCulloch, *Thomas Cranmer* (Yale University Press, 1996); George Bernard, 'The Fall of Wolsey Reconsidered', *Journal of British Studies* (1996), *Power and Politics in Tudor England* (Ashgate, 2000) and *The King's Reformation* (Yale University Press, 2005); Geoffrey Gibbons, *The Political Career of Thomas Wriothesley* (Mellon, 2001) Greg Walker, 'Rethinking the Fall of Anne Boleyn', *Historical Journal* (2002) and *Writing Under Tyranny: English Literature and the Henrician Reformation* (Oxford University Press, 2005); and Rory McEntegart, *Henry VIII, the League of Schmalkalden, and the English Reformation* (Boydell Press, 2002).

Many of the works listed above deal with the politics that created the Henrician Reformation, for which, in addition, there are Glyn Redworth, 'The Genesis and Evolution of the Act of Six Articles', *Journal of Ecclesiastical History* (1986); Paul Ayris and David Selwyn (eds), *Thomas Cranmer* (Boydell Press, 1993); D. G. Newcombe, *Henry VIII and the English Reformation* (Routledge, 1995); J. Christopher Warner, *Henry VIII's Divorce* (Boydell, 1998); R. W. Hoyle, *The Pilgrimage of Grace and the Politics of the 1530s* (Oxford University Press, 2001); Alec Ryrie, *The Gospel and Henry VIII* (Cambridge University Press, 2003); and Richard Rex, *Henry VIII and the English Reformation*, 2nd edn (Palgrave, 2006).

The great revisionist texts of English Reformation scholarship were J. J. Scarisbrick, *The Reformation and the English People* (Blackwell, 1984); Christopher Haigh (ed.), *The English*

Reformation Revised (Cambridge University Press, 1987); Eamon Duffy, *The Stripping of the Altars* (Yale University Press, 1992); and Christopher Haigh, *English Reformations* (Oxford University Press, 1993). Works which built upon or amended these include Glyn Redworth, 'The Henrician Reform of the Church', *History Today* (1987); R. N. Swanson, *Church and Society in Late Medieval England* (Blackwell, 1989); John A. F. Thomson, *The Early Tudor Church and Society* (Longman, 1993); Peter Marshall, *The Catholic Priesthood and the English Reformation* (Oxford University Press, 1994), *Reformation England 1480–1642* (Arnold, 2003), and *Religious Identities in Henry VIII's England* (Ashgate, 2006); Andrew D. Brown, *Popular Piety in Late Medieval England* (Oxford University Press, 1995); Diarmaid MacCulloch, 'The Impact of the English Reformation', *Historical Journal* (1995), and 'The Change of Religion', in Patrick Collinson (ed.), *The Short Oxford History of the British Isles: The Sixteenth Century* (Oxford University Press, 2002), and 'Putting the English Reformation on the Map', *Transactions of the Royal Historical Society* (2005); Clayton F. Dress, *Authority and Dissent in the English Church* (Mellon, 1997); Lucy E. C. Wooding, *Rethinking Catholicism in Reformation England* (Oxford University Press, 2000) (but see the reply by C. D. C. Armstrong in the *Journal of Ecclesiastical History* in 2003); Kenneth Carton, *Bishops and Reform in the English Church 1520–1560* (Boydell Press, 2001); Peter Marshall and Alec Ryrie (eds), *The Beginnings of English Protestantism* (Cambridge University Press, 2002); Ethan Shagan, *Popular Politics and the English Reformation* (Cambridge University Press, 2002); Marjo Kaartinen, *Religious Life and English Culture in the Reformation* (Palgrave, 2002); James Clark (ed.), *The Religious Orders in Pre-Reformation England* (Boydell, 2002); Felicity Heal, *Reformation in Britain and Ireland* (Oxford University Press, 2003); and Karl Gunther and Ethan H. Shagan, 'Protestant Radicalism and Political Thought in the Reign of Henry VIII',

Past and Present (2007). The best work to put the English Reformation in the context of the European whole is Diarmaid MacCulloch's blockbusting *Reformation* (Allen Lane, 2003).

Most of the earlier local studies that revised the traditional view of the Henrician Reformation are absorbed into the titles above. Most influential since 1980 have been Margaret Bowker, *The Henrician Reformation* (Cambridge University Press, 1981); John Davis, *Heresy and Reformation in the South-East of England 1520–1559* (Royal Historical Society, 1983); Norman P. Tanner, *The Church in Late Medieval Norwich 1370–1532* (Pontifical Institute of Medieval Studies, 1984); Diarmaid MacCulloch, *Suffolk and the Tudors* (Oxford University Press, 1986); Robert Whiting, *The Blind Devotion of the People* (Cambridge University Press, 1989); Susan Brigden, *London and the Reformation* (Oxford University Press, 1989); Beat A. Kumin, *The Shaping of a Community: The Rise and Reformation of the English Parish c. 1400–1560* (Scolar, 1990); Martha C. Skeeters, *Community and Clergy* (Oxford University Press, 1993); Ronald Hutton, *The Rise and Fall of Merry England* (Oxford University Press, 1994); Patrick Collinson and John Craig (eds), *The Reformation in English Towns 1500–1640* (Macmillan, 1998); Caroline Litzenberger, *The English Reformation and the Laity* (Cambridge University Press, 1999); Eamon Duffy, *The Voices of Morebath* (Yale University Press, 2001); and Robert Lutton, *Lollardy and Orthodox Piety in Pre-Reformation England* (Boydell Press, 2006).

Chapter 3 – The Mid-Tudor Regimes

Many of the titles listed above under Henry VIII's reign are also valuable for this period, especially Guy, *Tudor England*; Rex, *The Tudors*; Marshall, *Reformation England*; Haigh, *English Reformations*; Duffy, *The Stripping of the Altars*; MacCulloch, *Thomas Cranmer*; and my own *Rise and Fall of Merry England*.

The basic outlines of recent thought upon it were set out in Jennifer Loach and Robert Tittler (eds), *The Mid-Tudor*

Polity (Macmillan, 1980) and Jennifer Loach, *A Mid-Tudor Crisis* (Historical Association, 1990), and are reviewed with a special eye on school classes by Stephen J. Lee, *The Mid Tudors* (Routledge, 2007). The traditional admiring view of Somerset's regime was demolished by M. L. Bush, *The Government Policy of Protector Somerset* (Arnold, 1975). David Loades, *John Dudley, Duke of Northumberland* (Headstart History, 1996) is a sound narrative study, and Jennifer Loach, *Edward VI* (Yale University Press, 1999) important though limited by the author's tragically premature death. The Edwardian Reformation is gloriously portrayed in Diarmaid MacCulloch, *Tudor Church Militant* (Allen Lane, 1999), supplemented by Catherine Davies, *A Religion of the Word* (Manchester University Press, 2002). Edwardian political culture is treated by Stephen Alford, *Kingship and Politics in the Reign of Edward VI* (Cambridge University Press, 2002). Arguably, David Loades, *Mary Tudor* (Blackwell, 1989) does not engage sufficiently with revisionist views of her reign, while Linda Porter, *Mary Tudor* (Portrait, 2007) does so too readily. Mary's Church has recently been intensively studied in John Edwards and Ronald Truman (eds), *Reforming Catholicism in the Church of Mary Tudor* (Ashgate, 2005); Eamon Duffy and David Loades (eds), *The Church of Mary Tudor* (Ashgate, 2006); and William Wizeman, *The Theology and Spirituality of Mary Tudor's Church* (Ashgate, 2006).

Chapter 4 – Interlude: Rebellion in Tudor England
The original textbook that formed the subject was Anthony Fletcher, *Tudor Rebellions* (Longman, 1968), which went into its fifth edition in 2004, updated by Diarmaid MacCulloch. The latter's famous revisionist article was 'Kett's Rebellion in Context', which appeared in *Past and Present* in 1979, while the snapshot of the Earl of Arundel at work was provided by Lawrence Stone, 'Patriarchy and Paternalism in Tudor England', in the *Journal of British Studies* (1973–4).

Several of the titles already listed are important for this subject, especially Shagan, *Popular Politics and the English Reformation*; Bernard, *The King's Reformation*; Hoyle, *The Pilgrimage of Grace*; and Cooper, *Propaganda and the Tudor State*. Individual rebellions are studied in Michael Bush, *The Pilgrimage of Grace* (Manchester University Press, 1996); K. J. Kesselring, *The Northern Rebellion of 1569* (Palgrave, 2007); and Andy Wood, *The 1549 Rebellions and the Making of Early Modern England* (Cambridge University Press, 2007), which is the most sophisticated examination of a Tudor uprising yet made. The best overall recent reflection on the subject is also by Andy Wood: *Riot, Rebellion and Popular Politics in Early Modern England* (Palgrave, 2001).

Chapter 5 – Scotland

The most recent survey book is Jane Dawson, *Scotland Re-Formed 1488–1587* (Edinburgh University Press, 2007), though Jenny Wormald, *Court, Kirk and Community* (Arnold, 1981) and Alexander Grant, 'Crown and Nobility in Later Medieval Britain', in Roger Mason (ed.), *Scotland and England 1286–1815* (John Donald, 1987) still have bite. The kings are covered by Norman Macdougall, *James III* (John Donald, 1982) and *James IV* (John Donald, 1989), and his pupil Jamie Cameron, *James V* (Tuckwell, 1998), while other leading politicians get biographies from Margaret Sampson, *Cardinal of Scotland: David Beaton* (John Donald, 1986) and Pamela Ritchie, *Mary of Guise in Scotland, 1548–1560* (Tuckwell, 2002). Particular episodes are tackled by Alec Ryrie, *The Origins of the Scottish Reformation* (Manchester University Press, 2006); Peter Reese, *Flodden* (Birlinn, 2003) and Marcus Merriman, *The Rough Wooings* (Tuckwell, 2000).

Chapter 6 – Elizabeth I

The most detailed study of the reign since 1960 has been in the three successive volumes by Wallace MacCaffrey: *The Making of the Elizabethan Regime* (Jonathan Cape, 1969); *Elizabeth and the Making of Policy 1572–1588* (Princeton University Press, 1981); and *Elizabeth I: War and Politics 1588–1603* (Princeton University Press, 1992), followed by his one-volume digest, *Elizabeth I* (Arnold, 1993). Christopher Haigh's sparkling revisionist study is *Elizabeth I*, 2nd edn (Longman, 1998), while his edition of essays, *The Reign of Elizabeth I* (Macmillan, 1984) contains contributions on several aspects of the subject which still matter. John Guy (ed.), *The Reign of Elizabeth I* (Cambridge University Press, 1995) makes an important consideration of the final one and a half decades. David Starkey, *Elizabeth: Apprenticeship* (Chatto & Windus, 2000) is a bestselling account of her formative years, and Susan Doran, *Monarchy and Matrimony* (Routledge, 1996) is the classic work on her courtships. The 400th anniversary of her death brought Patrick Collinson's portrait in the *Oxford Dictionary of National Biography* (Oxford University Press, 2004); Carole Levin, Jo Eldridge Carney and Debra Barrett Graves (eds), *Elizabeth I* (Ashgate, 2003); David Loades, *Elizabeth 1* (Hambledon Continuum, 2003), and a set of essays in *History Today* (May 2003); all useful. The 2004 volume of *Transactions of the Royal Society* was dedicated to papers reviewing the reign, and an analysis designed for school students has appeared from Stephen Lee, *The Reign of Elizabeth I* (Routledge, 2007). Elizabeth's reputation has been studied in Patrick Collinson's essay, 'Elizabeth I and the Verdicts of History', in *Historical Research* (2003), and Susan Doran and Thomas Freeman (eds), *The Myth of Elizabeth* (Palgrave Macmillan, 2003). Some more general works already mentioned, Guy, *Tudor England*, and Rex, *The Tudors*, have interesting things to say about the reign. 'My' Elizabeth is closest to Christopher Haigh's, with some resemblance to those of Susan Doran and David Starkey.

The queen's main ministers and courtiers have all been well studied: Lord Burghley by Michael Graves, *Burghley* (Longman, 1998) and Stephen Alford, *Burghley* (Yale University Press, 2008); the Earl of Leicester by Simon Adams,

Leicester and the Court (Manchester University Press, 2002); and the Earl of Essex by Paul Hammer, *The Polarisation of Elizabethan Politics* (Cambridge University Press, 1999).

There has been little on the machinery of Elizabethan government in recent years, as historians have been more interested in political culture, and for overall surveys readers need to go back to Penry Williams, *The Tudor Regime* (Oxford University Press, 1979), and Guy, *Tudor England*. Between 1985 and 1992 there was a flurry of important publications on Parliaments: Michael Graves, *The Tudor Parliaments* (Longman, 1985); G. R. Elton, *The Parliament of England 1559–1581* (Cambridge University Press, 1986); D. M. Dean and N. L. Jones (eds), *The Parliaments of Elizabethan England* (Blackwell, 1990); Jennifer Loach, *Parliament under the Tudors* (Oxford University Press, 1991); and T. E. Hartley, *Elizabeth's Parliaments* (Manchester University Press, 1992). Conrad Russell's survey of developing administrative problems is found in *The Causes of the English Civil War* (Oxford University Press, 1990). The best books on Elizabethan political culture are all from Cambridge University Press: Stephen Alford, *The Early Elizabethan Polity* (1998); Anne N. McLaren, *Political Culture in the Reign of Elizabeth I* (1999); and Natalie Mears, *Queenship and Political Discourse in the Elizabethan Realms* (2005).

Some books cited earlier are very important for Elizabethan religion: MacCulloch, *The Later Reformation in England*; Haigh, *English Reformations*; Heal, *Reformation in Britain and Ireland*; Wooding, *Rethinking Catholicism*; and Marshall, *Reformation England*. Peter Lake, *Anglicans and Puritans?* (Allen and Unwin, 1988) has also been relevant to this section, as has Diarmaid MacCulloch's pamphlet, *Building a Godly Realm* (Historical Association, 1992) and Susan Doran, *Elizabeth I and Religion* (Routledge, 1994). More recently, we have Susan Doran's essay, 'Elizabeth I's Religion', *Journal of Ecclesiastical History* (2000); Peter Lake and Michael Questier (eds), *Conformity and Orthodoxy in the English Church c. 1560–1660*

(Boydell, 2000); and Brett Usher, *William Cecil and Episcopacy 1559–1577* (Ashgate, 2003).

The classic revisionist works on Catholicism were John Bossy, *The English Catholic Community 1570–1850* (Dalton, Longman and Todd, 1975), and Christopher Haigh, 'The Continuity of Catholicism in the English Reformation', *Past and Present* (1981). The recent works of reintegration include Alexandra Walsham, *Church Papists* (Boydell Press, 1993); Michael Questier, 'What Happened to English Catholicism after the English Reformation?', *History* (2000); Peter Lake with Michael Questier, *The Anti-Christ's Lewd Hat* (Yale University Press, 2002); and Ethan Shagan (ed.), *Catholics and the Protestant Nation* (Manchester University Press, 2005).

The 400th anniversary of the Spanish Armada saw a spate of important publication on Elizabethan warfare and foreign policy: Andrew Pettegree, 'Elizabethan Foreign Policy', *Historical Journal* (1988); Colin Martin and Geoffrey Parker, *The Spanish Armada*, 2nd edn (Mandolin, 1999); Simon Adams, *The Armada Campaign of 1588* (Historical Association, 1988); and Felipe Fernandez-Armesto, *The Spanish Armada* (Oxford University Press, 1988). Since then we have Loades's *The Tudor Navy*, and the relevant chapters in Doran and Richardson (eds), *Tudor England and its Neighbours*, plus Susan Doran, *Elizabeth I and Foreign Policy* (Routledge, 2000); Mark Charles Fissel, *English Warfare 1511–1642* (Routledge, 2001); and Paul Hammer, *Elizabeth's Wars* (Palgrave Macmillan, 2003).

For Scotland in the late sixteenth century, as earlier, Wormald, *Court, Kirk and Community*, and Dawson, *Scotland Re-Formed*, represent excellent old and new syntheses. The Queen of Scots continues to attract biographers in large numbers, and readers are invited to compare Jenny Wormald, *Mary, Queen of Scots* (George Philip, 1988); Michael Lynch (ed.), *Mary Stewart, Queen in Three Kingdoms* (Blackwell, 1988); John Guy, *'My Heart is My Own': The Life of Mary, Queen of Scots* (Fourth Estate, 2004); Retha M. Warnicke,

Mary, Queen of Scots (Routledge, 2006); Susan Doran, *Mary, Queen of Scots* (British Library, 2007); and Kristen Post Walton, *Catholic Queen, Protestant Patriarchy* (Palgrave Macmillan, 2007). Just for the record, my own favourites among these are Wormald and Guy, the former as a magnificent example of hostile polemic and the latter as a triumph of the biographer's art.

Steven G. Ellis's thesis was set out most clearly in *Tudor Ireland* (Longman, 1985); 'Economic Problems of the Church', *Journal of Ecclesiastical History* (1990); and 'The Collapse of the Gaelic World, 1450–1650', *Irish Historical Studies* (1999). A huge number of recent monographs have been synthesized in S. J. Connolly, *Contested Island: Ireland 1460–1630* (Oxford University Press, 2007). Of slightly older work, Bruce Lenman, *Engand's Colonial Wars 1550–1688* (Longman, 2001), and Alan Ford and John MacCafferty (eds), *The Origins of Sectarianism in Early Modern Ireland* (Cambridge University Press, 2005), retain distinction, to which should now be added David Edwards, Pádraig Lenihan and Clodagh Tait (eds), *Age of Atrocity: Violence and Political Conflict in Early Modern Ireland* (Four Courts, 2007).

Chapter 7 – Post-Reformation Britain
The classic textbooks of early modern English social history are Keith Wrightson, *English Society 1580–1680* (Hutchinson, 1982); Barry Reay, *Popular Cultures in England 1550–1750* (Longman, 1998); and J. A. Sharpe, *Early Modern England*, 2nd edn (Arnold, 1997). For religious and magical belief, the canonical work is Keith Thomas, *Religion and the Decline of Magic* (last reprinted by Weidenfeld, 1997). There are no real equivalents for Scotland and Wales, the nearest being T. C. Smout, *A History of the Scottish People 1560–1830* (Collins, 1969); R. A. Houston and I. D. Whyte (eds), *Scottish Society 1500–1800* (Cambridge University Press, 1989); and Glanmor Williams, *Recovery, Reorientation and Reformation: Wales c. 1415–1642* (Oxford University Press, 1987).

Interest in popular rioting and protest burgeoned among historians after 1968, when contemporaries in the Western world took up the same activities on a large scale. Especially relevant to the present book are Buchanan Sharp, *In Contempt of All Authority* (University of California Press, 1979); Keith Lindley, *Fenland Riots and the English Revolution* (Heinemann, 1982); K. J. Lindley, 'Riot Prevention and Control in Early Stuart London', *Transactions of the Royal Historical Society* (1983); David Underdown, *Revel, Riot and Rebellion* (Oxford University Press, 1985); Anthony Fletcher and John Stevenson (eds), *Order and Disorder in Early Modern England* (Cambridge University Press, 1985); and Roger Manning, *Village Revolts* (Oxford University Press, 1988). During the 2000s, interest revived in the topic, this time influenced by anthropology and represented by Alison Wall, *Power and Protest in England 1525–1640* (Arnold, 2000); Andy Wood's *Riot, Rebellion and Popular Politics*, mentioned earlier; Tim Harris (ed.), *The Politics of the Excluded c. 1500 and 1640* (Palgrave, 2001); and John Walter, *Crowds and Popular Politics in Early Modern England* (Manchester University Press, 2006). It was allied to a growing interest by historians in the nature of governance, typified in this context by Ian W. Archer, *The Pursuit of Stability* (Cambridge University Press, 1991); Paul Griffiths, Adam Fox and Steve Hindle (eds), *The Experience of Authority in Early Modern England* (Macmillan, 1996); Steve Hindle, *The State and Social Change in Early Modern England c. 1550–1640* (Macmillan, 2000); Michael J. Braddick, *State Formation in Early Modern England* (Cambridge University Press, 2000); and Michael J. Braddick and John Walter (eds), *Negotiating Power in Early Modern England* (Cambridge University Press, 2001).

The classic textbook on crime is J. A. Sharpe, *Crime in Early Modern* England, 2nd edn (Longman, 1999). Alan Macfarlane, *The Justice and the Mare's Ale* (Blackwell, 1984) was very influential in its time and still matters, and other important works on the subject include Lawrence Stone,

'Interpersonal Violence in English Society 1300–1980', *Past and Present* (1983); Cynthia B. Herrup, *The Common Peace* (Cambridge University Press, 1987); Malcolm Gaskill, *Crime and Mentalities in Early Modern England* (Cambridge University Press, 2000); and K. J. Kesselring, *Mercy and Authority in the Tudor State* (Cambridge University Press, 2003). The major publications on the place of alehouses are Peter Clark, *The English Alehouse* (Longman, 1983) and Keith Wrightson's essay in Eileen and Stephen Yeo (eds), *Popular Culture and Class Conflict 1590–1914* (Harvester, 1982). A. L. Beier, *Masterless Men* (Methuen, 1985) is the staple work on vagrancy, and Paul Slack is the main historian of poor relief, in *Poverty and Policy in Tudor and Stuart England* (Longman, 1988) and *From Reformation to Improvement: Public Welfare in Early Modern England* (Oxford University Press, 1999). Knowledge of the poor law has been greatly extended by Steve Hindle, *On the Parish? The Micro-Politics of Poor Relief in Rural England c. 1550–1750* (Oxford University Press, 2004). To the information in these can be added Richard M. Smith (ed.), *Land, Kinship and Life-Cycle* (Cambridge University Press, 1984); A. L. Beier et al. (eds), *The First Modern Society* (Cambridge University Press, 1989); Ian D. Archer, 'The Charity of Early Modern Londoners', *Transactions of the Royal Historical Society* (2002); and Paul A. Fideler, *Social Welfare in Pre-Industrial England* (Palgrave, 2006). The groundbreaking study of Scottish feuding was Keith Brown, *Bloodfeud in Scotland 1573–1625* (John Donald, 1986).

Research into crisis mortality has languished since 1995, so we depend still upon the famous studies made before then: Andrew B. Appleby, *Famine in Tudor and Stuart England* (Liverpool University Press, 1978); John Walter and Roger Schofield (eds), *Famine, Disease and the Social Order in Early Modern Society* (Cambridge University Press, 1989); E. A. Wrigley and R. S. Schofield, *The Population History of England 1541–1871* (Cambridge University Press, 1989); Paul

Slack, *The Impact of Plague in Tudor and Stuart England*, 2nd edn (Oxford University Press, 1990); David Palliser, *The Age of Elizabeth*, 2nd edn (Longman, 1992); and R. A. Houston, *The Population History of Britain and Ireland 1500–1750* (Cambridge University Press, 1995).

Popular religion is treated in Christopher Durston and Jacqueline Eales (eds), *The Culture of English Puritanism* (Macmillan, 1996); Christopher Marsh, *Popular Religion in Sixteenth-Century England* (Macmillan, 1998); John Spurr, *The Post Reformation* (Pearson, 2006); and Christopher Haigh, *The Plain Man's Pathways to Heaven: Kinds of Christianity in Post-Reformation England* (Oxford University Press, 2007). My thoughts on the impact of the English Reformation were worked out in various conversations with Jack Scarisbrick. The famous Scottish equivalent to the English cultural histories is Margo Todd, *The Culture of Protestantism in Early Modern Scotland* (Yale University Press, 2002), though Michael Lynch's essay in Menna Prestwich (ed.), *International Calvinism 1559–1638* (Oxford University Press, 1985) is still a useful overall survey.

The pioneering study of witch trials and beliefs in England was Alan Macfarlane, *Witchcraft in Tudor and Stuart England*, (2nd edn (Routledge, 1999), and the Scottish equivalent was Christina Larner, *Enemies of God* (reprinted by John Donald, 2000). James Sharpe subsequently became the leading expert on the English material, with *Instruments of Darkness* (Hamilton, 1996) and *Witchcraft in Early Modern England* (Longman, 2001), while Malcolm Gaskill provided a full-length study of the Matthew Hopkins episode in *Witchfinders* (John Murray, 2005). Larner's work has been followed up most productively to date by the Survey of Scottish Witchcraft project, with its website and two collections of essays, Julian Goodare (ed.), *The Scottish Witch-Hunt in Context* (Manchester University Press, 2002) and Julian Goodare, Lauren Martin and Joyce Miller (eds), *Witchcraft and Belief in Early Modern Scotland* (Palgrave Macmillan, 2008).

Family and gender history is well considered in some of the works listed above, but much augmented by Roy Porter and Sylvana Tomaselli (eds), *Rape* (Blackwell, 1986); Martin Ingram, *Church Courts, Sex and Marriage in England 1570–1640* (Cambridge University Press, 1987); Alan Bray, 'Homosexuality and the Signs of Male Friendship in Early Modern England', *History Workshop* (1990); Amy Louise Erikson, *Women and Property in Early Modern England* (Routledge, 1993); Anne Laurence, *Women in England 1500–1750* (Weidenfeld, 1994); Ilana Kraussman Ben-Amos, *Adolescence and Youth in Early Modern England* (Yale University Press, 1994); Amanda Shephard, *Gender and Authority in Sixteenth-Century England* (Keele University Press, 1994); Jenny Kermode and Garthine Walker (eds), *Women, Crime and the Courts in Early Modern England* (University College London Press, 1994); Anthony Fletcher, *Gender, Sex and Subordination in England 1500–1800* (Yale University Press, 1995); Garthine Walker, *Crime, Gender and Social Order in Early Modern England* (Cambridge University Press, 2003); and Alexandra Shepard, *Meanings of Manhood in Early Modern England* (Oxford University Press, 2003).

Kenneth R. Andrew has been the great authority on Elizabethan seafaring and the foundation of the First British Empire, in a series of books stretching from *Elizabethan Privateering* (Cambridge University Press, 1964) to *Trade, Plunder and Settlement* (Cambridge University Press, 1984). To these need to be added N. A. M. Rodger on the navy, in *The Safeguard of the Sea* (HarperCollins, 2004), and Susan Ronald, *The Pirate Queen* (HarperCollins, 2007), who is very good on the Elizabethan explorers and privateers, though more shaky in understanding their general context. Richard Helgerson, *Forms of Nationhood* (University of Chicago Press, 1992) is a fine all-round, though excessively optimistic, assessment of the Elizabethan cultural achievement. For the impact of print and plays, especially in London, see Joad Raymond, *Pamphlets and Pamphleteering in Early Modern England* (Cambridge

University Press, 2003); Lake and Questier, *The AntiChrist's Lewd Hat*; and Peter Lake and Steve Pincus, 'Rethinking the Public Sphere in Early Modern England', *Journal of British Studies* (2006).

The 'British Problem' was formulated and examined in 1990 in a series of collections of essays: Ronald Asch (ed.), *Three Nations: A Common History?* (Arbeitskreis Deutsche England-Forschung, 1993); Steven G. Ellis and Sarah Barber (eds), *Conquest and Union: Fashioning a British State* (Longman, 1995); Alexander Grant and Keith J. Stringer (eds), *Uniting the Kingdom? The Making of British History* (Routledge, 1995); Brendan Bradshaw and John Morrill (eds), *The British Problem c. 1534–1707* (Macmillan, 1996); Brendan Bradshaw and Peter Roberts (eds), *British Consciousness and Identity* (Cambridge University Press, 1998); and Glenn Burgess (ed.), *The New British History* (Tauris, 1999). The last of these was Allan Macinnes and Jane Ohlmeyer (eds), *The Stuart Kingdoms in the Seventeenth Century* (Four Courts, 2002). Steven Ellis's ideas have been most recently summed up in his survey work written with Christopher Maginn, *The Making of the British Isles* (Pearson Longman, 2007).

Chapter 8 – The Early Stuarts

Four different textbooks complement each other in covering English political history in the period. In an ideal world, newcomers should start with Barry Coward, *The Stuart Age*, 3rd edn (Pearson, 2003), which covers the years 1603 to 1714 and provides the basic facts with a balanced historiographical perspective. Then should come Derek Hirst, *England in Conflict* (Arnold, 1999), providing a more detailed narrative and analysis of the events of 1603 to 1660 from a post-revisionist viewpoint. This can be compared, where they overlap, with Austin Woolrych, *Britain in Revolution* (Oxford University Press, 2002), a dense narrative study of the period from 1625 to 1660. Finally, there is Jonathan Scott's *England's Troubles* (Cambridge University Press, 2000), which is a clever maverick reinterpretation of the Stuart age, 1603 to 1714, best read by those who are familiar with the period. Important essays by John Morrill and Conrad Russell were published in Anthony Fletcher and Peter Roberts (eds), *Religion, Culture and Society in Early Modern Britain* (Cambridge University Press, 1994). David Underdown's lectures, *A Freeborn People* (Oxford University Press, 1996), cover popular politics in the early to mid-seventeenth century, and Kevin Sharpe, *Representations and Revolutions* (Yale University Press, 2009) the way in which regimes portrayed themselves, in print and visual image, during the same period.

Jenny Wormald's pioneering revisionist essay on King James was 'James VI and 1: Two Kings or One?', *History* (1983), and this can be compared with her more measured assessment in the *Oxford Dictionary of National Biography* (Oxford University Press, 2004). Maurice Lee's view is summed up in *Great Britain's Solomon* (University of Illinois Press, 1990), and Pauline Croft's in *King James* (Palgrave Macmillan, 2003). In addition the 400th anniversary of his accession produced Glenn Burgess, Rowland Wyther and Jason Lawrence (eds), *The Accession of James I* (Palgrave Macmillan, 2003) and Diane Newton, *The Making of the Jacobean Regime* (Boydell Press, 2005), followed by Ralph Houlbrooke (ed.), *James VI and I* (Ashgate, 2006). Particular aspects of the king's rulership are covered in W. B. Patterson, *King James VI and I and the Reunion of Christendom* (Cambridge University Press, 1997) and Michael Young, *James VI and I and the History of Homosexuality* (Macmillan, 2000).

The early Stuart royal courts are treated in two essays in David Starkey (ed.), *The English Court from the Wars of the Roses to the Civil War* (Longman, 1987), and three in John Morrill, Paul Slack and Daniel Woolf (eds), *Public Duty and Private Conscience in Seventeenth-Century England* (Oxford University Press, 1993). The court of James is the subject of Linda Levy Peck (ed.), *The Mental World of the Jacobean Court* (Cambridge University Press, 1991), Linda Levy Peck,

Court Patronage and Corruption in Early Stuart England (Unwin Hyman, 1990), and Alastair Bellany, *The Politics of Court Scandal in Early Modern England* (Cambridge University Press, 2002). The key biographies of Jacobean ministers are Roger Lockyer, *Buckingham* (Longman, 1981) and Linda Levy Peck, *Northampton* (Allen and Unwin, 1982).

The best overall textbooks on early Stuart English religion are Susan Doran and Christopher Durston, *Princes, Pastors and People* (Routledge, 1991), and Andrew Foster, *The Church of England 1570–1640* (Longman, 1994), while with a lighter touch Peter Marshall, *Reformation England* is as good on that period as he is on the Tudors. Kenneth Fincham and Nicholas Tyacke, *Altars Restored* (Oxford University Press, 2007) is a detailed survey of worship in the established Church from 1547 to 1700. Key works upon the early Stuart Church of England are Nicholas Tyacke, *Anti-Calvinists* (Oxford University Press, 1987); Peter White, *Predestination, Policy and Polemic* (Cambridge University Press, 1992); Kenneth Fincham (ed.), *The Early Stuart Church* (Macmillan, 1993); Anthony Milton, *Catholic and Reformed: The Roman and Protestant Churches in English Protestant Thought, 1600–1640* (Cambridge University Press, 1995); and Judith Maltby, *Prayer Book and People in Elizabethan and Early Stuart England* (Cambridge University Press, 1998). To these should be added Christopher Durston and Jacqueline Eales (eds), *The Culture of English Puritanism 1500–1700* (Macmillan, 1996); John Spurr, *English Puritanism 1603–1689* (Macmillan, 1998) and *The Post Reformation* (Pearson Longman, 2006); Darren Oldridge, *Religion and Society in Early Stuart England* (Ashgate, 1998); Peter Lake and Michael Questier (eds), *Conformity and Orthodoxy in the English Church, c. 1560–1660* (Boydell Press, 2000); and Peter Lake, *The Boxmaker's Revenge: 'Orthodoxy', 'Heterodoxy' and the Politics of the Parish in Early Stuart London* (Manchester University Press, 2001). For James's Church, there are Kenneth Fincham, *Prelate as Pastor* (Oxford University Press,

1990); Peter McCullough, *Sermons at Court* (Cambridge University Press, 1998); James Doelman, *King James I and the Religious Culture of England* (Brewer, 2000); and Charles Prior, *Defining the Jacobean Church* (Cambridge University Press, 2005). For Charles's, there are Julian Davies, *The Caroline Captivity of the Church* (Oxford University Press, 1992); and Kenneth Fincham, 'William Laud and the Exercise of Caroline Ecclesiastical Patronage', *Journal of Ecclesiastical History* (2000).

The whole debate between revisionists of early Stuart political history and their opponents and successors is told in the first chapter of Ronald Hutton, *Debates in Stuart History* (Palgrave Macmillan, 2004). Those who want to follow some of their more recent manifestations should read Conrad Russell, *Parliaments and English Politics 1621–1629* (Oxford University Press, 1979), *Unrevolutionary England* (Hambledon, 1990) and *The Addled Parliament of 1614* (University of Reading, 1992); Richard Cust, *The Forced Loan and English Politics* (Oxford University Press, 1987); Thomas Cogswell, *The Blessed Revolution* (Cambridge University Press, 1989); L. J. Reeve, *Charles I and the Road to Personal Rule* (Cambridge University Press, 1989); Richard Cust and Ann Hughes (eds), *Conflict in Early Stuart England* (Longman, 1989); Glenn Burgess, *The Politics of the Ancient Constitution* (Macmillan, 1992) and *Absolute Monarchy and the Stuart Constitution* (Yale University Press, 1996); Kevin Sharpe's essay in Robert Smith and John S. Moore (eds), *The House of Commons* (Manorial Society, 1996); the discussion in the *Journal of British Studies* (1996); Paul Christianson, *Discourse on History, Law and Governance in the Public Career of John Selden* (University of Toronto Press, 1997); J. P. Sommerville, *Royalists and Patriots* (Longman, 1999); Alan Cromartie, 'The Constitutionalist Revolution', *Past and Present* (1999); Kevin Sharpe, *Remapping Early Modern England* (Cambridge University Press, 2000); Chris Kyle (ed.), *Parliaments, Politics and Elections 1604–1648* (Camden Society, 2001); D. Alan Orr, 'Sovereignty, Supremacy and the Origins of the English Civil War', *History* (2002); Thomas Cogswell, Richard Cust and Peter Lake (eds), *Politics, Religion and Popularity in Early Stuart Britain* (Cambridge University Press, 2002); and Nicholas Tyacke (ed.), *The English Revolution c. 1590–1720* (Manchester University Press, 2007). Significant recent studies of early Stuart politics and political culture include Pauline Croft, 'Libels, Popular Literacy and Public Opinion in Early Modern England', *Historical Research* (1995); Adam Fox, 'Rumour, News and Popular Political Opinion in Elizabethan and Early Stuart England', *Historical Journal* (1997); Stephen Lucas and Rosalind Davies (eds), *The Crisis of 1614 and the Addled Parliament* (Ashgate, 2003); Andrew McRae, *Literature, Satire and the Early Stuart State* (Cambridge University Press, 2003); and Glyn Redworth, *The Prince and the Infanta* (Yale University Press, 2003).

There is no full-length, properly researched biography of Charles I in print. Important shorter studies of the king in recent years have been provided by Brian Quintrell, *Charles I 1625–1640* (Longman, 1993); Michael B. Young, *Charles 1* (Macmillan, 1997); Christopher Durston, *Charles I* (Routledge, 1998); and (especially) Richard Cust, *Charles I* (Pearson Longman, 2005). All these are more or less hostile. Kevin Sharpe's works, listed above and below, are kinder, and for many years Mark Kishlansky has been working towards a full biography which is likely to be the most favourable of modern times. Milestones on the way to that are his articles 'Tyranny Denied', in the *Historical Journal* (1999), and 'Charles I: A Case of Mistaken Identity', in *Past and Present* (2005).

Kevin Sharpe's great book on the 1630s is *The Personal Rule of Charles I* (Yale University Press, 1992). Replies and additions to it are common in more general works cited above. Also relevant are J. F. Merritt (ed.), *The Political World of Thomas Wentworth, Earl of Strafford* (Cambridge University Press, 1996); Alexandra Walsham, 'The Parochial Roots of Laudianism Revisited', *Journal of Ecclesiastical History* (1998); David Cressy, 'Conflict, Consensus and the Willingness to Wink',

Huntington Library Quarterly (2000); and Kenrik Langeluddecke, '"I Find All Men and my Officers soe unwilling" : The Collection of Ship Money 1635–1640', *Journal of British Studies* (2007). Christopher Haigh, *The Plain Man's Pathways to Heaven*, mentioned above, is an important intervention in this debate.

Three huge books cover between them major aspects of the crowded years 1637 to 1642: Conrad Russell, *The Fall of the Stuart Monarchies* (Macmillan, 1991); David Cressy, *England on Edge* (Oxford University Press, 2006); and John Adamson, *The Noble Revolt* (Weidenfeld, 2007). The military aspects of Charles's contest with the Scots were considered in Mark Charles Fissel, *The Bishops' Wars* (Cambridge University Press, 1994). John Adamson's essay in Niall Ferguson (ed.), *Virtual History* (Picador, 1997), is a valuable exploration of what might have happened had Charles decided to attack the Covenanter army in 1639.

Some of the works above also cover Scotland, Ireland, or all three kingdoms, but the literature that deals with these is mostly separate. The collections of essays listed above as dealing with the 'British Problem' under the Tudors are all equally relevant to it under the Stuarts. Newcomers seeking an introduction should read Jenny Wormald (ed.), *The Short Oxford History of the British Isles: The Seventeenth Century* (Oxford University Press, 2008). The best overall textbook for Scotland in the latter period is still Keith Brown, *Kingdom or Province?* (Macmillan, 1992). The Covenanter rebellion and its background is dealt with in David Stevenson, *The Scottish Revolution* (David and Charles, 1973); Peter Donald, *An Uncounselled King* (Cambridge University Press, 1990); John Morrill (ed.), *The Scottish National Covenant in its British Context* (Edinburgh University Press, 1990); Allan I. Macinnes, *Charles 1 and the Making of the Covenanting Movement* (Donald, 1991); Keith Brown, 'The Scottish Aristocracy, Anglicisation and the Court, 1603–1638', *Historical Journal* (1993); Julian Goodare, 'The Scottish

Parliament of 1621", *Historical Journal* (1995); *State and Society in Early Modern* Scotland (Oxford University Press, 1999); and 'The Admission of Lairds to the Scottish Parliament', *English Historical Review* (2001); and Julian Goodare and Michael Lynch (eds), *The Reign of James VI* (Tuckwell, 2000). All these are hard on Charles I and get tougher on James. Ireland in the same period is best covered by Nicholas Canny, *Making Ireland British 1580–1650* (Oxford University Press, 2001), together with the last section of Connolly, *Contested Island*, recommended above. These can be supplemented with the essays in Ciaran Brady and Jane Ohlmeyer (eds), *British Interventions in Early Modern Ireland* (Cambridge University Press, 2005), and Victor Treadwell, *Buckingham and Ireland 1616–1628* (Four Courts, 1998). The anniversary of the great Catholic rebellion generated Brian Mac Cuarta (ed.), *Ulster 1641: Aspects of the Rising* (Queen's University of Belfast, 1993) and M. Perceval-Maxwell, *The Outbreak of the Irish Rebellion of 1641* (McGill-Queens University Press, 1994). Scotland and Ireland are linked by John R. Young (ed.), *Celtic Dimensions of the British Civil Wars* (John Donald, 1997).

Chapters 9 and 10 – Civil War and Revolution; The Commonwealth and Protectorate

The most detailed overall narrative for the period 1642 to 1660 is Austin Woolrych, *Britain in Revolution*. The military side is currently best handled by Ian Gentles, *The English Revolution and the Wars in the Three Kingdoms 1638–1652* (Pearson, 2007), alongside which should still be read the essays by different experts in John Kenyon and Jane Ohlmeyer (eds), *The Civil Wars* (Oxford University Press, 1998). Clive Holmes answers a series of major questions concerning it, with a style ideal for students and general readers, in *Why Was Charles I Executed?* (Hambledon Continuum, 2006). Michael Braddick, *God's Fury, England's Fire* (Allen Lane, 2008) is a dense history of England in the 1640s, especially good on intellectual, political and cultural affairs. For the 1650s, those who want a quick account and analysis of the period are welcome to my own *The British Republic,* 2nd edn (Macmillan, 2000). Those who would like a more detailed treatment of the Protectorate should use Barry Coward, *The Cromwellian Protectorate* (Manchester University Press, 2002). The most accessible overall account of the neglected last two years of the republic is in the first part of my book *The Restoration* (Oxford University Press, latest reprint 1993).

Clive Holmes's disagreement with Malcolm Wanklyn over the outcome of the Great Civil War was voiced in his *Why Was Charles I Executed?*, and directed against Malcolm Wanklyn and Frank Jones, *A Military History of the English Civil War 1642–1646* (Pearson Longman, 2005), which is the best current work on its subject. The overall causes were considered in three successive and differing books of the 1990s: Conrad Russell, *The Causes of the English Civil War* (Oxford University Press, 1990); Ann Hughes, *The Causes of the English Civil War,* 2nd edn (Macmillan, 1998); and Norah Carlin, *The Causes of the English Civil War* (Blackwell, 1999), of which the first has been by far the most influential or provocative. John Morrill, *The Nature of the English Revolution* (Longman, 1993) brings together a series of important studies of the war and its context by this key historian. Its ethnic dimension is well treated in Mark Stoyle, *Soldiers and Strangers* (Yale University Press, 2005). The local aspect, so prominent in the period between 1965 and 1985, is still represented in recent years by Mark Stoyle, *Loyalty and Locality: Popular Allegiance in Devon during the English Civil War* (University of Exeter, 1996); A. R. Warmington, *Civil War, Interregnum and Restoration in Gloucestershire 1649–1672* (Boydell Press, 1997); Thomas Cogswell, *Home Divisions* (Manchester University Press, 1998) (On Leicestershire); John Morrill, *Revolt in the Provinces* (Longman, 1999) (a famous general survey); John Walter, *Understanding Popular Violence in the English Revolution* (Cambridge University Press, 1999) (on Colchester); and Lloyd

Bowen, *The Politics of the Principality: Wales c. 1603–1642* (University of Wales Press, 2007). Most publications on the wars pay more attention to the Parliamentarians, but the Royalists get some from my own monograph *The Royalist War Effort*, 2nd edn (Routledge, 1999) and Jason McElligott and David. L. Smith (eds), *Royalists and Royalism during the Civil Wars* (Cambridge University Press, 2007). Parliamentarian politics are surveyed in the more general works listed above, and in Ian Gentles, *The New Model Army* (Blackwell, 1991); D. E. Kennedy, *The English Revolution* (Macmillan, 2000); and Michael Mendle (ed.), *The Putney Debates of 1647* (Cambridge University Press, 2001).

The question of how far the wars in the three kingdoms should be treated as a whole was debated by Jane Ohlmeyer and John Adamson in *History Today* (November, 1998). Important works that take the holistic approach include David Scott, *Politics and War in the Three Stuart Kingdoms 1637–1649* (Palgrave Macmillan, 2003); Allan I. Macinnes, *The British Revolution 1629–1660* (Palgrave Macmillan, 2006); and John Morrill's contribution to Wormald (ed.), *The Short Oxford History of the British Isles: The Seventeenth Century.*

Blair Worden's groundbreaking essay on the meaning of toleration in the period was published in W. J. Sheils (ed.), *Persecution and Toleration* (Oxford University Press, 1984). Religious politics in it have been recast by a series of articles by J. C. Davis: 'Puritanism and Revolution', *Historical Journal* (1990); 'Religion and the Struggle for Freedom in the English Revolution', *Historical Journal* (1992); 'Against Formality', *Transactions of the Royal Historical Society* (1993). Most recently there is Christopher Durston and Judith Maltby (eds), *Religion in Revolutionary England* (Manchester University Press, 2006). The role of pamphlet propaganda during the 1640s and 1650s has been well considered by Jason Peacey, *Politicians and Pamphleteers* (Ashgate, 2004)

The establishment of the republic has been revisited in a set of short studies: Sean Kelsey, *Inventing a Republic* (Manchester

University Press, 1997); Jason Peacey (ed.), *The Regicides and the Execution of Charles I* (Palgrave Macmillan, 2001); and Sean Kelsey, 'The Death of Charles I', *Historical Journal* (2002) and 'The Trial of Charles I', *English Historical Review* (2003). Republican and quasi-republican writing in early modern England has been the focus of three books from Cambridge University Press: Markku Peltonen, *Classical Humanism and Republicanism in English Political Thought 1570–1640* (1995); David Norbrook, *Writing the English Republic* (1999); and Jonathan Scott, *Commonwealth Principles* (2004). An overview of the subject is provided by John McDiarmid, *The Monarchical Republic of Early Modern England* (Ashgate, 2007).

The Protectorate has been re-examined in detail in Patrick Little (ed.), *The Cromwellian Protectorate* (Boydell, 2007); the period of the Major-Generals in Christopher Durston, *Cromwell's Major-Generals* (Manchester University Press, 2001); and the ecclesiastical settlement in Jeffrey R. Collins, 'The Church Settlement of Oliver Cromwell', *History* (2002). Foreign policy gets a rare treatment from Steven Pincus, *Protestantism and Patriotism* (Cambridge University Press, 1996). The five best recent biographies of Cromwell are Peter Gaunt, *Oliver Cromwell* (Blackwell, 1996); Barry Coward, *Oliver Cromwell*, 2nd edn (Longman, 2000); J. C. Davis, *Oliver Cromwell* (Arnold, 2001); Martyn Bennett, *Oliver Cromwell* (Routledge, 2006); and John Morrill's entry for him in the *Oxford Dictionary of National Biography* (2004), which has since been issued as a short book by Oxford University Press. To these should be joined the still significant collection of essays in John Morrill (ed.), *Oliver Cromwell and the English Revolution* (Longman, 1990). The final stages of the republic remain neglected: there is a useful but unfortunately polemical monograph by Ruth Mayers, *1659: The Crisis of the Commonwealth* (Boydell Press, 2004).

There is no new panoramic study of Ireland in the period, but instead a remarkable recent explosion of essays and monographs by different authors: Micheál Ó Siochrú, *Confederate*

Ireland 1642–1649 (Four Courts, 1999); Jane Ohlmeyer (ed.), *Political Thought in Seventeenth-Century Ireland* (Cambridge University Press, 2000); Micheál Ó Siochrú (ed.), *Kingdoms in Crisis: Ireland in the 1640s* (Four Courts, 2001); Padraig Lenihan, *Confederate Catholics at War, 1641–49* (Cork University Press, 2001); Padraig Lenihan (ed.), *Conquest and Resistance: War in Seventeenth-century Ireland* (Brill, 2001). Tadhg Ó hAnnracháin, *Catholic Reformation in Ireland* (Oxford University Press, 2002); and Robert Armstrong, *Protestant War* (Manchester University Press, 2005). In this group is Edwards, Lenihan and Tait, *Age of Atrocity*, mentioned earlier. After 1653, however, everything suddenly goes quiet, and nobody has succeeded T. C. Barnard, *Cromwellian Ireland* (Oxford University Press, 1975). There is nothing comparable for Scotland in the whole period, no work having yet really replaced David Stevenson's classic books, *Revolution and Counter-Revolution in Scotland, 1644–1651* (Royal Historical Society, 1977) and *Alasdair MacColla and the Highland Problem in the Seventeenth Century* (John Donald, 1980), and F. D. Dow, *Cromwellian Scotland* (John Donald, 1979). John Grainger, *Cromwell against the Scots* (Tuckwell, 1997) is at least a new history of the English conquest, and Patrick Little, *Lord Broghill and the Cromwellian Union with Ireland and Scotland* (Boydell Press, 2004) brings a three-nation perspective to the 1650s.

INDEX